An Untraditional Fire

OTHER BOOKS BY
HARRY A. MITCHELL III

Work. Pray. Bless.
Discovering Your Work in God's Mission

The Wandering Life:
A Wayward Journey to Understand My Work,
Calling & Mission

Reflections:
Embracing God's Call for Your Latter years

Good Job:
Developing A Biblical Perspective of Your Work

An Untraditional Fire

The Extraordinary Ministry of Rocellia Johnson

Harry A. Mitchell III

AWordDigital.com

An Untraditional Fire: The Extraordinary Ministry of Rocellia Johnson

ISBN – 978-0-578-85773-2 (Hardcover)

Published by A Word Digital at www.awordigital.com.

Cover design by Harry A. Mitchell III

Amazing effort! Harry did an amazing work of gargantuan size to capitalize the life of this giant of humanity – Dr. Rocellia Johnson. I am grateful that I was allowed to be a part of this work.

Pastor Lester Heath
Mt. Olive Missionary Baptist Church
Los Angeles, CA

This book, *An Untraditional Fire* by Harry A. Mitchell III captures the mind, mood and message of Dr. Rocellia Johnson, our modern-day mentor. Dr. Johnson had the rare ability to stand with giants and still not lose his common touch. You will find in this book testimonies of colleagues by which a matter shall be established (2 Cor. 13:1).

Brother Harry Mitchell is to be applauded for his detailed and time-consuming efforts to bring to us An Untraditional Fire, which is a compilation of many thoughts of Dr. Johnson detailing the true purpose of the Christian church from its inception.

Reginald Pope
Pastor Emeritus, Bethel Missionary
Baptist Church of South Los Angeles
Los Angeles, CA

This tenacious labor of love on the part of my friend and brother Harry Mitchell is an excellent read both for those who knew Dr. Rocelia Johnson, and those who did not. It captures the mind-set for ministry of our late beloved organizing Pastor, Dr. Rocellia Johnson. Those who read this work are in for a major blessing. Happy reading.

Dr. L. A. Kessee
Senior Pastor, Bethany Baptist Church of West Los Angeles Los
Los Angeles, CA

This book is more than a historical document. It is a documentary for other young pastors to learn from. Pastor Johnson was a man who followed the dictates of the Holy Spirit and not other preacher's information. He did what God wanted him to do, the way He wanted Him to do it. So, he stands alone in his life's work as Pastor.

Pastor William Turner
Senior Pastor, New Revelation Baptist Church
Pasadena, CA

I want to express my gratitude to Brother Harry Mitchell, and all who helped to write the story of Dr. Rocellia Johnson. Dr. Johnson was my mentor who provided counsel, encouragement and helpful suggestions that have helped to shape my ministry and pastorage for more than 50 years.

Bishop Sylvester Washington
Senior Pastor, Pleasant Hill Baptist Church
Los Angeles, CA

Harry Mitchell has captured the phenomenon that I had the privilege to experience in the person of Pastor Rocellia Johnson.

GOD could not have given me a more effective ministry mentor than Rocellia Johnson. He was a dynamo who sparked a movement for small and mid-sized congregations to embrace follow-up and follow-through evangelism, and his story can help any pastor who desires to meet the Great Commission.

Rev. Richard Williams, III
Pastor and Teacher Victory Institutional Baptist Church,
Hawthorne, CA

Contents

Foreword

An Untraditional Fire is the exciting story of Dr. Rocellia Johnson, his pastoral prose of the Bethany Church of West Los Angeles, California, and the birth of the National Evangelism Movement. This book is appropriately named, giving us a brief glimpse of the life and legacy of one of the greatest pioneers of modern-day Christian education. I am honored beyond words as a "boomer" to have fostered a personal relationship and partnership with one of the greatest founder/ teacher/ pastor/preachers of all times. If you knew Dr. Johnson, you knew it was hard to separate the man from the movement.

In fact, you are tremendously blessed if in your lifetime, you get to experience up close and personal a life like his, a life that transcends generations and leaves a lasting impact on churches and church leaders throughout the country.

I grew up in the traditional Baptist church and early on as a pastor, I grew tired of the tradition. I began pastoring in 1991, and I quickly realized how outdated methods of the past would not help our church maximize our potential in the present or the future.

I looked around for help and I could not find anything or anyone at the time with the right equipment for launching us into the future. It is a fact that churches and church leaders, for whatever reason, do not change or keep up with the times, rapidly or easily. Just like the church in the Book of Acts, usually it only happens when there is tragedy such as persecution. Dr. Johnson, a man before his time, developed a process that literally threw out tradition. He embraced tools for local churches that met practical needs and spurred real church growth and health.

Harry A. Mitchell has done a superb job in helping us to once again get a glimpse at that greatness. Someone once said that "all of our lives began in obscurity, and we don't know how it will end in history." On December 17, 1922, during the time of the great migration and the Great Depression in Broken Arrow, Oklahoma, God gave the world, and the church, someone who now belongs in a rightful place of history. This book is more than a biography. It is a historical sketch of the man and the movement that changed many lives.

Pastor Ray D. Brown, Sr.

Lead Pastor, Resurrection Baptist Church

[12]

Dedication

This book is dedicated to the legacy of Rocellia Johnson and all the members of Bethany from its inception to the present day. It is dedicated to all the members known and unknown, every auxiliary and pew seat member, active or quiet, who faithfully responded to God's urging and the preacher's voice down through the years. It is dedicated to those who joined not knowing the Lord but became one of his disciples, to those with Christian experience who came to serve, to the new members who opened their homes to receive the gospel, and to those who sacrificed their finances, time, and energy to be a blessing. It is dedicated to the loving community you have all become, which has transcended the church building and the weekly gathering to leave a lasting legacy. And it is dedicated to all of you who have gone home to rest and peace in glory. You have become members of that great crowd of witnesses. You will never be forgotten.

Special Tributes

Sarah Alexander	Ruthie Bollin Peete
Sidney Beach	Annie Petty
Daniel Dawson	Julia White
Marilyn Menefee	

A portion of the proceeds from the sales of this book will be donated to the Bethany Baptist Church of West Los Angeles.

Acknowledgments

Let me begin by first acknowledging thanks to Almighty God for answering my prayer in allowing the story to be written about the legacy of an "Untraditional Fire" materializing into this awe-inspiring book.

To be perfectly honest, I didn't know where to begin on my quest, but there is a certain scripture that my mother instilled in me from a small child which is embedded in my heart and mind – Proverbs 3:6: "In all thy ways acknowledge Him, and He shall direct thy paths."

In October 2008 my beloved mother, Dorothy Jeanne Johnson, had finished her course and was called home to be with the Lord. Needless to say, that was an enormous, unspeakable loss for me and my family, as well as for Bethany; but, especially, for my father (they had shared almost 57 years of marriage). Ten years later in September 2018, having experienced the monumental loss of my father – now with both parents gone – it became my mission and purpose to ensure that this historical legacy would never be forgotten and would be shared across the globe and preserved for generations to come.

I had been praying and asked that the Lord would guide me to whoever would be the right person to accomplish such an extensive and endeavoring task. I remember it being a few months after the passing of my father that I had shared in conversation with Rod Miles about my aspirations of having a book published as a means to share the history and legacy of my Dad's ministry.

Coincidentally, around February 2019, Harry had been talking to Rod Miles and made mention to him how he felt inspired and compelled to write about Pastor Johnson's ministry and his teachings. Rod Miles was the common denominator that put us in contact. Shortly thereafter, Harry reached out to me and shared his expertise. I could hear in his voice the genuineness, elation, and enthusiasm through the phone as he talked about his memories of "Pastor Johnson" and what he meant to him. I felt in my heart that this was the answer to my prayer.

I am deeply indebted and eternally grateful to Harry Mitchell III for the undertaking of this unique and extraordinary project. Not only does he have the qualifications and experience as a writer, but he was a very studious, impassioned and involved young minister and Bible student under the leadership and teaching of Pastor Johnson for many years. Thank you, Harry, for the many sacrifices that you have made throughout this journey to accomplish this goal.

To all who participated in this project, I want you to know that I am eternally grateful and deeply moved by your contributions, the sacrifices you made in giving your time, providing interviews, sharing memories of past experiences and momentous moments, donating writings, sermon notes and preserved video and audiocassette tapes, which served to culminate memories of a 50-plus-year legacy and history of Dr. Rocellia Johnson and First Lady Dorothy J. Johnson.

I would like to extend my heartfelt thanks and give special recognition to Emilie Duncan, Charlee Kessee, Edward Russell, Daisy Stewart, Cecile Johnson Simmons, and Pastor Greg Tyler. This project could not have come together the way that it did without your hard work, commitment, dedication, and consistency throughout. For this, I am exceedingly grateful.

I wish to personally thank The Bethany Baptist Church of West Los Angeles for over 50 years of infinite love shown to my mother and father and our family in countless ways. Let there be no doubt that they both loved Bethany with all of their heart and soul. Thank you from the bottom of my heart for the way that YOU loved them.

I want to convey my profound gratitude and sincere appreciation to Pastor Ray Brown, Pastor Lovely Haynes, Pastor Lester Heath, Pastor L.A. Kessee, Pastor Emeritus Richard Kessee, Pastor Emeritus Reginald Pope, Pastor Warren Stewart, Pastor Sylvester Washington, Pastor Richard Williams III, Rev. Paul Peete, Rev. Bruce Emerson and Rev. Brian Skinner for taking time out of your busy schedules to share your contributions to this book, as you flashed back through the archives of your memories, reflecting upon Rocellia Johnson and the many ways that his teaching and leadership has impacted and enhanced your ministry.

Last, but not least, I would like to acknowledge a special thank you to my husband, Vonnell Adams, who knew more than anyone else just what this project meant to me. I am so blessed and grateful for your constant support and encouragement.

It is my fervent prayer that the Bethany Baptist Church of West Los Angeles will once again emerge as that purpose-driven, thriving organism that flourishes as a beacon light, winning souls for Christ ALL to the Glory of God.

I sincerely hope that you find this book to be enjoyable reading and will cherish the stories and many wonderful memories that encompassed the preaching and teaching of our dedicated and beloved Servant of God, Pastor Rocellia "Rocky" Johnson.

Love and Blessings Always,

Rosalyn K. Adams
Daughter of Dorothy and Rocellia Johnson

Special appreciation for support and assistance
that made the book possible:

Rosalyn Adams   Cecile Simmons
Ed Russell   Daisy Stewart
Emilie Duncan   Pastor Greg Tyler
Rod Miles   Charlesetta "Charlee" Kessee

We are blessed and grateful for the many people that
were willing to share their memories and insights
of Pastor Johnson and Bethany:

Pastor Sylvester Washington   Pastor Lee Arthur Kessee
Pastor Richard Williams   Pastor Emeritus Richard Kessee
Deloris "Dee" Berry   Pastor Ray Brown
Keith Williams   Pastor Emeritus Reginald Pope
Rev. Paul Peete   Pastor Lester Heath
Rev. Edward Berry   Pastor Lovely Haynes
Vicki Kelley   Rev. Eddie Cole
Hazel Shipp   Laura Cole
Karen Butler   Anthony Jefferson
Pastor Warren Stewart   Rhonda Wilson
Ann Woodmore   Mary Evans
Barbara Mitchell   James Mitchell
Cathy Mitchell   Rev. Brian Skinner
Family of Brenda Williams   Herman "Billy" Turner
(Charise, Jamise & Victor   Terri McNeal
Williams)   Cheryl Warren
Family of Sarah Alexander   Rev. Reginald Williams
(Angela Alexander-Rogers)   Deborah Augborne-Allen
Shelia Tolan   Christine Wallace
Lula Hines   Bruce Emerson
Annie Emerson   Pastor William Turner
Daniel Dawson   Erma Daniels
Huns Lee   Margaret Williams
Thera Lee   Pastor Kerwin Lee
Ronelle Damon

Preface

On September 25, 2018, a great man of God finished his race and transitioned to his eternal resting place. His name was Dr. Rocellia Johnson, the founding pastor of the Bethany Baptist Church of West Los Angeles. The people that he had spent his life guiding were now, for the first time, left to suffer through the impact of his loss and continue their lives of faith without his leadership. He was celebrated as a hero, but that one day set apart by the congregation to praise God for his life and to say goodbye didn't seem like it was enough. The celebration of his life in that Homegoing Service could have lasted a week and that may not have been enough either. There just couldn't be enough time to adequately recognize the magnitude of his spiritual impact on his members through the fifty-one years that he pastored, the hundreds of churches around the world that he impacted by the movement that he started and the thousands of other Christians that were reached and blessed by his work.

That is why I felt led to take up my "pen" and tell his story in this book. I felt there needed to be a lasting record of this beloved and unique man of God's life and ministry. I was privileged to call Dr. Rocellia Johnson my pastor for seventeen years. I came to know Christ, to become a disciple of Christ and to be called to the ministry under his pastorage. He was my father in the ministry that taught me, counseled and guided me in the service of God. Because of his great impact on me, I just couldn't let that Homegoing Service be the last word on the impact and ministry of Pastor Rocellia Johnson. Therefore, I reached out to his daughter Rosalyn to offer my assistance which eventually became an idea for a book and we became partners in this endeavor.

My goal was not just to write a book. Reaching out to Rosalyn was more significant than that. I had no idea what was on her heart. I just felt that God was calling me to undertake some effort to ensure that the world knew the stories of Rocellia Johnson and the Bethany Baptist Church of West Los Angeles. This required me to make emotional, spiritual and financial sacrifices that required me to pour myself into this project for the legacies of Rocellia and Bethany. This project required a person with a unique history, knowledge and devotion of these two subjects to complete this book with little info and flawed memories. I began this project knowing that I was the person that God had uniquely equipped me for this important task. So, I took on the burden and responsibility on behalf of Bethany to tell these stories and do it in a way that I hope would make Pastor Johnson proud and that represents Bethany's history and her people.

The truth is, there was so much to his life and ministry and impact that it has been challenging to tell that story even in a book. It is probably impossible to capture all the insights and meaningful moments in Pastor Johnson's life, but I have done my best. I hope that all those who knew Pastor Johnson will, in their reading of this book, have many, "Yes, that was Pastor Johnson!" moments, accompanied by warm smiles and warmer hearts; and that all who did not have the privilege of knowing him and sitting under his ministry will have the pleasure of "meeting" him through these pages and in the process grow closer to the Lord he loved and served with his whole heart.

In writing this book, I had the pleasure of reaching out to some fifty individuals who knew Pastor well – family members, current and former members of Bethany, fellow pastors who served with and learned from him, National Evangelism team members, auxiliary leaders and others who could provide helpful insight. In addition to the many interviews, my research included access to dozens of Pastor Johnson's sermons, on CDs and cassettes, as well as historical church documents, original programs from the Workshops, and hundreds of photographs and newspaper archives from over the decades. Most of these resources were made available by Rosalyn Adams, Emilie Duncan, Brenda Williams, Daisy Stewart, Rod Miles and Sarah Alexander. This project could not have been completed without their contributions.

I hope you enjoy this lovingly painted portrait of my former pastor, Dr. Rocellia Johnson.

Introduction

I n 1958, an African-American pastor named Rocellia Johnson founded a Baptist church that for fifty-one years carried on a ministry of Bible-based discipleship and evangelism, a ministry that grew into a Bible college and a national movement that reached and helped hundreds of pastors and churches. It was a ministry and movement that required a unique personality with an unconventional approach to ministry, and Rocellia Johnson provided both. My goal in this book is to introduce you to this remarkable man and his extraordinary ministry.

Rocellia Johnson founded a local church and instilled within it a devotion to evangelism and discipleship. Through his teaching and pastoral witness and through the work of the Holy Spirit, God built into its DNA the will to witness for Jesus Christ. Rocellia taught and commissioned his congregation on behalf of Christ to be intentional, not just about their faith, but in living out the mission of Christ to be His witnesses throughout the world. Thus, his local congregation became a church that was sent by God to do the missions of evangelism and discipleship and became a sending church.

Rocellia Johnson

His accomplishments are especially significant because in general the black Baptist church community is steeped in history and tradition. Sometimes Pastor Johnson's unconventionality was viewed negatively, but it was this unconventionality that perfectly suited him for the task that God had assigned to him, the task of confronting the barriers to adopting an evangelistic focus. The word "unconventional" means "not bound by or conforming to convention, rule, or precedent; free from conventionality." He devoted himself and his ministry completely to teaching, witnessing and discipling in ways that challenged the traditions of the church he knew. As a result, he became a revolutionary figure that helped re-shape the honored traditions of the black church.

Unconventional is a quirky word to describe someone's approach. It leaves room for a variety of interpretations that can be positive and negative. However, there may not be a better word to describe the full scope of his character or personality and approach. There's probably not a person that spent time with him, who did not feel an indelible impression made upon their faith and ministry. They were either challenged by his authority or disarmed by his kindness. He was a man that possessed a clear and positive sense of himself, but never a negative or arrogant sense of who he was.

Of course, he was a Christian pastor in the truest sense, one that shepherds God's people. He was a remarkable preacher, not for his exegesis or whoop (the celebratory and rhythmic style of preaching often used by black preachers in the closing of a sermon) or singing, but more for his forthrightness. He was also an innovator, because he had a sense of tradition, but was able to innovate without negatively affecting tradition. More than anything else, he was a teacher. Rocellia was so much of a teacher that he taught in every aspect of who he was and what he did as a pastor, teacher and counselor.

The more you learned more about him, the more you were likely to be in awe of him, as E.V. Hill once asked Reverend Lee Arthur Kessee, the pastor that followed Pastor Johnson at Bethany, "Who is this guy?" Therefore, the best way to know him requires an introduction by people that knew him best. So, one of the questions to be answered in this book is, "What manner of man is this?"

As you reflect on his work, you will begin to truly understand that he was a one-of-a-kind minister with a one-of-a-kind ministry. Thus, one of the goals of this book is to look at each aspect of his ministry, which includes his pastoring, his preaching, teaching, evangelism, the Bible institute that he launched, as well as the unheard of 24-Hour Gospel Marathon, all of which affirmed his uniqueness. To accomplish this, this book will share many stories from the many people that knew him best and loved him most. We'll start that introduction with the words of his grandchildren – Angel, Blaze (Ebony) and Vaughn, which they shared at their grandfather's Homegoing Service.

At that packed, upbeat and historic service, Rocellia's granddaughter Angel spoke first among the three grandchildren. Angel tearfully shared her remarks, trying to hold back tears as she spoke clearly in a soft, almost fragile tone. She said, "Papa was the epitome of a man. When I think of what a man looks like, it looks like my Papa. He had the perfect mixture of confidence and humbleness. He added the perfect amount of pure love on top of tough love. He was patient. He was sincere. He was noble. He was selfless…He was beyond your typical street smart or book smart man." She said, "Papa was Bible-wise. He knew without a doubt that he could do all things through Christ. He never showed any worry, doubt or fear. Papa trusted the mysterious ways God works. He truly had a rapport with God. This was proven by his discernment, his demeanor. His actions said it all." She continued, "Papa was a man of the cloth, but took his role as man of the family just as seriously." She continued, "He did everything with all his might. He added value to all that he touched."

After Angel spoke, his oldest granddaughter Blaze spoke more intimately of her relationship with her grandfather Rocellia. She mentioned that as a baby she went on Workshops and was passed from arms to arms. She reflected on her fond memories of Vacation Bible School (VBS) and church picnics in the summers at Bethany. She shared that regardless of what happened, "He was my rock … He never judged me or got mad at me. He loved me through everything."

Rocellia's grandchildren speaking at his Homegoing Service. Above: Angel.

Blaze (Ebony) above and Vaughn below.

His grandson Vaughn stepped forward after Angel and Blaze to share a couple of memories. He began by acknowledging that everyone in attendance was part of his grandfather's journey. Vaughn shared, "My grandfather was a thinking man and he was also a man of action. He always stressed knowledge, knowledge, knowledge mixed with, 'Get up off your behind and go make something happen.' ... He loved to teach. He loved to learn and was an avid reader." Vaughn also told the story of once seeing his grandfather reading from Proverbs 23:7, which says, "For as he thinks in his heart, so is he" (NKJV). Many years later when Vaughn was older, he went to Rocellia for guidance. Vaughn said Rocellia said to him in his raspy, scratchy, but somehow incredibly smooth voice, "Bud, if you want things to change, you gotta change your thinking." Vaughn at that moment remembered that verse from Proverbs. Vaughn said that his grandfather knew that "your most prevalent thoughts affect your beliefs, which affect your actions, which yield some type of result; and when you come back around full circle, that picture you're looking at is your life, and it starts with your thinking." Vaughn explained that this was why his grandfather was a man of action because he knew that you could think something and have faith, but "unless you put in that work, you won't have much."

Rocellia built his ministry on the faithful pursuit and obedience to two New Testament scriptures, Matthew 28:18-20, which is Christ's Great Commission and mandate to the Christian church to evangelize and make disciples, and Ephesians 4:11, which speaks of God calling and gifting evangelists, pastors and teachers to equip all Christians for the work of ministry—this was the impetus for his teaching ministry.

This book is separated into two main sections: "The Minister" and "The Ministry." Each section provides insight into Rocellia Johnson and his service to God. The "Minister" section begins in Chapter 1 with a comprehensive list of descriptions of the man in his many roles—minister, pastor, teacher, evangelist, innovator and more. This chapter also provides descriptions of him by some of the people that knew him best. Also, throughout the book, stories of the people that were blessed by Pastor Johnson will be shared, because his story is part of their story. As their paths were divinely orchestrated to cross with his, God used him to provide guidance and encouragement for their lives.

The "Ministry" section begins in Chapter 2 with a discussion of his views and theology of the local church and its work. Chapter 3 chronicles the history of the Bethany Baptist Church of West Los Angeles, the inception of "little Bethany" in 1958, then the move to "big Bethany" and the introduction to his approach as a pastor. Chapter 4 shares a little about the unique people of Bethany and their unique faith as a result of Pastor Johnson. Chapter 5 shares the story of Bethany's music ministry and how their work was shaped and guided by God's word and a call to Christian service. Following that chapter, Pastor Johnson's unique and sacred approach to communion will be described in Chapter 6. One of the most untraditional and unconventional events inaugurated in Pastor Johnson's ministry was the 24-Hour Gospel Marathon, which will be discussed in Chapter 7. Chapter 8 will discuss the teaching ministry of Bethany, born of a desire to evangelize and make disciples, and a ministry that grew into the Bethany Christian Training Institute (BCTI) and the National Evangelism Movement (NEM). Chapter 10 concludes the book with the story of the evangelism movement and the phenomenon of the Workshop.

Let's now continue the introduction to Pastor Rocellia Johnson.

THE MINISTER

1

Rocky

Rocellia possessed paradoxical qualities about his nature. He could display a level of seriousness about God's work that gave him a sense of piety. Yet, he could also be earthy and ordinary. He enjoyed playing dominoes, fishing and drinking his coffee. He enjoyed people, meaningful conversations and teaching. Yet, on every occasion, he could be engaging and friendly, but he never got silly. He could also be loveable and warm, but not usually cuddly. He was tough, intimidating and demanding, but he was never negative or mean. He seemed to understand that his work required that he challenge, cajole and prod people to be obedient to God's calling and work. In all, he was always able to be himself. He was comfortable in who he was and in what he thought God was calling him to do, even if that made you uncomfortable.

Reverend Brian Skinner described Rocellia by these three qualities – humility, initiative and truthfulness. Skinner said Rocellia demonstrated humility because he recognized who he was supposed to become. He courageously took initiative on the things of God. He was true to his character. These qualities were significant because, in all of his religious education, he didn't try to show off his piety.

Pastor Rocellia "Rocky" Johnson on the balcony at big Bethany with Bethany's current location across the street behind him.

In his early years with his thin, wiry frame, he looked like anything but a "Rocky." His niece Cecile said the family called him "Uncle Cheety" and "Uncle Dud." His slender frame and glasses made him look more like a Rocellia, than a Rocky. His first name Rocellia was a little ambiguous and a little disarming if you didn't know him. On paper you couldn't know how to pronounce it, nor could you tell if it referred to a man or a woman. It expressed a type of ambiguity that made people unfamiliar with the name and the man stumble either in their pronunciations or expectations of the person they were speaking of. He has a niece that bears his unique name. Once you met him, you'd realize that the name Rocellia was simply unique and unconventional, but not unusual. Rocky, on the other hand, was very clear. Rocky expressed a sense of strength, manhood and determination, but it was not combative. And he was both – unconventional and strong. So, people that knew him may have called him "Rocellia," but others knew and admired him as "Rocky."

There was an incident that best described the duality of Rocellia and Rocky. In 1982, when he was at least sixty years old, Rocellia had met with a few of the men of the church for their usual Saturday morning friendly, but spirited, game of dominoes in a classroom at the church. The story was that some kids threw rocks at the window of the classroom where they were playing dominoes. It was the first classroom on the ground floor of the building where all the classes were located, which was separate from the church building and sanctuary. The room sat over a parking stall that was underneath, which meant that the room was high above the ground and the window was about fifteen to twenty feet above the slightly declining parking stalls. Pastor took offense to the rocks being thrown at the window, but instead of running out the door and down the five of six stairs outside the classroom to get to the parking lot and the offenders, he attempted to climb (or jump) out the window to get to them. Unfortunately, the ring finger on his right hand got caught on the window trim and tore off the top half of his ring finger. Yet, he didn't miss any time. He showed up for church with a bandage and never mentioned anything publicly. No sympathy. No pity. This story characterized the scope of who he was – the friend that enjoyed his time with the church brethren in a casual and intimate environment was Rocellia, but "Rocky" was the one that was "not gonna back down" or "take any stuff off anyone." This incident provides a window into the nature of this complex man.

The name "Rocky" inspired images of strength, toughness and invincibility. But he didn't look like a Rocky in his early years as a pastor. The nickname was not assigned to him based on any of those physical qualities, but because it characterized his aura of confidence, courage and determination, mixed with a sense of warmth and kindness that attracted people to him and him to them. It was these qualities that also made people want to follow his leadership. In a way, his nickname was a metaphor for his spiritual strength, toughness and determination. The more you knew him, the more you understood that he was a "Rocky."

He always dressed nicely, usually in a suit and tie, but with a penchant for white short-sleeve shirts under his suit coat. Yet, he wasn't someone that was concerned about being known by his wardrobe, car or anything else related to his outward appearance.

Rocellia had a swagger about him that people recognized. Ann Woodborne, a one-time co-teacher with Pastor Johnson in Evangelism, when asked to describe him, referred to his walk. Ann was a member of St. Mark Baptist Church, a student at Bethany's Bible College and had been recommended to teach with Pastor Johnson, which despite her nervousness, she considered it as a blessing for her learning. When asked about her first impressions of Pastor Johnson, Ann said that he had a "sway about him, a coolness about him," because he knew what he wanted to do and did that." Ann added that he was calm, cool and collected and that she "loved his walk." It was more of a strut, which was more an expression of his self-confidence than a type of cockiness based on a person's appearance, ego or sense of achievements. Ann's description brings to mind the walk of George Jefferson from the 1970s situation comedy show "The Jeffersons." The main character George Jefferson was remembered for his proud, macho stroll to characterize his rise in society or as the show theme song blared, "Moving on up to the Eastside. We finally got a piece of the pie." The actor described his character's walk as the way he would walk around South Philadelphia when you think you're important. However, Pastor's walk didn't actually resemble George's walk in any physical or visual way. They were only similar in the aura of confidence that they both expressed.

Rocellia announced his call to the ministry in 1948 when he was twenty-six years old. Ten years later God called him to start his church that he would name the Bethany Baptist Church of West Los Angeles. The church site was near Fifth Avenue and 15th Street in Los Angeles and was affectionately referred to as "Little Bethany," after it had become too small. Little Bethany was already a small church building when it was first acquired with a few members. There were no classrooms. The Sunday School classes were taught in various sessions of the pews. The young adult class met in the choir robe closet. On some occasions there could be standing room only. As the church membership grew, it became even smaller. So, with all the growth the church experienced, they moved a larger campus farther south to the corner of Hillcrest Avenue and Santa Barbara Boulevard, which was later renamed Martin Luther King Boulevard. The new, larger location was referred to as "Big Bethany." It was known for its striking stain-glass window with rows of the star of David in red, yellow and purple glass that formed a glass wall that rose at least forty feet from floor to ceiling and reached the length of the sanctuary.

Johnson Family picture on
Wedding Day of Rocellia and
Dorothy on October 25, 1951.

(Right side) Front row: (Dad in inset). Orienthia, Lily (Mom), unknown woman, Georgia. **Back row:** Ulysses, Willa, Lawrence, unknown man, Rocellia, Dorothy, Leon and E.C.

Pastor Heath, the Pastor of Mount Olive Baptist Church in Los Angeles, met Rocellia while he was a student at Bethany. Heath described Rocellia Johnson as the most unique person he'd ever met. He said that their first encounter was when he sat at his desk in an Evangelism 101 class, which was taught by Pastor Johnson when he watched Johnson stand and recite the entire fifty-third chapter of Book of Isaiah verbatim. According to Mary Evans, quoting Isaiah 53 was a requirement that her brother J.P. Evans and Rocellia were given at their ordination service. It was a practice that Rocellia would faithfully honor through his sixty years of ministry. Heath said that one of the things that stuck out to him, which he admired most about Pastor Johnson, was that he knew who he was and was comfortable in his own skin. He said, "He didn't try to put on any airs. He didn't have to try to impress you. He knew who he was and his goal in life was to share as much as he could with other believers" through the Evangelism Movement. He added that, "Pastor had a love for people that could accept you just as you are."

To illustrate this point, Pastor Heath shared the story when Rocellia was speaking one night at a church service and the power in the building went out and there were no lights to see or electricity to power the microphone. Normally in that situation, people would say, "The lights are out. It's time to go home." Heath said that when this happened, somebody in the audience yelled out, "We don't need no lights to hear you – go on with it!" And Pastor Johnson kept speaking despite the darkness and without the aid of the microphone. That amazed Heath, because not everyone would or could do that. It wasn't a big thing, but the significance was that people can take little things like that and make them a big problem. This situation reinforced Rocellia's approach that he wasn't going to let anything stop him from doing his work of sharing the gospel. It was in those kinds of adverse situations that Rocellia wanted God's people to know that there's nothing that's supposed to stop them from doing God's work.

Rod Miles, the Executive Director of the Baldwin Bethany Community Development Corporation, which was inspired by the vision of Pastor Johnson, initially got to know Pastor through some personal matters and as a student in his Evangelism 101 class, where Phyliss Leftwich was the co-teacher. In that class, Rod said that he got to know Pastor Johnson from a different perspective, which Rod admitted was new for him. Rod said, "I'd never experienced anybody sharing Christ about you sharing Christ. That was all brand new to me." He observed that Pastor Johnson's mannerisms were different in the classroom than they were in the pulpit, which helped him to understand the importance of salvation. In the pulpit, Rod said, "Pastor was emotional and charismatic, etc., but in the classroom, he focused on the details and was less emotional." According to Rod, this made the student want to open up and want to understand more about sharing the gospel. He also remarked that Pastor Johnson had a high energy level. This made him wonder, "Is this cat like this every day?" To him it is was amazing to see Pastor Johnson "with that same fire Monday night, Tuesday night, Wednesday night," as he displayed in the pulpit on Sunday. Rod appreciated Pastor's consistency because as a man that hadn't been very involved with church and didn't have a positive perception of preachers, Pastor Johnson was unique.

One of the members of Bethel Baptist Church in South Los Angeles, where Pastor Reginald Pope was the Pastor was friends with Evelyn ("Aunt Bae"), the sister of Nat King Cole that was a member of Bethany at the time. Through her friend at Bethel, Evelyn encouraged Pastor Pope to meet Pastor Johnson and get involved in the Evangelism ministry. Eventually, the two men met. Pastor Pope said that on first impression Pastor Johnson "looked like a mean man if you didn't know him." Pastor Haynes shared a similar impression. He wondered if Rocellia was approachable or not. This was partially due to Rocellia's serious-minded nature. Rocellia was a serious-minded man of confidence, but not arrogant, prideful, or boastful in any way. You could say that he possessed strong humility. Pope admitted that once you got to know him, he was a kind and gracious man. As Pastor Haynes put it, "Doctor Johnson was Doctor Johnson. Amen." He was one of a kind.

This uniqueness wasn't simply an attribute of his charismatic personality. He expressed fresh thoughts and approaches to ministry that were uncommon for black pastors at that time. These qualities made him unusual and unconventional in his preaching style, his emphasis on teaching, his passion for evangelism, and his ability to be innovative in his approach to ministry. Of course, it began in his approach to being a pastor.

Humble Beginnings

Rocellia was born on December 17, 1922, during the time of the Great Migration. The Great Migration was the period in the United States from 1916 to 1940 when the first wave of over one million African Americans left the South to the Northeast and Midwest for cities like Chicago, Detroit and New York. He moved to Los Angeles in 1941 at the beginning of the Second Migration. This Second Migration began in 1940 and proceeded through World War II, a period during which five to six million more African Americans moved in pursuit of better-paying jobs, a better quality of life and to get away from the violence and the Jim Crow laws of the South. Los Angeles and Western cities were popular destinations during this second migration.

Rocellia was from Broken Arrow, Oklahoma. Broken Arrow was named for a community settled by Creek Indians who had been forced to relocate from Alabama to Oklahoma in the 1830s. It is the largest suburb of Tulsa, located in the northeastern part of the state where an estimated 100 to 300 black residents were killed in a horrible Tulsa massacre by whites in what was called the single worst race riot in American history. He was born a year later to Monroe and Lillie Johnson.

Monroe and Lilly (or "Gram") were Oklahoma farmers of partial Cherokee descent. Rocellia seemed to have inherited the thin frame and serious demeanor of his father and the warmth and friendliness of his mother. Rosalyn remembers her "Gram" as sweet and kind, a great cook and a deeply-rooted Christian woman, to whose prayers Rocellia credited his life. Monroe and Lillie had ten children, five girls and five boys – Mable, Ethylene, Emma Dale, Ada, Orenthia, E.C. (Ernest Cornell), Leon and Lawrence (twins) and Rocellia, who was the baby. Another son not named here passed away. Despite his citified sophistication, Rocellia was raised on a farm in the 1920s and 30s. His daughter Rosalyn said he'd talk about life on the farm all the time.

In the 1920s the average farm size was about 160 acres with many that were under fifty acres. For most families, the farm was the family's business, upon which everyone, including the children, would work. Rosalyn said her father Rocellia used to tell her how growing up on a farm they always had to keep count of their livestock – the exact number of hogs, chickens and horses – in order to manage the family finances and survive. Certainly, those childhood skills caring for and keeping account of the animals helped make him the Pastor-Shepherd that he was to become.

His older brother E.C. and his youngest sister Orenthia moved to Los Angeles as part of that Second Migration from the South to flee the violence, racism and discrimination of the Jim Crow era and to find better opportunities and a better life. Auntie Rent, as Cecile called her, found a wartime job and her father and mother did domestic work for the same family. E.C. had also worked with the U.S. Civilian Conservation Corps.

As a nineteen-year-old, Rocellia followed E.C. and Orenthia to Los Angeles to begin his adult life. He arrived in Los Angeles at a time when the I-10 that reaches from downtown Los Angeles to Santa Monica was under construction. This new construction, which would pass near little Bethany and connect it to downtown and the beach, didn't open until eight years after little Bethany was founded. The Brooklyn Dodgers hadn't yet moved to L.A. The Los Angeles Lakers didn't arrive until 1960, two years after little Bethany opened its doors. Disneyland wouldn't open for fourteen more years, only three years before little Bethany.

It is hard to comprehend that by the time he got to Los Angeles as a teenager he had already grown up in the Great Depression and lived through World War II, segregation, Jim Crow and other forms of legal discrimination before the advent of the civil rights movement. Yet, witnessing his aspirations, optimism and determination, you would never have known the difficulties that he had seen or experienced.

Upon arriving in L.A., Rocellia worked as a probation officer and was one of the first black bus drivers in Los Angeles. In fact, for some period of time he maintained a full-time job while pastoring the church. He attended Los Angeles Business College, earned his bachelor's degree at Preacher's and Teachers Training School and earned three Masters degrees: at Fuller Theological Seminary (in theology) in 1975, at the American Institute of Family Relations (in pastoral psychotherapy) and the University of La Verne (in family counseling).

Young Rocellia in the pulpit (above)
and seated with Mt. Gilead ushers (below).

Cecile remembered Rocellia's maiden [first] sermon. She said, "Unc preached for a solid hour without stopping." She remembered that he "was on it" theologically and there didn't seem to be any question that he had been called to be a preacher. Part of the tradition in the black church is that congregations tend to make their own assessment of a preacher's calling based on their first sermon. This congregation thought it was funny that he preached for an entire hour, but they certainly sensed that he had been called to preach. Cecile was quick to clarify that an hour-long sermon was not unusual for him, but during that time an hour for a maiden sermon was a long time. Otherwise, he was one of the young ministers at the church. However, when it was his turn to preach, Cecile said, "We knew that if Uncle Rocellia took the pulpit we were gonna be in there a couple of hours. He never cut his speaking time down. He kind of stepped on that hour and stepped up some more. Even the grandkids would say I don't wanna go. They knew he was gonna speak forever." Yet, Cecile admitted that for him to stand up there and preach for an hour on his first sermon said a whole lot about that man Rocellia.

In an article for the *Los Angeles Sentinel* newspaper in 2015, Pastor Johnson said that when he arrived in Los Angeles, he joined the Metropolitan Baptist Church, which was under the leadership of Dr. George H. Washington, Jr., whom he considered as his mentor as a young minister. E.C. and Rocellia both attended the Los Angeles Preachers and Teachers Training school under Dr. George H. Washington, Jr., whom they called "Doc Washington." Greater Metropolitan Baptist Church, in South Los Angeles, was the Johnson family church at that time. Cecile said Washington was a "very strict man," with little patience, but was very endearing. Overall, Dr. Washington was a "[heckuva] man" and it was no surprise that Rocellia and all the other ministers would consider him their mentor. E.C. and Doc Washington were also close friends. Both preachers remained members at Greater

Metropolitan until E.C. became the pastor of Mt. Gilead Baptist Church. E.C. had been a student at the school years before Rocellia, but there was a time when they were students there together.

One Sunday each month at a 3:00 o'clock service, Doc Washington would have a service where he would show off his ministers. He would pick out one or two ministers to speak at the 3:00 o'clock service and critiques these ministers. When it was time for them to end their sermons, he'd tell them "C'mon in, c'mon in," which meant that they end their sermon. He would then critique them in front of the audience. Through this method, Cecile said he turned out some great preachers. Cecile added, "They didn't preach off the top of their heads." They had to study.

According to Cecile, Dr. Washington was more of a teacher than a preacher and this must've been the influence that he had on both men. Cecile said that they all taught from this long chart that illustrated the dispensations of the church from creation to the Judgment. This was the chart that used to be on the wall in the room called "the Small Chapel" at Big Bethany. That chart came from Dr. Washington. This is another example of his influence on their ministries.

Rocellia later served as a minister at Mount Gilead Baptist Church on South Normandie Avenue in South Los Angeles under his brother and Pastor Rev. E.C. Johnson. Pastor Johnson's niece Cecile, the daughter of E.C., who was able to provide some early memories, said that her father E.C. Johnson was "Big Rev" or "Uncle Preacher" and Rocellia was "Lil' Rev." E.C. also had a tremendous influence on his younger brother and Rocellia greatly respected his big brother.

It's important to mention here that if there hadn't been a Mount Gilead, there would not have been a Bethany. Mt. Gilead wasn't just the church home of Rocellia and E.C., it was the place of his spiritual formation. It was the place where he recognized his calling. It was where he first noticed his future wife as she played the piano. So, it was the gathering place for Rocellia, Dorothy and her parents, Reverend Little and Mama Rosa, and Brenda Williams and her mother Gigi Washington, as well as Rev. Broxton and Rev. George Hall and his wife Orenthia. They all eventually joined Bethany under Rocellia's leadership. They formed the original community of Bethany and made Bethany a church built on family and relationships.

Mary Evans was another longtime member of Bethany that had also been a member of Mt. Gilead with her mother and brother in 1957, then she and her mother joined Bethany. She continued to be an usher and became one of the first graduates of the church's Bible school. According to Mary, Rev. Dennis Broxton, Rev George Hall, Pastor Johnson and her brother Rev. J.P. Evans were all were members of Mt. Gilead and were among the group of young ministers under the tutelage of E. C. Johnson. Eventually, all of them left to start their own churches. Broxton and Evans started Florence Mission Church before Broxton went on to join Bethany. Hall started Philadelphia Baptist Church before he later transitioned to Bethany, and, of course, Rocellia Johnson started Bethany. In the remainder of this chapter you'll be introduced to Rocellia as shepherd, leader, preacher, teacher, evangelist, pastor of pastors, theologian, visionary and innovator, which characterize his gifts to the church.

His Christian Anthropology

Rocellia didn't typically speak about his history, personal story, or testimony. He didn't tell stories about the farm in Broken Arrow, his days as a young preacher, what shaped his philosophy of ministry or his theology. He also never really revealed what led him to his calling. However, he would talk a little about his various professions and his many sacrifices to pastor Bethany. If there was a story that he'd readily tell, it was the story of Bethany – the first four members, that $21.50 and meeting in Tiny's living room. Every once in a while, when he was preaching and got happy he'd sing, "Without God, I could do nothing."[1] That wasn't just his favorite song. It was actually a clue to who he thought he was and what he could do apart from Christ. Nothing.

This song helped reveal his Christian (or theological) anthropology. An anthropology refers to the study of a person's origin. A Christian anthropology describes how a Christian deals with how they are in their humanity and how they relate to God from a biblical perspective. So, to understand Rocellia's testimony, you must understand his anthropology, his origins and his perspective with God. So, that song identified who he was based on who God is to him.

Of course, he was created in the image of God, but he came out looking and acting like Rocellia. He was without piety, comfortable with his own imperfections and without any concerns for religiosity. Yet, he was adorned in a biblical humanity fully committed to being a servant of God. That's who Rocellia was and how he lived out his special calling to God. He was himself for the Lord. God had made him be Rocellia because that's the type of man God needed to reach a particular group of pastors and churches with the Movement. God needed a Rocky.

This framed Rocellia's humanity in Christ Jesus. Rocellia was one of God's many pastoral masterpieces, created in Christ Jesus to do good things that God had planned long ago (Eph. 2:10). Black coffee, fishing, dominos, relationships and ministry are what he enjoyed, but were uniquely him. He was a man that God found his entire being and purpose in God's word. That is what inspired and instructed him through his life. In God's word, he recognized his calling and authority to teach, to preach and to minister. All of these things came out of his relationship with God. Like Paul said to the men at Areopagus in Acts 17:28, Rocellia understood that in Christ he lived and moved and had his being.

His relationship with Christ shaped his human story. Like all of us, he was conceived out of nothing by the mind of God, but was formed from the dirt of the grown. Yet, he recognized that despite his mother's faith he had been born in sin and shaped in iniquity. However, by his faith in Christ, he received salvation through God's grace, redemption and reconciliation and was given hope for victory and eternity. God had awakened him and called him not just to any particular task, but to the mission of evangelism and discipleship in his own unusual ways. And because he knew that God was serious about His mission that Jesus gave his life for, so did Rocellia. He devoted his life to that work. Therefore, this work for God made him who he was and shaped how he lived his life. In all of this, God had equipped Rocellia with a long list of gifts to be the pastor of a church that was intentional about fulfilling the mandate.

His Gifts for the Church

Rocellia was a man of many gifts, all of which he used effectively to fulfill his work as a pastor. He was a teacher, a preacher, an evangelist, a pastor of pastors, a theologian and an innovator. Among all these talents, one of the first to acknowledge was his gift as a good shepherd. The Bible defines a shepherd as a person that took complete care of a flock of sheep. The task of the shepherd was to find grass and water for the sheep for them to eat and drink, to protect them from wild animals, to find and restore those the sheep that strayed (Ezek. 34:8; Mt 18:12), to lead the flock out of the fold each day, and to return the flock to the fold at the close of the day (John 10:2–4).[2] God was considered the Shepherd of Israel and his people (Jer. 31:10). That's why David could say, "The Lord is my Shepherd" (Psa. 23:1). God also assigned earthly shepherds to care for and lead his people (Jer. 3:15). As such, Jesus is the Good or Great Shepherd who gives his life for the sheep (John 10; Heb. 13:20; Rev. 7:17). Isaiah 40:11 said, "He will tend his flock like a shepherd; he will gather the lambs in his arms; he will carry them in his bosom, and gently lead those that are with young." Three times he encouraged Peter to "Feed my sheep" (John 21:17). The Apostle Paul wrote that God assigned pastors to his church; they were special leaders given to the church by God to care for God's people as a shepherd cares for his sheep, leading and teaching them in the ways of God.[3]

One of the primary responsibilities of pastoral care is the feeding of the flock, that is, instructing it in the word of God and giving attention to its needs in the whole economy of life. The word for "feed" often referred to the shepherd's general care for the sheep.[4] In this regard, Christian shepherds are to imitate Jesus as the Chief Shepherd.[5] These leaders had to be strong, devoted and selfless.[6] Pastor Johnson was one of those strong, devoted and selfless shepherds that honored his call to feed God's sheep and faithfully cared for the people of God, feeding them God's word and helping them grow to maturity.

Pastor Johnson took his job as shepherd and undershepherd very seriously. As a shepherd for Christ, Pastor showed great care for the people that God had entrusted to him. Pastor Johnson didn't lead by what allowed people to be comfortable. He led by what he thought God was telling him and what God wanted. Where he thought God was leading him to superseded everything else. This was something that his members had to mature to understand. Pastor Johnson would try to serve his people as a good shepherd would, but he was always trying to please the Lord. The serious manner that he embraced this aspect of his calling was evident in how he led leaders in his church and other pastors and churches through the National Evangelism Movement.

As an example of his love for people, Emilie shared the story of two men that sat on the bus stop across the street from the church near Hamburger City. They'd sit there to talk and maybe drink a little, peering across at the church as if it was their entertainment as the members came and went. They sat there so often that they eventually became known by the church members. One day one of the men died. The news reached Rocellia. He directed one of the ministers on the staff to contact the other man to find out about the funeral arrangements for his friend. When that was done, Pastor Johnson had the church make plans for Bethany to host the funeral services for the man. His family was able to attend. He also made sure that Bethany's choir was present. They sat in the center section side, while the other man and his family sat on the left side nearest the stained-glass windows. Those two families didn't know each other, but were able to celebrate the man's life and his friendship thanks to Pastor Johnson.

Then there was also Erma and her family. In 1966, Erma was a married seventeen-year-old that joined Bethany because she lived within walking distance to little Bethany. Only a year later, Erma lost both of her parents, first her father then her mother, to cancer only months apart. These losses left her seven preschool-to-school age siblings in Columbus, Georgia, without any parents. Although she was married, her husband told her that her siblings could not move in with them because it was too many. The following Sunday, after the invitation, Erma went down to the front of the church to ask for prayer. She stood before the congregation to ask for help. She had been a member for less than a year and was only a teenager herself. After she told her story, she said that Pastor Johnson stood over the pulpit and told the church, "We're going to help this family." This gave Erma the support to send for her seven siblings, Eva Mae, Roosevelt, Bessie, Kenny, Elizabeth, Willie and Amanda. She was their older sister by only a few years, but they grew up calling her "Mom."

As a teenager herself, Erma didn't qualify for government assistance, so, she says, "Bethany raised my family." According to Erma, the church rallied to support her and her siblings. A member of the church rented them an apartment and Bethany paid her rent for their first year. She said Pastor Johnson and the trustees would give her a check for food, bills and clothing on Sundays. The church also made sure that they were well taken care of during Thanksgiving and Christmas. Erma credited the church with financially supporting them for at least five years.

The family's support also included financial assistance through the C.E.E.A. program for college tuition for Roosevelt to attend Bishop College in Dallas, Texas, after he had become a minister. In those days, Bishop was a black college renowned for educating and graduating historically popular black preachers and scholars like Manuel Scott Sr., E.K. Bailey and Lee Arthur Kessee. Before Roosevelt left for college, he would spend time around the church and Pastor Johnson would mentor him in things related to ministry. Kenny and Willie also received support through the C.E.E.A. program for college. Kenny was able to receive his degree in criminal justice and later became a minister at Bethany.

As she shared her story, Erma remembered some of the other Bethany members that helped her like Rick and Gerri Landry, Daisy Stewart, Cecelia and Thomas Day, Louis Moore, Annie Jefferson and Phyllis Leftwich. Sister Leftwich, Erma said, bought Roosevelt five suits and five pairs of shoes for college. In fact, all of Erma's siblings grew up and never got in any trouble and had long-term careers.

Erma eventually graduated from college, married Charlie Daniels and they had two sons named David and Douglas. She became a school principal at a nearby West Angeles Church's elementary school and was celebrated in an area newspaper in 1976. This is a remarkable story that shows not just how Pastor cared for his people, but it provides a picture of the remarkable character of Erma and her helpers at Bethany. This is who Pastor Johnson and Bethany were. Caring. Supportive. Loving. Servants.

From the conception of his pastorship, Rocellia took complete care of his flock. His initial task was to feed them with the teaching of the gospel and the Word of God. He developed a systematic instruction of God's word to make sure they were eating and drinking properly. As such, his flock could know that they understood the essence of God's grace and were assured of their salvation through the "follow-through" counseling and teaching. He prayed for them and taught them to become prayer warriors through the Prayer Workshops and to become fishers of men and women witnesses through the Evangelism ministry. He nurtured a family of disciples that shared the love of Christ and to this day that has not changed. Most of the church membership that sat under his leadership have gone on to experience their eternal rest. The others that have scattered still live with the blessings of his leadership and instructions. He guided every member with his teaching to become a disciple of Christ and to share the message of the gospel.

A Natural Leader

It seems obvious and unnecessary to say that Rocellia was a good, strong leader. He exemplified all the expected qualities of an effective leader. He was able to communicate his vision. He inspired. He encouraged. He could build a consensus. It would've been impossible for him to be a good shepherd without also being a good leader. So, the reason for this section is not to state the obvious, but to describe what made him a good leader. Three qualities that made him so effective. He led with a sense of authority. He led through adversity. He gave people the confidence to follow him.

One obvious thing was that he was in charge. There was an authority that he exhibited that seemed to exude from his sense of calling, as they said of Jesus, "he taught as a man of authority." He led out of his calling from God to do the things that God sent him to do. It gave him the power to make decisions and the ability to lead people through difficult moments.

It was probable that many of the people that came to Bethany were either seeking something, maybe God, or fleeing something, maybe God. In either case, there were experiences and moments in life that they were having to deal with. Spiritually, they may have been lost in need of a Savior or struggling in their Christian experience or dealing with some other issue of adversity that they struggled to understand and overcome. Rocellia could preach, teach or counsel people through those awkward, painful moments in their lives. Like a Joshua, he led people to cross those Jordan type episodes into a relationship with Christ as faithful disciples.

You could think of him as a general. Although he was not militaristic, egotistical, or narrow-minded. The had a strong-minded determination that inspired trust that he would succeed and accomplish the mission and that what he was proposing was good and right, which made you believe in him and the mission. So, it gave you the confidence to follow him and if he said take the hill, you did. To say that differently, if he said take (i.e., teach) a class, you did; if he said to travel to a Workshop or host a Workshop, you did.

A Gospel Preacher

Pastor Johnson was a gospel preacher. This should not be understood as a cliché because almost all Christian preachers would consider themselves gospel preachers when in fact they rarely speak of Jesus' sacrificial death, resurrection and ascension. Rocellia was a gospel preacher because he preached the gospel – the birth, witness, ministry, death, burial and ascension and coming again of Jesus Christ. Even if he took a topic that did not begin with Jesus, he made certain that it ended at *the cross*. He also placed great importance on giving his listeners an on-the-spot opportunity to know Jesus and become a disciple of Christ. He taught and preached the message of Jesus Christ because he understood that message to be the power of God that was sufficient to provide salvation to the person that responds by faith to its words.

As such, he was a great preacher, in part because there was an honesty, a sincerity and a clarity to his style of preaching. He employed topical and expository styles of preaching. Dan Dawson, a long-time faithful member of Bethany, had promised his big sister Annie that he would join the church. His sister Annie V. Dawson was one of the founding members of Bethany. At the time, Dan was living with her and, according to him, his sister was "bugging" him to attend her church. He eventually visited Bethany and decided to become the 23rd member of Bethany. Dan said of Rocellia's preaching style, "I saw Rocellia with an exceptional amount of knowledge in understanding the word of God, but he didn't know the Greek or the Hebrew language, yet he could break scripture down into where the wayfaring man could understand it." In any case, Rocellia always managed to successfully preach with a truthful and forthcoming style.

Brian Skinner said that when he first attended Bethany, the first sermon he heard Pastor Johnson preach was about the Rich Man and Lazarus, which Jesus spoke about in Matthew 19:23-30, which Skinner said was about "a man who learned something in hell that he could not have learned in the church house." He said that message scared and stirred him up. He came back a second time to hear another message which explained that "you're either saved, or you're not, and you can't be on both sides of the fence." He remembered being stirred up once again. He said that on his third visit he sat closer to the front, being more comfortable with the greetings and the fellowship, and heard the message "if Christ be not risen" from Matthew 28:1-10. Skinner felt that Rocellia was preaching words that he could comprehend and believe and felt that his words "cut me to my stomach." He felt that Pastor Johnson could reach out and connect with his listeners, which "allowed Pastor Johnson to transcend the culture to meet the people that were there."

Rocellia modeled his preaching style in the traditional homiletics of the black preacher without spending much time in unnecessary platitudes or getting too bogged down in the theatrics that made many preachers popular. He also didn't preach for effect, emotion, or shouts from the pews. He was most concerned about how you'd respond to the truth of God's word in your life. So, in that way, there was nothing really extraordinary about his homiletical style, like a Chambers with his dramatic delivery or a Morton with his singing voice. He didn't preach a sermon based on three main points as Kerwin Lee would famously do. He didn't have any exceptional ability of oratory. He didn't have a particularly great speaking voice or the ability to incorporate song into his delivery like a Kessee or a Washington. He also wasn't known as a storyteller, like a Kenneth Ulmer or a Kerwin Lee. Nevertheless, he never tried to preach like anyone else, but himself. Like elsewhere, he was also an original in the pulpit. He had his own particular gestures and delivery style that seemed unique to him.

Rocellia always seemed to preach comfortably within his own nature and personality. He typically started with a slow deliberate delivery then expounded on his topic with an urgency and a seriousness that made you know that what he was describing was important and worth hearing. So, if you heard him often, you'd know to get yourself ready for what was coming. The thing that made his style so refreshing, memorable and effective was that he was a truth-teller.

Those truths that he shared might be something about the world, society, or life that God needs you to hear. He may put it to you in a way that you either didn't like or that made you uncomfortable, but as far as he was concerned that was your problem, not his. It could be something that helped you and your family, friends, or co-workers. They could also be those personal private things that made you wonder how he knew and who told him your secret. In all cases, Rocellia always told the truth about Jesus, salvation, grace and eternal life as he understood it. This truth-telling garnered him respect, admiration and followers from pastors and churches around the globe. His messages struck you with the truth that had a way of cutting through all the clutter of life and made you listen to and remember what he said. He said of his forthrightness:

> There was a time that I was somewhat noted for people remembering what I said. And I believe that's partially true today. In other words, at the end of the message you don't have to spend the rest of the night trying to figure out what it is I was talking about or trying to say. And if you remember long enough some things that you hear at a point in time will be understood later down the road. I had somebody to say to me just a few days ago, "Pastor, now I remember and understand what you were saying twenty years ago." While I appreciated that statement, that observation, that remark, I don't have twenty years left for you to understand. You need to understand tonight. You need to understand as I speak.[7]

There were three Services on Sunday at Bethany, at 8 a.m., 11 a.m., and 6 p.m. Of course, there were times when Rocellia preached a series of messages or preached a message multiple times on the same day, but rarely did he preach the same sermon at all three services. In most cases, each sermon was unique for that time and audience.

He placed great importance on words and how they were communicated. In a meeting with the ministers of the church, he took time to explain that when you are preaching you couldn't pronounce "God" as any ordinary word. He emphasized that whenever you said "God," it had to be pronounced based on His majesty and the reverence due Him coupled with your experience with God. In other words, you had to say it as you've been through something with Him and the people need to be able to hear that experience when you said His name. This showed that he was always serious about the importance of God's Word and the message of the gospel. So, whether it was preaching, teaching, or evangelizing, his ultimate focus was on the gospel of Jesus Christ. Here is how he stated the importance of the gospel in one sermon:

> Far too often we go out there to bring folks to church and we have the wrong message. It's often we go out and try to persuade people to hear the choir or certain groups, saying, "My preacher can preach. He's the best preacher in the world." That sounds good, but it is not the mandate [of the believer]. See when he is instructing us to go back into the world and all the world he didn't tell us to go out there and try to impress the world with our talent and our abilities. He said go back into the world with the gospel. You see the gospel is the only thing that God left on this green earth for the purpose of giving lost folk the saving knowledge of Christ. That's why Paul said I'm not ashamed of the gospel of Christ,

because it is the power of God unto salvation to everyone that believeth.[8]

Perhaps the most notable thing about his preaching was that he'd preach until he was done. He was never in a rush to finish a sermon nor did he ever try to squeeze a sermon into a thirty- or forty-five-minute window to keep a schedule or accommodate his listeners, whether he was preaching at Bethany or elsewhere. This meant that whenever he preached, the services were always open-ended. They began when he started talking and ended when he was finished. Sometimes, he finished and extended the invitation to the church. Sometimes, he'd think of something else and resume his message after having taken his seat and hop up to continue. In any case, he felt that if the Lord gave him something to say, he was going to say it.

Of all the preachers, Pastor Johnson was usually the only one that would grab the microphone from its holder. Most of the Bethany preachers would stay stationary in front of the mic and speak into it. Pastor Johnson needed to walk around and occasionally turn his back to the congregation and turn to speak to the choir or leave the pulpit and go down to the floor to speak to the congregation. So, when Rocellia preached, there were two important, but not so obvious, tasks that had to be undertaken in the pulpit.

One of the tasks took place when Pastor Johnson would leave the pulpit to go down to the floor in front of the two main sections of pews to finish his whoop or to extend the invitation. The challenge here was that the pulpit area and choir area were on a platform that was about two feet above the floor where the members sat. In addition to the raised platform, the podium which the preacher would speak behind was another four feet tall and at the top of this sacred desk, where the preacher's Bible would lay, was the place where the microphone was plugged in. So, when

Pastor Johnson was on the floor with the microphone, someone would have to hold and guide the twenty-foot-long microphone cord, so it didn't become unplugged, and to make sure that Pastor didn't get entangled as he moved about. It was like going fishing and having a large fish pulling on your fishing line as you fight not to let it go or break your line. This was a difficult task, that there was no way to be trained for. It was one of those things that you could only learn from observation.

The second task was when Pastor was down on the floor, he'd work up a sweat. He'd beckon up to the pulpit, usually to the minister navigating the cord, to hand him a dry handkerchief, which was also an important duty. Paul did a good job of handling these odd duties. Lastly, not as a duty, but something to know was that when Pastor Johnson seemed to be done and took his seat, he probably wasn't finished. He'd typically hop back up from his high-back middle chair to continue and elaborate on another important point. Sometimes that second mini sermonette could last as long as someone else's entire sermon. Bethanites knew that these continuations were just as important as the earlier part of the sermon. No matter how long Pastor spoke, they knew to sit faithfully and patiently until he was finished and the invitation for people to accept Christ or to join the local church had been extended.

One of his favorite sermon illustrations regarding knowing Christ was as follows:

> There is such a thing as knowing Jesus and he not knowing you. He said they shall come in that day, and say, "Lord, Lord we did this in your name. We were at a Workshop in your name," and the Lord will look somebody right in the face and say, "Depart from me. I don't know you." Sometimes I brag about the folks I know. I brag about I know Ronald Reagan. I brag about I know Castro. I brag about I know Gorbachev.

I brag about some of the other dignitaries I know. When it comes to Reagan, Gorbachev and Castro, I know 'em very well, but not one of them knows me. So, until Jesus knows you, and Jesus is not gonna know you until you accept him as Savior, Redeemer and Lord.[9]

Of course, there were times when the mood was lightened elsewhere in the congregation. There were memorable and humorous occasions when Pastor was preaching that Reginald Shaw, the church's organist, got happy. When Reggie got happy, he'd do his version of a happy dance. He'd get emotional, shout and throw his arms up, then begin to flail about on his seat. People near him would start moving out of the way. Because Reggie was a big, heavy man, one of the ushers and an L. A. City fireman named Anthony Jefferson, who joined little Bethany with his family in late 1963 or early 1964, was one of a few members that had the strength and willingness to grapple with Reggie. Anthony would anticipate the issue and make his way from the back of the church to the front to stand by Reggie.

Just when Reggie was on the verge of falling off his bench, Anthony would grab him in a bear hug until Reggie was done. One time, in his excitement, Reggie's dentures popped out of his mouth. Anthony picked them up and set them on top of the organ. When Reggie returned, he put them back in his mouth and resumed playing. Oddly, that wasn't the only occurrence. Anthony said that there were other times when Reggie would get so happy that his dentures would either hang out of his mouth or risk causing him to choke on them and Anthony would have to pull them out of his mouth and either hand them to one of the Mothers of the church or set them on the organ.

Of course, like most black preachers, he would whoop. Sometimes, he'd do it out of formality or tradition and then there were times when he did it because he was feeling good. He would rare back with the microphone to his mouth, his head reared back, with one knee extended forward as if to kneel and shout out the climax of his message. There were also times, usually, when he was especially happy, he'd sing his favorite song. He'd sing in his raspy voice in a slightly offbeat tone,

> Without God, I could do nothing,
>
> Without God, you know my life would fail,
>
> Without God, life would be rugged, Oh Lord
>
> It'd be like a ship
>
> Without a sail.[10]

Pastor Johnson didn't sing it exceptionally well, but you knew what it meant, and it usually provoked the listeners to cheer him on with a hearty, "Sing, preacher!" Or a "Go ahead, Doc!" In any case, his style was memorable and impactful. You didn't leave feeling a certain way, as much as you left thinking differently.

Overall, his sermons were memorable, not because of his style, but because regardless of his topic, he always took you to Calvary to make sure that you heard the message of the gospel. It's also important to know that he put almost as much emphasis on extending the invitation to salvation to those who have not accepted Christ. He'd make the offer after every sermon and sometimes during. He considered the invitation as a sacred, prayerful time, so he was also patient. He'd warmly make many appeals to the people in the pews as if to offer an appeal for every person or situation that might be present.

A Diligent Teacher

Being a teacher was not just something Pastor Johnson did. Teaching is who he was. Therefore, teaching was a very evident and vibrant aspect of his ministry. When asked about this, Ed Russell, a member little Bethany since May 1963, said that Rocellia was more of a teacher than a preacher. He thought that Rocellia's focus was more on training than it was evangelism. His focus was on training the church for ministry, which included evangelism. So according to Dan Dawson, "Although I'm not sure there was a written rule, if you didn't involve yourself in Bible study you wouldn't be on Rocellia's team."

In a *Los Angeles Sentinel* newspaper article announcing his Homegoing Services, the newspaper quoted Rocellia explaining his lifelong commitment to teaching and training God's people. They quoted him saying, "I believe in the stronghold of the church. James 1:22 says, 'But be ye doers of the Word, and not hearers only, deceiving your own selves.' Also, I was moved by the Biblical mandate to witness to the lost and to train the saved for service. For Jesus said in Matthew 7:26, 'and everyone that heareth these sayings of mine and doeth them not shall be likened unto a foolish man, who built his house upon the sand.'"[11]

The idea of Bethany's Bible school was never about building a school or an institution. It was about creating a place where each individual Christian could develop as a Christian learner concerning the gospel mandate and the need to ensure growth within each believer and each church. Ed Russell said that one day Pastor Johnson announced the end of the Tuesday night Bible class because he felt that a single, weekly class had served its purpose. He said that by people listening to him on Tuesday night there was no way he could tell if any learning was taking place. Ed said that Rocellia wanted systematic Bible instruction. With an emphasis on Christian education that allowed people to be held accountable for their learning and Christian growth. Ed said that this eventually gave way to the Bethany Christian Training Institute (BCTI), which was needed to fulfill the mandate and to fulfill the need for a systematic curriculum and to do that he had to get away from one-night-a-week Bible study. This signified his attitude on teaching and paved way for the expansion of teaching that helped Bethany to grow and that became an important emphasis in the National Evangelism Movement.

A Committed Evangelist

"Evangelists" are missionaries who pioneer outreach in areas where the faith has not as yet been proclaimed.[12] Rocellia was an evangelist and missionary sent to other pastors and churches to proclaim the mission of evangelism and discipleship. There was a mandate for evangelism, but it was expressed in two different ways. In Matthew 4:19, Jesus said, "Follow Me, and I will make you fishers of men." The Apostle Paul said, "And He Himself gave some to be apostles, some prophets, some evangelists, and some pastors and teachers, for the equipping of the saints for the work of ministry, for the edifying of the body of Christ." Being an evangelist was about preaching the gospel, which meant making the truth of the gospel known. So being an evangelist emphasized the Good News and being a fisher of men was about catching or winning the souls for Christ. Pastor Johnson did both. He told a Workshop audience in Nova Scotia, Canada:

> If anybody is interested in catching some fish, it only makes sense if you go where the fish are. You're not gonna catch any fish on dry land. You're not gonna catch them in the parking lot. You're not gonna catch them on the mountain top. You're gonna have to go down to the water where the fish habitat, where they live, where they abide. Hallelujah! What I'm saying is that if the church is interested in bringing the lost to the saving knowledge of Christ, the Workshop is about getting prepared to go fishin.'[13]

Rocellia loved to fish. In the States, Paul Peete, a member of Bethany since 1968 and one of the senior ministers at big Bethany, said they'd go fishing at lakes like Lake Pyramid in Nevada, Lake San Antonio in California between L. A. and San Jose, Lake Vail in Southern California near Temecula and other lakes nearby. Rocellia would also go fishing at Workshops when the schedule allowed. Was he a good fisherman? Paul Peete said that Rocellia was a good fisherman, but Ed Berry, one of the initial evangelism team members disagreed. Paul also told the story that once Rocellia, Ed Berry and he were fishing when one Pastor's casts hooked Ed in the face and they had to take Ed to the doctor to get the hook removed.

Ed Berry said they were at one of their favorite fishing spots at Lake Pyramid. It was about one or two o'clock in the afternoon. Rocellia was on one end of the boat fishing for catfish, which was his preferred fish and Paul and Ed were at the other end fishing for bass. He said that you'd have to watch Pastor when he'd get to swinging his fishing rod around. So as Rocellia was swinging his rod, in the motion of casting his line, he said he'd caught on something. Ed replied, "Yeah, you hooked my face." Rocellia hooked Ed in the face, just below his eye, worm and all. Initially, Ed thought the hook had taken his eye out. They couldn't remove the hook, so they cut the line. There was very little bleeding, so Ed suggested that they keep fishing. So, they continued until their usual quitting time, which was around five o'clock with the hook still in his face. They didn't want to let a perfectly good fishing trip go to waste. After fishing, they found a hospital near Castaic which was at least twenty-five miles away. The doctors were able to get some wires and pliers to cut the hook to remove it, then gave him a couple of stitches.

There was another occasion when Pastor and Ed were fishing together when each of them caught a fish. Ed caught a catfish and Rocellia caught a bass. Both fish were of equal size. The problem was, Ed preferred bass and Rocellia preferred catfish. Pastor wanted Ed's catfish and Ed wanted that bass. Instead of just doing a quick swap, they negotiated for at least three hours over those two fish. Each man was determined to gain some leverage on a potential trade by catching more fish. Yet, they continued fishing, but now as more of a competition of sorts. Now they were determined to out-fish the other. Ed was intent on catching his bass and Pastor on catching some catfish, which would solve the stalemate. When the day was done, neither man caught another fish. The only two fish that they'd caught the entire day was that catfish and that bass. So, at the end of the day, when it was time to go home, they finally traded fish and each man got the fish he wanted.

Ed confirmed that fishing was Rocellia's way of meditating and gaining reflection. He said, "It wasn't always about catching fish. It was about being on the lake." Ed explained that being on the lake was soothing to his mind. There were times when they would go an entire day without catching fish, then leave and Rocellia would say, "Had a good time, didn't we?" It was a quiet time. Sometimes they'd talk for just a few minutes out of the day and other times when they talked for hours straight. It allowed you to think about life and whatever serious stuff was going on. It allowed you to think about things that you might not be able to think about at home on a typical day and that was one of the reasons that Rocellia enjoyed it. It gave him a chance to talk and think about things, and at times he'd even develop some sermon ideas on the lake. "We'd be talking and he'd say that's a pretty good sermon right there," Ed said. Fishing was the one therapy that they both enjoyed together.

In all, Pastor Johnson was an evangelist. He was tactical in his approach at winning souls by using the gospel as the hook. He cast his widest net at the Workshops to win pastors and churches to the ministry of evangelism. And it can be said, according to

Paul and Ed, with firsthand testimony that Pastor Johnson was truly a fisher of men.

A Pastor of Pastors

Pastor Johnson had a way of developing and encouraging young pastors, which made him a "pastor of pastors." In the process of writing this book, several of the pastors, which were all young pastors when they first met Pastor Johnson, shared strikingly similar stories of how Pastor Johnson mentored them. In his relationships with these pastors, it's as if Pastor Johnson was discipling them, which in the pastor world back then was another one of those unconventional things that he did. Pastors would disciple one of their sons in the ministry from their church, but for one pastor to take it upon himself to pastor another pastor was pretty remarkable in its own right. Yet, Pastor Johnson seemed to do that very comfortably. It wasn't anything initiated by their efforts or their ambitions, but Pastor Johnson remarkably would take the initiative to reach out to disciple them.

Pastor Sylvester Washington is the Pastor of Pleasant Hill Baptist Church and the current National Director of the National Evangelism Movement that was founded by Pastor Johnson. Reverend Washington had only been a pastor for about two years when he met Pastor Johnson at Fuller Theological Seminary in Pasadena, California, in 1972. They car-pooled together to school for a while with several other pastors that were also attending Fuller. At that time, Pastor Washington was challenged with his church building that had been damaged in a recent earthquake that prevented his continued attendance.

In their time together, Washington discovered that "What was unique about him was that he saw a young man that he didn't think would get very far without the assistance of someone with more experience than what I had. So, he took me on." He said,

"I didn't know exactly why he did that at the time. He started to talk about Christian Education, which was a mainstay of his since I met him. He was very concerned about Christian Education." Washington realized later as he became involved in the Movement that Pastor Johnson had adopted him as a spiritual son. Many years later, while reflecting on Pastor Johnson's contribution to this book, Sylvester Washington became a little emotional as he remembered the fact that Pastor Johnson had sought to become his teacher and mentor. Washington admitted, "What I know in ministry and how I move about in my ministry comes from Rocellia Johnson. He indirectly taught me some things and he taught me some things directly."

Pastor Haynes shared the story that his brother told him about the classes at Bethany and he told his brother, "Aw man, ain't no way I'm going over there." Haynes said, "Low and behold I became a student," at Bethany and eventually credited Pastor Johnson for expressing confidence in him as a young pastor. This began when Pastor Johnson asked him to teach at the church's school in 1989 when Haynes was preparing for a trip to Israel. He said that Rocellia approached him and asked him if he would teach the Gospel of John class. Haynes was shocked by the request because he said he didn't think that Pastor Johnson knew enough about him to make that type of request. In those days, Pastor Haynes considered himself an introvert that has since made himself an extrovert and would not have imagined himself in front of a group of people teaching, but Rocellia did. In some ways, Pastor Johnson didn't have to know you personally or intimately. In reply to Pastor Johnson's request, Haynes said, "I've never done this before." To which Rocellia quipped, "Well, you're preachin', aren't you?" Haynes said this caused him to study and grow. He went on to teach that course with Minnie Russell and began to travel with the Evangelism team. Haynes admitted, "I wasn't thinking of teaching at all. He did."

This was not an insignificant pairing in traditional Baptist church settings. Ordinarily, the idea of partnering a pastor and a woman to teach a Bible class together would not be acceptable. This was a common strategy with Pastor Johnson. Plus, Minnie was an excellent teacher and the perfect partner for the new teacher. She had a long resume of Christian service since becoming a member of Bethany. She was a member of the Executive Choir and one of the voices of the Bethaniares. She taught Sunday School and the Gospel of John for thirty-four years. In addition to being a teacher, Minnie was also Director of Teacher Training for seventeen years. For ten years, she was a Teacher Instructor in the Evangelism Movement. Minnie's experience as a teacher, her meticulous organizational skills and proven expertise in teaching methods provided Pastor Haynes the perfect structure to succeed. Pastor Haynes thought of Minnie as an impeccable lady and spoke well of their camaraderie and friendship.

"He loved young preachers and he loved people," noted Pastor Haynes. He said that Pastor Johnson had confidence and a charisma that attracted people to him. Haynes said that Pastor Johnson "invested his time, his talents, his money. He poured himself into you as an individual." Haynes said that it was because Pastor Johnson had poured so much into his life that he wanted to become a part of Rocellia's ministry. When asked about some of the initial impressions that Rocellia was making on him as a young pastor," Haynes responded, "He was like my pastor."

In all, there was something unique about Rocellia in that he could see something intangible within a person that had not yet developed within a person, especially these young pastors. He saw the potential within them before they saw it in themselves. He didn't have to know your characteristics or your preferences or comforts because he didn't spend a lot of time on what you thought you could do or what you thought your skills were. His primary concern was what God wanted from you.

Pastor Heath told the story of how Rocellia helped provide wisdom to new pastors. At Workshops, Pastor Johnson often led breakout sessions for newly assigned pastors to help them understand the Workshop and ask questions. In one of those sessions, Heath said, "I remember he had an insight into things you don't think about. In one of those sessions, a pastor asked, 'How do I take control [as the pastor of the church]?' Pastor Johnson responded, 'It'll take about seven years before the church makes you the pastor. You can wear the title, but you have to wait until the church says you're the pastor.'" In an annual church meeting at Bethany in 1985, Rocellia explained his comment to that pastor about when you can become a pastor to the people. He said,

> Now, I've been called pastor for thirty-something odd years in the Bethany Baptist Church, but don't let nobody fool you, I haven't been pastoring that long. I've been preaching all that time and I've been going under that banner [of pastor] all that time but I haven't been a pastor all that time. When you become pastor, it means to a great extent that people are accepting the gift of the ministry, that gift [of a pastor] that God gives to the church.

Haynes shared that because Pastor brought him into Bethany's teaching ministry, "There was a certain discipline that I had to have in my life. I knew that that was a no-no because I had to respect my leader. I had to respect this ministry. I had to honor his trust and confidence in me." At one point in the conversation, Haynes jested, "Maybe I was Titus or Timothy or something." For all these ministers the answer was yes. They were a sort of protégé for Pastor Johnson, not to succeed him, but to replicate and continue his work within their flocks.

Yes, it certainly appeared that Rocellia modeled the Apostle Paul in the ways that he mentored some of these preachers that were newer to the role as pastors, like Heath, Haynes and Washington. Like Paul chose Timothy to travel on his second missionary journey, Rocellia chose these men to teach and to travel with him in Bethany's evangelism ministry. In this work, they were challenged to expand their ministry outlook to include teaching and discipleship (1 Ti. 1:2). Rocellia also encouraged and impressed upon them the need for personal and ministerial accountability (1 Ti. 4:16). They were also inspired to remain faithful to the things that they had been taught (2 Ti. 3:14). In all this, they were his mentees or his disciples, and they became part of Rocellia's legacy.

A Practical Theologian

As much as any other ministerial attributes, Rocellia was a practical theologian. When he was preaching, Pastor Johnson would call some of the points that he was making and say of that point, "That's good theology!" "Good theology," in Pastor Johnson's view, was basically about what God likes, thinks and wants, which will work in your life. His views of the church ministry, evangelism and discipleship were based on "good theology."

Theology is the study of what the Bible teaches about the nature of God, his dealings with his creation and the practice of Christian thought and faith. It is important because it frames what God says about a topic. Practical theology is that area of Christian theology that examines and reflects on the study of God in theory and practice. Its focus is to be practical and to practice the teaching of Scripture in a way that should affect the way we live and how Christian leaders minister and equip the church for ministry. In his book *Practical Theology for Black Churches*, Dale Andrews explains that "practical theology" bridges the chasm between living in the world and living in faith and is best understood by what it does. It is the process of engaging theology, theory and practice.[14] Rocellia was able to navigate this chasm by teaching the truth of God's word for ministry and life, without ever separating the two.

In an article on the Black Church, Dennis Wiley explained practical theology this way, "Since theology is always done by human beings, it always emerges in some practical human question, problem, issue or concern."[15] Rocellia recognized that good theology must be inherently practical for human life. One tragic example of practical theology occurred when Reverend Brian Skinner's son was killed, and he was deeply heartbroken, anguishing the loss of his son. When Rocellia heard from Skinner that it was true, he asked the grief-stricken father, "How's your theology?" Rocellia wasn't asking about some deep theological understanding of the tragedy. He was asking Skinner about his understanding of God in these matters because inside a good, practical theology that grief-stricken father would be able to find the source of his strength and comfort for his time of bereavement.

Those designations of "good theology" by Rocellia added clarity and validation to the biblical truth he'd share. Oddly, he said that a preacher once told him that he wouldn't make it with that approach. Rocellia exposed proper thinking about the church, church traditions, teaching, evangelism, servanthood and ministry. His entire ministry was evidence of good theology, which shaped his worldview, his ideas and his approach to ministry. The fact was, Pastor Johnson didn't get his theology from someone else's theology nor was it something he picked up in someone's book. He proclaimed something good and practical as God had revealed it to him.

Rocellia's theology for the church was that God is alive and present in the lives of people, therefore the church should be open and accessible. For good preaching, the preacher should always proclaim the truth of God into the lives of people. Teaching must be done because Jesus mandated it and because the mission required it. Evangelism is essential because God's people are commissioned to share the gospel and to tell the story of Christ and Calvary. The Movement is a blessed work of God because it is obedience to God's call and instructions to teach and make disciples. He told a group of BE-101 teachers, "Every church should have a class in systematic theology."

Systematic theology seeks to understand God within particular categories of study by topic, such as Christology the study of Christ, ecclesiology the study of the church, eschatology the study of future events, hamartiology the study of sin, pneumatology the study of the Spirit, soteriology the study of salvation, missiology as the study of mission or eschatology the study of the last days. However, he chose not to speak in lofty theological doctrines or terms that could go over the head of the typical churchgoer. He spoke with an earthy, practical style that made his preaching and teaching helpful for the real-life issues that people were dealing with and he always seemed to provide a word from God for those situations. Dan Dawson said that "He was a seminarian but did not preach or teach like someone from the seminary. It was not important for him to speak in Greek or Hebrew."

Rocellia would speak of end times or the last days, not of "eschatology." He spoke of Jesus as the Son of God, without calling it "Christology." When he was talking about the sin he didn't call it "hamartiology." The Holy Spirit was spoken of as the Spirit of God and the Holy Ghost, without being addressed as "pneumatology." When he talked about salvation, it was about coming to the knowledge of Jesus and his sacrifice, payment for sin and the cross at Calvary, not "soteriology." The church was the people of God and the bride of Christ and not referred to as "ecclesiology." The mission of God was always His mission, evangelism, discipleship and the Movement and never defined as "missiology."

"He thought biblical, but talked secular," is how Reverend Skinner put it. Skinner said that "Pastor Johnson could disrobe himself of any pious gestures and religiosity to take on the humanness of Christ to make himself able to use evangelism to speak into a person's humanness in a way that made the gospel come alive within you."

Overall, Rocellia presented God's word and the message of the gospel in a way that could be understood, in a way that made you think and apply it to your life. This meant that his pragmatic, but relevant, manner not only helped people to understand what he taught, it also helped them to move from knowledge to action based on what he taught.

A True Visionary

The Bible speaks of prophets as spokespersons for God, and as such, they often have the ability to predict the near as well as the distant future. Sometimes for this ability, they are called "seers," "one supernaturally enlightened to see things which God only can reveal."[16] They had the divine ability to become aware of and comprehend God's urgings and to envision future events as described by God. To see the classrooms and the school before there was a school, to see a national evangelism ministry before he got to Seaside and to see the church or school across the street, while the property is occupied – all involved a unique vision that could only be given by God to Rocellia. These things didn't involve just regular seeing things, but allowed Rocellia to see God's dreams in such a way that he could take action and build them.

Rocellia had visions of a church that studied God's word, was committed to evangelism and discipleship and put its faith in action.[17] So when he was starting at little Bethany and told God that he would teach his word, he saw classes, a Bible college and a national teaching ministry, just not all at once. It was more like he knew it over time as he continued to be faithful to God and this allowed him to gradually see his vision more clearly. Yet, it was in the work of ministry that he did the leading, teaching and discipling, that allowed him to see more and more of what God wanted him to do. It wasn't that others could see his vision, which is what made him so unique, but that people would follow him because they put their trust in the vision that he saw. For example, who else saw in the future what starting a few Bible classes could do? His special gift and calling were not just to see what God showed him. He could take those abstract ideas and goals from God, to acquire the people and resources and organize all the necessary pieces to implement God's plan.

"People talk about him being a visionary, he was that a man of faith, he was definitely was, but I think about him being an investor. He invested in our lives," was how Charlesetta "Charlee" Kessee described Rocellia. Charlee, now wife of Pastor Lee Arthur Kessee, Bethany's current pastor, eventually joined Bethany in January 1971, initially because she wanted to be in Bethany's Young Adult choir, which she loved hearing. Charlee said, "I'm talking about he invested nuggets, gave me words of wisdom, gave you guidance, had an open-door policy, as he sat there studying with his door open."

At Rocellia's Homegoing Service, Pastor Richard Kessee (Charlee's brother-in-law and older brother of Pastor Lee Arthur Kessee), also spoke of how Rocellia had invested in his life and ministry. Pastor Richard Kessee considered Rocellia a friend, brother, father and teacher. They had initially met in the summer of 1962 before Richard was called to the ministry when he was visiting little Bethany where his family were members. He and Rocellia became friends. After he'd been called to the ministry the following year at St. Andrews Baptist Church in 1963, Pastor

Kessee said that "Pastor Rocellia Johnson supported me and my ministry at the Mary Magdalene Church," where he pastored for seven years, "and when I left Mary Magdalene and went to Second Baptist Church," for another seven years, which is the oldest black church in Santa Ana. After Pastor Kessee left Mary Magdalene in 1980 and founded Saint James Missionary Baptist Church, he said that in 1981 Pastor Johnson and Bethany Baptist Church team came to Santa Ana and did the evangelism Workshop at Saint James Missionary Baptist Church. Kessee added that as a result of that Workshop and their commitment to evangelism, St. James "grew by leaps and bounds." Haynes said that he "loved Rocellia's spirit, his personality and thought he was an excellent man."

The point was that Rocellia was a type of seer. In the Old Testament, a seer was a person gifted by God with the ability to see future outcomes and to speak predicatively of those events. Rocellia could also see into people what they could become, how and where God could use them. This "investing" happened with almost everyone that knew him, especially with people like Pastors Heath, Haynes and Pope when it might begin with a challenge to do something they'd never done like teach a ten-week class, join the Evangelism team or lead a breakout session or implement evangelism at their churches. It could also be where he gave people a task with almost no instruction so that they can discover their gifts and talents for ministry. This allowed him to make the appropriate investments into the lives of the people that he was equipping for ministry.

He was also a man with a vision. Part of the discipleship and equipping of Pastor Johnson was to "Catch the vision." The vision meant seeing and embracing the mandate of evangelism and discipleship. So regardless if you were a pastor, teacher, or ministry leader at a church, whatever role you played in the church's ministry, he wanted you to see, understand and pursue

God's mandate for evangelism. He wanted everyone to see what he saw.

Pastor Lovely Haynes, the Pastor of St. Mark Baptist Church in South Los Angeles, considered Rocellia a man of trust and integrity. Yet, he also described him as a total radical. "He was radical in his approach to ministry. Radical in establishing his approach to the Movement," said Haynes. At his Homegoing Service, Pastor William Turner described him as a radical pastor. He said that he was Radical when he organized Bethany. He stepped outside of the box. He heard the voice and saw the vision God gave him. He was radical in building the church. He followed the direction of the Holy Spirit, which was a radical move (because he did not follow church tradition). He never had a vote in his church, which was radical. He followed scripture and the people followed him.

Pastor William Turner, the pastor of New Revelation Missionary Baptist Church in Pasadena, California, and a longtime friend of Rocellia, described him as radical: "Rocellia looked beyond his own tenure, because he knew that Bethany needed strong leadership and he invested in his successor." On the first Sunday night in December 1964, Pastor Johnson named an eighteen-year-old preacher to be his successor. That was radical because, as Turner said, "Men today are not really concerned about who comes after him."

Lee Arthur preached at Bethany for the first time on that first Sunday night in December during the Communion service. After preaching his sermon, Pastor Johnson stood and announced to the congregation that L.A. Kessee would be the next pastor of Bethany. "I was shocked," Lee Arthur said about the announcement. Before that time, Lee Arthur said he didn't have a relationship with Rocellia to speak of beyond Pastor and member and attended one of the evening courses that Pastor

Johnson taught. "I had never even considered being a pastor. I had only been preaching one year," Lee Arthur explained. He said that Pastor said, "We're gonna give this boy some money," so the church raised $1,300 that night to send him to the historic Bishop College in Dallas, Texas. When asked how Bishop was decided upon, it was Pastor Johnson's urging. According to Lee Arthur, he planned to go to Los Angeles and get rich. He didn't have any plans to go to college. One Sunday evening, weeks after he had preached, Pastor Johnson happened to walk into the area where the class was taught, coincidentally only Lee Arthur was present, walked up to Lee Arthur and said, "You need to get your butt ready to go to Bishop College. You got too much on the ball to sit around here on that little job you got." Lee Arthur responded, "Yes, sir." That's when he decided he was going to Bishop College.

They didn't even really know each other. Lee Arthur had only been a preacher for about fifteen months, but his older brother Richard and his father were also preachers. He had only known Rocellia for about six months when he visited and joined Bethany for the first time on the fifth Sunday in May 1964. His family members, which included his older sister, her husband, and his cousin all sang in the choirs and were already members. He said that before his arrival in Los Angeles his family had already determined that he would join Bethany and sing in the choir, so that's what he did.

Lee Arthur admitted, "I had never met a man like him." Rocellia had made a tremendous impression upon Lee Arthur by that time. Lee Arthur said that as a teenager, "I was scared to death of him. He was the most authoritative [fellow] I had seen in my life. I had never seen anybody who just barks out and issues orders, 'that you do this, you do that' and people did what he said do." Lee Arthur said that his idea was, "I thought that this guy has something [on] between him and God and what he said do was what God was commanding you." His parents and pastor back home had talked to Lee Arthur about college, but they didn't "bark it as an order" as Rocellia did.

Here's another example of Pastor Johnson investing in someone. According to Lee Arthur, Rocellia had strongly encouraged him to attend Bishop College after being at Bethany for six months. So, part of his ministerial formation was from Pastor Johnson and the other part was from his experiences and friendships at Bishop College. Lee Arthur shared, "I credit him for all that I've been ever able to do ministry wise, places I've ever gone, my ministry, people who I've met, the great preachers that I became friends with over the years, and I [contribute] it all to Preacher." While he was at Bishop, they'd talk occasionally, and he'd always visit Pastor Johnson at Bethany when he was in Los Angeles. Immediately out of college, before graduating, he was called to be the pastor of True Vine Baptist Church near Los Angeles. In his role, as a new pastor, he maintained fellowship with Pastor Johnson and Bethany. He was there when they marched into big Bethany. He later hosted a Workshop at his church in Port Arthur, Texas. He preached in some of the Marathons until he formally agreed to reunite with Pastor Johnson and Bethany around Thanksgiving and was announced as the Executive Pastor in January 1994.

A Ministry Innovator

Pastor Johnson recognized "the reality in the Black church," and admonished the evangelism team leadership to "be aware of the kind of things that we are up against, what we must overcome in this particular movement."[18] He was able to understand and anticipate some of those challenges would come from the tension between the seeming newness of the National Evangelism Movement, church traditions, or what Pastor Johnson commonly referred to as church rituals. He also recognized the need for change because he saw the church as a change agent. All of this made him a ministry innovator.

Innovation is not just about ideas and new things. It's also about thinking differently about an issue to solve it. Rocellia understood and appreciated church tradition. He also recognized that sometimes you have to innovate church tradition to solve problems that were negatively affecting the ministry of the local church. Rocellia saw the church as a change agent. In a message at a Workshop in Port Arthur, Texas, he explained that in many ways the church has been bogged down in traditions without any signs of change. He said that God is depending upon the church to bring about the kind of change that He expects in the earth.[19]

By "church" he was not talking about one particular local church. He thought the church had to embody the change and sense of renewal and reconciliation that it represented. Ray Brown, the Lead Pastor of Resurrection Baptist Church in San Antonio, Texas, shared that early on as a pastor, he'd grown tired of the traditional church himself. He said, "I grew up in the seventies and so you know all the things that were more traditional back then and I just thought they were outdated coming into the nineties. Even the conventions were traditional. During the nineties, I saw in other pastors too, a disconnect from the local church to the convention. The local church could come to the convention and participate with your finances, but you could not take anything back. I just thought it was a waste of my time and money to go to the convention and there's nothing I can bring to my church from the convention. It was different in the earlier years, but now it is not a criticism of the convention. It's just something that happens in Christianity, churches, conventions, they don't change with the times rapidly or easily. So, the first thing that I saw with this process through Dr. Johnson, was that he was continually adapting to the powers. His thing was to throw out tradition and to set up things in your churches and even in your preaching things that meet practical needs."

Pastor Johnson spoke often against church traditions and rituals, but the truth was he was not against tradition. He enjoyed his church anniversaries with his pastor friends on those 3:30 p.m. church services and the traditions of preaching and other things. Overall, he respected tradition, but he saw how it could stifle the work of ministry. Rocellia had actually embraced a "traditioned innovation" perspective to solve ministry problems within the church, particularly the black church when it came to taking new approaches to teaching and discipleship. There was no tension between them in his mind, between tradition and change.

Tradition refers to the passing of customs or beliefs from generation to generation, or the fact of being passed on in this way. They are all things that you do because "that's the way it's always been done." However, there are times when some of these traditions need to be examined and changed when they prevent the mission of Christ to be fulfilled or cause problems. This is what Rocellia recognized. He had the discernment to see and point out areas where many churches were putting too much emphasis on programs.

In the New Testament, Jesus' teaching was considered irreverent and radical. However, he proclaimed that his approach was not to destroy the Old Testament teachings, but to fulfill them (Luke 24:44). However, it required a newness. Jesus required that the people rethink how things were to work, make it new again, renovate it.

Pastor Johnson operated from a theology of God's church that understood and wanted to fulfill its mission. The main point is that innovation doesn't always signify a break in the old way of doing things. "Traditioned innovation" describes a way of thinking and living that points toward the future in light of the past, a habit of being that requires both a deep fidelity to the tradition that has borne us to the present and a radical openness to the innovations that will carry us forward in the work of ministry to equip the saints that Paul discussed in Ephesians 4:11-12, where Paul wrote, "And He Himself gave some to be apostles, some prophets, some evangelists, and some pastors and teachers, for the equipping of the saints for the work of ministry, for the edifying of the body of Christ."[20] Rocellia understood this distinction.

Although he didn't use the word "innovation" often, he clearly understood the need for change, saw the church as an agent of change and recognized that many people were uncomfortable with change. Yet, in his usual manner, he addressed it head-on. He told a group at a Workshop,

> If you don't think change is threatening, if you do not think change will upset you, brethren who are married tonight, go home and sleep on the other side of the bed. Sister you just come home and sit in your husband's favorite chair. Don't give him his regular spot at the table. Don't give him his regular cup that he usually drinks coffee or tea out of, just change. And I guarantee you will get some reaction.[21]

So Rocellia recognized that the change from tradition to innovation could be more difficult for some than it is for others. His work often introduced a potentially uncomfortable change. The change he sought was to expand teaching in the church, to expand the duties of the local pastor from preacher to teacher, to establish teaching and counseling at the church, to extend the hours that the church is open, knowing that all of these things would be foreign and frightening to some preachers.

Ann Woodborne said that her former pastor and a close associate of Pastor Johnson was disinterested in the Evangelism Movement because he perceived it as some new fad. He said,

"We're not doing that new thing," as if evangelism was new and its perceived newness made it bad. On the contrary, the message of evangelism was not newly invented, however, there was a newness then for the Evangelism Movement because it was a fresh methodology for witnessing and discipleship that had been neglected in many local churches. That perceived newness left some church leaders unable to distinguish it from a church anniversary, musical, or some other program and made many pastors see it as untraditional and undesired.

Pastor Johnson understood the dichotomy that confronted the acceptance of the Movement. Some traditions might make his vision difficult to understand and accept. There were also material issues such as costs and resources. So as an innovator he built solutions within his efforts to address certain problems that he saw. To these types of concerns, Rocellia said,

> See, there were some programs in the church, that we tried to stimulate and energize and move the church on, that are man-made: Men's Day, Women's Day, Anniversaries, Annual Days and they're just what they say, a day. Men's day don't live all day long. It's superficial. Women's Day. I don't care how many people respond you are dealing with something God cannot bless. If God doesn't bless it, it's not going nowhere.[22]

Rocellia recognized that in some ways that some traditions served to frame how church was to be perceived and experienced, which could limit the work of ministry. So, he was conscious of how his work in the Movement was respectful, but he was not restrained or bound by tradition, nor was he afraid of change. He confronted this dichotomy of tradition and mission to help pastors and churches to understand its calling and focus. Yet, it was his desire and obligation to honor the Word of God, sound biblical doctrine, and good theology. Whether tradition or comfort or status quo, he refused to be restrained by anything that could lead him away or distract him from the work of the church. So, it was Pastor Johnson's respect for tradition and the need for change that helped him to orchestrate an approach that fit the context of his ministry.

In the Evangelism Workshops, he conducted sessions that addressed the specific roles and areas of ministry responsibility for people to learn the things that would be most specific to them at their church (Read Chapter 9). There were breakout sessions for returning and new pastors to help them understand their role, while also giving them a private forum to ask questions and discuss concerns. Pastor Johnson also made sure that people knew that there was no charge for these Workshops and materials.

Rocellia and his team developed an infrastructure that would support every pastor and church, at no expense to the church, which typically included sending teachers from Bethany to teach at a church to get them started. Lastly, he engaged the efforts of Pastors Washington, Haynes and Heath and others to be team members that were able to provide valuable roles of their own experiences and testimonies to pastors new to this topic.

This issue of tradition versus innovation raises the question of what would he do for the church today? This is something we could never know, but we can know that he would anticipate the problems and find ways to solve them. He'd probably call a meeting and listen to people. He'd respect traditions. One thing

Pastor Johnson and his daughter Rosalyn in his office at big Bethany.

for sure, he would never remain in the status quo.

As a minister, he was a shepherd, a preacher, teacher, evangelist, pastor, visionary and innovator. In all these roles, God used Rocellia not just to lead an untraditional ministry but to shape a unique congregation of devoted and gifted disciples. Much of which was formed by his thoughts on the role of the local church and her pastor. The church was to go teach and make disciples and the pastors were to equip the saints for the work of ministry. In the next several chapters you'll be introduced to his unusual ministry, beginning with his theology of the church and a glimpse into the history of Bethany, the people of Bethany and how they did church and ministry.

THE MINISTRY

2

A Theology of Church

I n his book *Religious Education in the African American Tradition: A Comprehensive Introduction*, Kenneth Hill wrote, "The church, as the central institution in the Black community, has carried forth its educational ministry to form, inform, and transform people in Christ," which "created an environment of spiritual awareness" that has contributed to forming "communal identity."[23] There was a perception held by Rocellia that many Black churches began to adopt a long list of traditions and practices that were not truly congruent with the church's evangelistic mission. So, he modeled a church based on his theology of a local church – active, open and untraditional. In his views of the church, Rocellia seemed to think about the church, not the way churchgoers do about who we know, the sermons, the choir, where we like to sit, etc., but from God's perspective - what he said about her, her purpose and duties for God.

The Bible speaks of "church" as an assembly of people (Acts 19:32, 39), as a local place of worship or house of God (Matt. 21:13), and as a universal group of believers (1 Cor. 1:2) over whom Jesus is the head (Eph. 1:22; Col. 1:18). It refers to people "called out" for God's particular purpose, a purpose that includes the church's role in the world and its internal practices and traditions. Regarding the building, Rocellia said some people incorrectly saw it as a place where the people operate, instead, he saw the building as the base where the church operates from. This view helped shape his theology about mission and the church.

Theology is the study of the nature of God. There is a theology of the church called "ecclesiology," which is the name for the systematic study of the church according to scripture. Ecclesiology was not a term that Rocellia would use, as he liked to speak in down-to-earth words that anybody could understand, but his theology of the church was as well-developed as any seminary professors. As such, he was intent on developing a local church according to God's standards, a church not restrained by manmade rituals and traditions.

There was a common misconception among many local churches that their goal was to get people to come to the building as if that was the mandate of Jesus Christ, instead of going to be witnesses and introducing people to the saving knowledge of Jesus Christ. The goal was worship, not discipleship. In some churches, members were voted into the church to become members, despite the idea of "whosoever will let them come" from the Book of Revelation 22:17 that says, "And the Spirit and the bride say, 'Come!' And let him who hears say, 'Come!' And let him who thirsts come. Whoever desires, let him take the water of life freely" (Rev. 22:17, NKJV). Rocellia was so against the practice of voting in members that he wrote into Bethany's bylaws that "There shall be no vote." Churches would also sell barbeque and chicken dinners to raise money and he was against those approaches to fundraising also. He would always say that tithing among its members should be the way the church funds its activities. Churches would often define duties like singing in the choir, ushering and deaconing as Christian service, instead of recognizing the need for biblical ministry. Teaching was limited to the weekly Bible study by the pastor and Sunday School classes were conducted each week without an emphasis on systematic biblical instruction and disciple-making. So, throughout his ministry he confronted the various thoughts and misconceptions that had shaped many of these activities, "traditions and rituals," as he called them, that had affected the local churches outlook and approach to ministry. To these issues, Pastor Johnson said,

> There are many things that we are asking God to bless that he would have to go against himself. God can't be true to himself and bless some of the things we are asking him to bless.[24]

Pastor Johnson's emphasis on teaching the Bible, making disciples and training people to be witnesses gave him a unique theology of the church – what God says and thinks about the church. As such, Rocellia was keenly aware of the issues that he saw within local churches that prevented them from fully implementing ministry efforts and meeting Christ's mandate for ministry. As a practical theologian, he could see the church the way he thought God saw his church – being alive, accessible to people in need and doing the work of the ministry, which largely involved Christian education and evangelism. His criticism was often that the church had fallen asleep and he was concerned with the reliance on church programs to grow the church instead of a focus on Christian ministry.

In a teacher's Training workshop in Phoenix, Arizona in 1989, Rocellia said that,

> The strength of the church is discipleship not just going to church. Just because you are delivering a message, just because you are playing a religious role that is not conclusive in itself that you are being a follower of Christ. When it comes to being a follower of Christ you don't have

to guess and speculate as to what's involved in that process, because the Lord Jesus laid down the prerequisite for being a disciple, for being his followers.[25]

At one point in time at the start of the worship services at Bethany, the choir would march down the center aisle singing and as they reached the front of the church, the announcement from a minister in the pulpit was, "It's time to worship." Eventually, Pastor Johnson did away with that practice because he felt that "It was always time to worship, not just when you show up." He held the position that the doors of the church were always open, and the lights should literally never go out. He saw God's church as a living organism that should always remain open and never close. This meant that the church should be open and alive, active in the lives of people with people coming and going 'like a supermarket," as he once told Pastor Washington. His point was that God's church had a mandate and mission to fulfill. He once said it this way,

> There is evidence everywhere that the church is asleep. Our efforts over the years and over the times have been feeble in trying to arouse the church to serve. Not that we have not tried. We've tried but our efforts have been feeble and unsuccessful in waking the church. The Church of God is not a weak organization. The church is a giant. There's no place that the church can't go. There's nothing the church can't do. There is no service they can't be rendered by the church if the church was awake. Literally, we have a sleeping giant on our hands…But what we've been trying to wake the church with doesn't keep it awake. I'm just going to cut across the field and say it like it is. We've been trying to do mission work sitting around the table serving coffee and cake and soda crackers and soda water and trying to have a mission… We've been trying to wake the church up with

musicals and get all the choirs together where they stand and sing just like they're looking God in the face and the time they get through singing if you're not careful they get up and walk out... Then sometimes we tell them to stick around we might need you to sing. You don't come to church to sing you just sing because you come to church. You come to church because of who God is... And once we take mission out of the program category. Mission is not something you do on the side. Mission is not something you do if you have time, mission is not something you do if you can fit it into your program. The Church of God is mission. Mission is a mandate of the Church of God. You don't have no choice if we're going to do missions. There's no board that decides if we ought to have mission. No Mothers Board. It's not a program. So, we've been trying to keep the church awake on man-made programs. We've been trying to revive the church on man-made situations. See there's a difference between a program and a movement. In the Church of God programs are man-made, period. A movement is God ordained, God instituted, God-energized and God-directed. Until we get with that, mission ain't going nowhere.[26]

In some notes from a church meeting, he wrote:

Did you all know that perhaps 90% of the Baptist churches are closed. Not just Sunday nights but closed for most of the part of the week. Many times, when they'd open up it was for choir rehearsal and Wednesday night prayer meeting and Bible study. We open seven days a week but I'm praying that not just seven days a week but seven days a week and twenty-four hours a day. As long as there is somebody roaming the streets, somebody in trouble, somebody needs help, the Church of God ought to be and can be open.[27]

He provided remarks that were captured in a church meeting on January 23, 1977, to encourage and challenge the ministry leaders to catch the vision of the church:

> I want you to see beyond the walls of a forty-voice choir, three hundred members, ten ushers, ten deacons, half a dozen nurses and members sitting around just having church with no idea as to what God's program is for the church and I'm endeavoring to get you out of some of it. When you don't stand behind the overall total church program, I don't need you as a leader.[28]

In pastoral circles over the years, there have been many books, classes, and seminars about "growing the church," i.e., increasing its attendance and membership numbers. Pastor Johnson held unique opinions on this topic. At its peak, Bethany's membership had increased some 20,000% from its original four members, but that still did not make it a megachurch by today's criteria. However, Bethany was "mega" in its expansive outreach and influence: Through its Workshops and other ministries, Bethany interacted with and mobilized untold thousands of people each week in worship, Bible study classes, evangelism counseling and visits in churches all over the country.

Rocellia didn't measure growth by the number of seats filled each week. Church growth for him was not a numerical or quantifiable measurement. It was a spiritual measurement based on a believer's growth in Christlike maturity and Christian service. Thus, Rocellia always focused on the number of classes being offered, the number of students and the number of teams and visits that were being conducted each week. The number of churches involved within the Movement was also an important measure. These numbers mattered to Rocellia for they reflected Christian discipleship and service in action.

He seemed to take all these thoughts and concerns about the local church into consideration when he thought about the church God called him to launch. So, he founded a local church that would embrace worship and ministry the way God thought about it. His church would be an assembly of believers that lived out their collective calling to be witnesses for God. They would be devoted to worship, committed to studying his word and sent to share the Gospel. It would be a church alive to the needs of people and to the mission of evangelism, and open to responding in a way that honored God and fulfills His mandate. Rocellia took all those thoughts and concerns about the church into consideration when he thought about his church and named that church the Bethany Baptist Church of West Los Angeles.

3

Bethany: A Historicity

The Bible speaks of Bethany as a city that Jesus frequented. The story of why Rocellia chose the name Bethany was not reported, but it's important to understand the significance of Bethany in the Bible. Bethany was situated "at" the Mount of Olives (Mark 11:1; Luke 19:29), about fifteen stadia (i.e., 1 1/2 or 2 miles) from Jerusalem (John 11:18). It has been described as "remarkably beautiful, the perfection of retirement and repose, of seclusion and lovely peace."[29] It was known as the place where Jesus raised his friend Lazarus from the dead (John 11-12), where Jesus was anointed with oil by his friend Mary at the home of Simon the Leper (John 12:3), and perhaps more significantly as the place where he blessed his disciples before his final ascension (Luke 24:50-53). This chapter will attempt to provide a historicity - a factual historical accounting of the Bethany Baptist Church of West Los Angeles.

In its history, Bethany Baptist Church of West Los Angeles under Rocellia Johnson resided at three different locations. Each location seemed to illustrate a period of Bethany's growth and stages of ministry. Little Bethany signified its beginning and formation. Big Bethany, which was the church building that moved to the corner of King and Hillcrest, signified its maturity, which launched the Movement. Bethany's move across the street signified its restoration and the church where Pastor retired and said goodbye. In this chapter we will take a look at each phase, beginning with the origin and historical chronology of the Bethany Baptist Church of West Los Angeles. This chapter introduces the historical legend and phenomenon of the Bethany Baptist Church of West Los Angeles from its founding at little Bethany, to its growth and outreach at big Bethany to the rebuilding of the current church.

Little Bethany (1958-1971)

On October 24, 1978, at the Bethany Baptist Church, an annual church meeting was held. In those meetings, each night of the week Dan Dawson read from a document that provided a historical review of the Bethany Baptist Church. On the first night, Dan began with a greeting to the many guest churches in attendance, the preachers in the pulpit, Pastor Johnson and his older brother Pastor E.C. Johnson. Dan explained that it was a history that was compiled from the original minutes of the first organizing meeting on May 15, 1958, that came as Dan wrote: "in the channel of time." Dan spoke so eloquently of that historic day,

> On this date, God established another part of the vineyard, that a man could till the soil and bring forth fruit from the harvest. Many enjoy the comforts and beauty that surround us today. But it has not always been as you now see. Stained glass windows and all that meets the eye was yet future when God began to put together the Bethany Baptist Church of West Los Angeles.

From this, Dan provided a historical record of how God "during the time of the old economy" called and bestowed "gifts for services" through the Holy Spirit to men and women of His church. He went on to reference Ephesians 4:11 when he added that, to some the Lord gave the gifts to preach, to teach and to evangelize. He went on to speak about the "undershepherd," which was the Reverend Rocellia Johnson.

Pastor Johnson would also tell the story of the first official meeting of Bethany Baptist Church and the original members. The first meeting was held at 9:30 a.m. on that May 29th date at the home of Vernice "Tiny" Moore on South Van Ness Street, with a purpose to organize the church. Present at that meeting were Pastor Johnson and the other three founding members Kelly Bollin, Vernice "Tiny" Moore and Annie V. Dawson. Pastor's wife Dorothy was a very talented musician and choir director at Mt. Gilead. Dorothy was also from Tulsa, Oklahoma, with her parents Reverend John Little and her mother Rosa. They moved to Los Angeles in 1945. Reverend Little had pastored two churches before joining Mt. Gilead, then Bethany. At a church meeting that was conducted at her and Rocellia's home on July 7, 1958, Dorothy joined Bethany and committed her talents and service to the small church family.[30] She and Pastor had married in October 1951 and gave birth to their daughter Rosalyn in 1958, the same year that Bethany opened.

Despite her immeasurable contributions, Dorothy is mentioned somewhat sparingly in the book, incommensurate with her contribution to Rocellia's ministry or the ministry of the Bethany Baptist Church. So, it's important to take a minute here to acknowledge her contributions to Bethany. Throughout their marriage, Dorothy was a dignified, gracious and glorious complement to Rocellia and his ministry. Dorothy was blessed with a warm, open and engaging personality that allowed her to be approachable and to relate with people. She was also uniquely gifted in her own right as a singer, musician, choir director, prayer warrior and First Lady.

Above: First four members of Bethany from left to right: Pastor Rocellia
Johnson, Vernice Moore, Kelly Bollin and Annie V. Dawson.
Below: Rocellia and Dorothy on Bethany's first church Anniversary.

These giftings helped make Dorothy the ideal complement for Rocellia and First Lady for Bethany. She was a partner and had a voice in his decision-making. She opened her home to church meetings. She was present at those meetings, not just in attendance, but involved, offering her voice. She allowed families from the church to stay at her home when they needed a place to stay. She traveled with Rocellia in his work across the country. She played music for him when he preached and led the choir. She took the role of Prayer Coordinator. She was always supportive of him, the Bethany family and its community of churches. In all, Dorothy was able to minister as a Christian, as a wife and as a servant out of her personality, gifted with her own sense of calling to the Lord. It can be viewed this way: Bethany embodied Rocellia's doctrinal philosophies and Christian beliefs and Dorothy's warm, friendly personality. Overall, her commitment, sacrifices and contributions to the history of Bethany were immeasurable. Bethany could have never become the church known to many around the country without her support to her husband and service to the ministry of the church.

In that historical report, Dan said that the church joined together in song to sing "Jesus Keep Me Near the Cross," which he said had been their prayer. Pastor Johnson prayed and read from 2 Timothy 4:9, which says: "Be diligent to come to me quickly" (NKJV). The verse spoke to Pastor Johnson's recognition of the daunting nature of his task and that he would need the Lord to be present as his help.[31] They collected a total offering of $21.50. As Dan had recorded, Pastor Johnson and Deacon Kelley Bollin gave $10 each and Vernice Moore and Annie Dawson both contributed fifty cents apiece with fifty-cents unaccounted for. In their first four months, they had $125.09 in the church's treasury, enough to pay the $70 fee to incorporate in the state of California.

It was Dan Dawson that may have provided the most prophetic description of Rocellia, when he noted that Pastor Rocellia

Johnson as "an unusual kind of man." In looking back, he could see that Rocellia's calling was a special calling for a special job to get a special work underway for God."

In that historical record, Pastor Johnson was noted for his "unusual leadership." He was that "undershepherd who was called, placed in the position of leadership at Bethany to "till this portion of God's vineyard [and] would be the one who would hear the voice of God, understand the vision and carry the message of salvation."[32] Dan tells the story of Vernice Moore and Annie V. Dawson, two of those founding members, that weren't members of any particular church and when asked about their relationship with Christ, they said that they "loved the Lord, but if they were to join a church their desire was to be pastored by a man that they'd known because they long for his unusual leadership." They concluded that if they found that pastor, they would serve him with a willing heart. Pastor Johnson had a style that attracted members.

"Unusual" is an interesting word used to describe a pastor, but in Rocellia's case, it was a fitting description because of the way he approached his pastoral duties and philosophy in a way that was unconventional and untraditional. He was organized in his approach and decisions. On June 23rd of that same year, Pastor called a group together to complete the organizational structure of the church. In this meeting, they developed church policies, but they also had the wherewithal to look into the future of Bethany to see some potential "problem areas." It was in these discussions that Pastor Johnson addressed some of the "traditional church policies," which could become detrimental to the growth of the church.[33] These views would provide important themes in his ministry. Later as the church grew, Rocellia conceived of the idea of the Coordination Board.

Rocellia Johnson at little Bethany.

In 1960, the Coordination Board was introduced to establish and promote better communication and harmonious leadership among the various auxiliaries of the church. Pastor Johnson initially selected seven members –Oscar Harvey, William Calhoun, Howard Scott, Johnnie Starks, Annie Dawson and Carolyn Lewis with Pastor Johnson as the seventh member of the Coordination Board. Their jobs were to represent each of the auxiliaries of the church. The idea was to bring together each leader and group in ways that assisted with ministry coordination, shared information, addressed inter-departmental issues and provided spiritual support.[34] The Coordination Board would conduct periodic meetings with Pastor Johnson to provide a periodic forum and foster cooperation and a working relationship among the leadership and members of the church.

From its inception to 1978, the church had grown to at least fifty different departments. The expansion of ministries and departments represented a type of gathering at the church, but a scattering within it. This meant that there was a necessity to ensure organization within the church.

Five policies were recorded in the historical record. Several of the policies covered basic items, like the hours of service would start at 10:40 a.m. and end at 12:00 p.m., the pronouncement of an annual church meeting, and the weekly Bible study would be conducted at 8 p.m. to 9:30 p.m. each Tuesday night. Two other policies had much more significance. Top on the list was that "No member would be received into the Church by Roberts Rules of Order. There shall be no vote," because Jesus said "Whosoever will, let him come"(Matt. 8:34; Rev. 22:17).[35] The second noteworthy policy, as mentioned earlier, was that "There shall be no buying or selling for the support of the Church, because the Prophet Malachi said in Malachi 3:10 to God's people, "Bring all the tithes into the storehouse, That there may be food in My house, And try Me now in this," Says the LORD of hosts, "If I will not open for you the windows of heaven And pour out for you such blessing That there will not be room enough to receive it" (NKJV). These policies touched on local church traditions that Pastor Johnson spoke against often and was a central part of his theology of the church. Dan noted that "Pastor strove to remove the myths that had crept into our churches."

His unusual nature that was evident early in his ministry was also evident in several more public ways. The first unusual observation was that Pastor Rocellia was known to stand outside in his suit watering the grass around the church. Annie Walker (who would eventually marry and change her name to Emerson) was nine years old when she joined the church after hearing about the young church when some of the men of the church were passing out flyers, while she and her mother were at a nearby grocer. She told the story that on some afternoons Pastor Johnson was seen outside watering the grass of the church dressed in his full three-piece suit, white shirt, necktie and shined shoes. She said he would get odd looks from the people in the neighborhood because that was not a usual task or look for the pastor of a church.

In 1966 when Margaret Green (now Williams) had visited Bethany and one weekday happened to be driving around the church to take a closer look at the church, she saw Pastor Johnson outside sweeping the street. She decided then that was the church and pastor for her. In 1971, Billy Turner remembered seeing Pastor Johnson alone cleaning out some clogged sewage in the back of the building at big Bethany and just like Margaret, he decided to join Bethany because of that. Margaret said, "He'd tell pastors in the Workshops – 'Man, you gotta roll up your sleeves and let the people see you doing some of the work. You can't send people and you don't go yourselves'" He was about setting an example for others would follow.

Several decades later he explained his thoughts about this in a sermon. He said that even as pastor sometimes you have to sweep the floor. He explained that sometimes you have to show God you're grateful, by doing some things that you are not accustomed to doing. He continued to explain that sometimes in the ministry you have to do things that are not in your job description, but people may need to see you doing the work that you've been trying to get them to do. Rocellia jested, "I'm the organist. I'm the pianist. I am the director, but God knows I can't play. I can't sing. He already knows that I can't carry a tune in a suitcase. So, what does he do? If he sees you doing what you ought to do, God will send you somebody." He added that if you didn't have people to help you, then you have a different problem. He told the story that one day he was at Bethany dressed in his work clothes working in the yard of the church. He said,

> One time at the Bethany Baptist Church, I had on work clothes. I had on some big'ol coveralls. I was working. I was watering the lawn and trimming the grass and straightening up the flowers and what have you. I walked into a church and somebody asked me if they could use the facilities on that particular day and I was glad to make the facilities available to them, so I said sure. While I was working, I came into the sanctuary, in my work clothes. The people were just closing down their affair. There was a little lady there, as I was walking in, that had something tacked up on the wall and said [to me], "Hey would you get that down." I said sure. I got a chair, a ladder, or something, but by that time somebody else up walked in and said "Hey Pastor what are you doing [up there]. That lady liked a fainted. She had never seen a pastor dressed like that, doing menial work like that.[36]

The second seemingly unusual item was in his choice of Bethany despite its location. One Sunday afternoon, Pastor Johnson approached some men that had gathered and from their discussion became aware of a church building and a house on its property that was for sale for a $5,000 down payment. Pastor Johnson was excited about the opportunity because the church was outgrowing the living rooms where they had been meeting and needed a large stable place to worship. He went with his trusted friend Rev. George Hall and brother-in-law to see the building that would become little Bethany.[37]

Upon visiting the area where the church was located, they learned that the church resided in what was at that time an Asian community. As Dan told the story, "There was little to no black families that lived in those neighborhoods." Pastor and Reverend Hall went to the schoolyard and didn't see any black children playing in the schoolyard, which left them disheartened because they went trusting that this was where God wanted them to be. Pastor Hall turned to Rocellia to say, "Surely this was not the place." They drove home, but neither man spoke during the ride. When Pastor arrived home, Dan said that Rocellia said he heard God speak to him in that still small voice to say, "This place I give to you. Take it and work it and I will be with you." Pastor returned later but this time he didn't notice race or color, only the possession that God promised to give him. He made a vow to God saying, "God, if you give me this place, I will surely teach your word." This represented the birth of little Bethany and the ministerial approach of Rocellia Johnson. He would faithfully honor his commitment to the Lord and become a great teacher, lead a community of teachers and launch a Movement for God to teach other pastors and churches.

Despite Rocellia's covenant with God, when other people began to hear the news of the church opening, they thought it was foolish and doomed for failure and wanted no part of it because it was supposed to be a black congregation, but there were no black folks in the area.[38] It was understood that black churches in those days and even today reside in black communities because that is where the black folks were. So, this was considered unusual, maybe even nonsensical. Nevertheless, on the fourth Sunday of September in 1958, only six months after their initial meeting at Vernice Moore's home, they had acquired the church property. They were permitted to move in and take possession before they had closed escrow. The audacity of this young black pastor and his tiny membership! This was considered a signal to them that God was with them.

This decision was a deal. In many ways, the significance of this decision has been overlooked and certainly unappreciated. To appreciate the groundbreaking nature of this decision, it's important to recognize the historical context of this decision within the context of Black history. The Brooklyn Dodgers had moved to L.A. earlier that year. The Los Angeles Lakers wouldn't arrive until 1960, which was two years after little Bethany opened its doors. Disneyland was only three years old. Perhaps more importantly, in 1958, when Bethany opened, the vast majority of African American churches in Los Angeles were located South and East of the city crowded in predominantly black communities. When black folks migrated to Los Angeles they typically settled in communities south of the city, like Baldwin Hills, West Adams, Central, Exposition Park, South Vermont, Watts, and areas further east and south. This meant that the majority of its Black members would not live near the church.

It was a period in Los Angeles when the city was still recovering from the bombing, violence and burning crosses on the lawns of Black families south of Slauson Boulevard. White gangs were rioting in suburbs like Compton and fought integration to keep many black families from moving into the neighborhood. Residential covenants were established to continue to perpetuate segregation.[39] So Rocellia's decision to choose this area for his little church demonstrated bravery to make decisions and showed his faith that the people would come.

Above: Little Bethany. Below: Big Bethany.

There were very few, if any, Black churches north of Venice and west of Arlington Boulevard because those weren't considered black communities. To locate there could invite violent retribution. It's worth noting that even as of this writing there are still few if any predominantly black churches in that part of the city referred to as Arlington Heights. Now, it cannot be determined that Rocellia had this in mind. What can be determined with reasonable certainty is that his mind was not bound by demographic or social restraints or concerns. His mind and his faith allowed him to imagine such a move based on where he felt God told him to go.

Despite the possible dangers, the members of Bethany entered their new sanctuary without much pomp or ritual on that special and historic occasion. There were no news releases to announce the event. Dan noted that Pastor Johnson was the only minister in attendance along with a handful of members and a few well-wishers from Mt. Gilead. According to Dan, Rocellia sat alone as the music rang out through the small church for that first time.

When it was time for him to preach, he stood and took the title for that first historic sermon, "The Five Steps That Made Gideon Victorious" from the Book of Judges. The five steps were 1) A willingness to listen to the voice and command of God; 2) A willingness to follow divine guidance through human leadership; 3) A willingness to sacrifice for the task that lay ahead; 4) Complete and absolute organization; 5) Total dependency on God.[40] Pastor Johnson seemed to provide in that sermon the creed that would provide a baseline for how he would serve God throughout his ministry. Yet, the church continued to grow in members as a result of Pastor Johnson's preaching and teaching.

Despite its membership growth there was not enough money coming in to take care of the needs of the church. They fell six months behind on the mortgage and could not provide for Pastor

Johnson and his family. They were living on $40 per week from the church and it began to show on Pastor Johnson's appearance. His clothes began to look worn down. Annie shared that once she heard Pastor mention over the pulpit the holes in his shoes (probably commenting on his personal sacrifices for the church). She later asked him if he really had holes in his shoes and replied to her, "Well, baby, they do," then took off one of his shoes to show her the hole. This was the type of thing that made him so genuine and relatable. Yet, God remained faithful.

Dan read that, "God moved to relieve his servant that he would not be ashamed. The landlord, being moved by God's hand, cleared the debt and gave the pastor another start. A new auxiliary was formed called the "Pastors Aid" to assist the pastor in his needs. The leadership for this new ministry was filled by someone that loved Pastor Johnson dearly, Anne Lucas." To further assist the church in its financial obligations the C.E.E.A. auxiliary was also put into motion.

Big Bethany (1971-1994)

As little Bethany continued to increase in members, after thirteen short years, the membership began to outgrow its building. The historical record cited that the church continued to grow and they ran out of space. The number of auxiliaries had expanded, and each was full. The choir was filled. There were occasions during the Service where the aisles were full and people had to stand during the service. To make more room, they added an annex, the Pastor's office and a baptistry. By then they were able to pay all their bills and were able to have $18,000 in the bank. Dan noted that much of this money was contributed by Pastor Johnson because he never took the money that had been raised for him from the Pastoral Anniversaries. They had paid off their debts to position themselves to purchase a larger property.[41]

Pastor Johnson led the effort to find a new church building. He received a letter in the mail informing him about a larger church. The asking price for the building was $350,000. Dan explained that they wanted to take a look at the building. As they drove around the church this time, they saw black children playing in the schoolyard and the streets were busy. He said, "the building loomed in their sight" and they said to themselves, "This is it." It would eventually become "big Bethany."

The property probably looked like the perfect facility for the growing church and burgeoning teaching ministry. It had a sanctuary with a large choir stand and seated at least two hundred people. The north-facing wall of the sanctuary was stained glass from wall to ceiling. Next to the sanctuary, there was a large auditorium that when it's sliding door was opened it could expand the seating by almost another one hundred and fifty to two hundred more seats. There was a large spacious conference room and office space upstairs with a walk-out balcony that overlooked the areas across the street and beyond. In addition to this, annexed to the church building, there were three floors with three or four classrooms on each floor. There was also a parking lot on the property that could account for at least sixty to seventy vehicles. The church did need some painting, office and sanctuary furniture, but it was a great facility.

When they stopped to see the property, the doors were locked. Dan said he found a small unlocked door on the side of the stained glass wall near the front of the church. He was able to get in and make his way to the front door to let Pastor into the building. They asked themselves rhetorically, "Can we do it?" Their answer came to them immediately from Philippians 4:13, which says "I can do all things through Christ who strengthens me."

Above: Opening Day at big Bethany.
Below: Opening day crowd at big Bethany.

Pastor assembled the church Trustees to make plans to acquire the building. They met with bank officials that asked for a $100,000 down payment, even though they didn't have that amount of money. So, they began to figure out how to raise the money. On the following Sunday morning, Pastor Johnson made what Dan noted was an honest and sincere, but somewhat unusual prayer from his pastor. Pastor Johnson prayed something like, "Lord, make not a fool of your servant before these people. I have committed myself. I have gone out on your word. Don't make me a fool." Because they were young Christians, Dan said those words frightened them. Yet, as Pastor rose from his knees, with tears in his eyes, he began to call the names of members of the church and they came forward with $10, $20, $100, $500 and even $1,000 contributions that totaled $13,000 on that Sunday, all with a willing heart toward the new church.[42] With those contributions and God's help they were able to move forward to gather the funds to buy the new church property, but it wasn't easy. They were able to earn the $2,500 good faith money the brokers required. Yet, they were working with a pushy agent that was eventually replaced. Dan said that "God then placed another man there who was more understanding and who was tender towards this Church" that worked with them to close the deal.

Bethany still had to come up with the balance of their down payment. It seemed to happen as another expression of God's faithfulness that one morning, as Dan described, "Sullivan Lewis, the church's oldest Deacon, was at the bank and one of the bankers asked him if he knew of a church for sale. He answered, "Certainly. I know our church is for sale!" They sold little Bethany for $60,000 which put them in a position to buy the new church.[43] Again, God had favor on Bethany and allowed them to purchase this new property and continued to bless their ministry.

Pastor Johnson extending the invitation at big Bethany.

Bethany "Across the Street" (2008 – Present)

Pastor Johnson had long mentioned his vision to take possession of the property across the street from the church where the Page Four lounge, Hamburger City and a neighborhood grocery store were located. James Mitchell, an Evangelism teacher and member of the traveling Evangelism team shared the story of how one day Pastor Johnson was standing on the balcony looking across the street. He told James Mitchell that he had a vision of owning the property directly across Santa Barbara Boulevard (now Martin Luther King Boulevard) where the church was located at that time. Pastor L.A. Kessee also remembered a similar conversation in 1986, when Rocellia also told him that one day that property across the street would be the property of Bethany.

Ironically, on January 17, 1994, at 4:30 a.m. there was a 6.7 magnitude earthquake called the Northridge earthquake. There was no way to know that it would take an "act of God" in the form of an earthquake to make that happen. L.A. Kessee had just been announced as the new Executive Pastor and heir to Pastor Johnson just days before. Bethany was among the list of lost landmarks due to this quake. This event created a new story in the life of Bethany.

The church building suffered significant structural damage that could not be repaired, so the city of L.A. rendered the building non-occupiable and the church was forced to find a new home. This was an "act of God" that took down the church building that changed the history of Bethany forever. Everything had changed at that moment. Of course, the two biggest activities were the National Evangelism Movement and the Bible classes. Most people would have probably taken this as a sign to pause to regroup, to reflect and to restructure. According to Rod, "For Pastor Johnson this was business as usual…He made sure that the church never lost any traction with the school being closed, the worship or ministry ceasing because of that catastrophic event.

He was determined to make sure they continue.

Pastor Johnson called Ed Russel to meet him at the church to be the first to assess the damage to the building. The damage wasn't immediately obvious from the outside. On the inside, there were sections of the stained-glass window that stretched from floor to ceiling that were broken and left holes in the windows, as the glass littered the aisle. File cabinet drawers in the office were open and files covered the floor. In the choir stand, it looked like part of the ceiling had fallen and the chairs had been tossed about. Yet, according to Ed, Pastor didn't grieve or panic. He said that Pastor's chief concern was figuring out where they'd worship on Sunday. Other groups met prayerfully and tearfully to salvage as many items as they could before the building was taped off by the city.

Arrangements were made to rent the auditorium at Dorsey High school which was only blocks away for a month. On that initial Sunday after the earthquake the auditorium was full. Many of the people that were no longer attending Bethany showed up either out of curiosity or were pulled together by their shared grief. Ed remembered that some of the members were upset because Pastor Johnson announced that he was going to have church until his time was up. He paid until 2 p.m. and he intended to worship until 2 p.m. He wanted God to get his money's worth. Remember, it was his policy – "It's the Lord's day all day."

The congregation eventually moved from Dorsey High School because that arrangement didn't allow for them to have Sunday School. Since Ed Russell was an Assistant Principal at a nearby Junior High school at the time, named Audubon, he was able to make arrangements for the church to conduct their services at the school's auditorium on Sunday. At Audubon, they had use of the auditorium all day and were not only able to have Sunday School but other activities, such as the BCBC graduations. Bethany

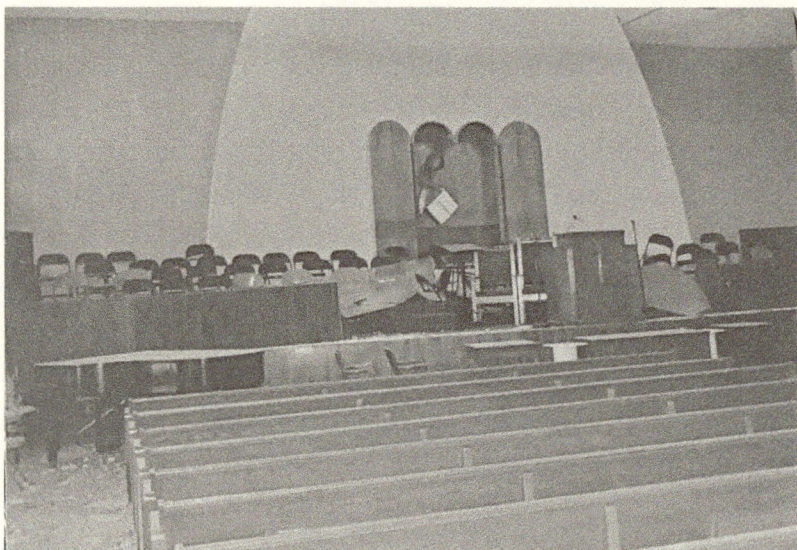

Above: Damage to the sanctuary windows.
Below: Damage to the church sanctuary.

Building demolition.

For the first time in its thirty-six-year history, Bethany had been displaced. This meant that regardless of their collective faith, this had to be difficult. There had to be a level of grief and shock that had confronted that congregation. All of them prayed and some cried. There is a theology of place throughout the Bible, which asserts that even though God is present everywhere, place has a unique significance in how God deals with his people. God creates places for his people to have a relationship with Him. This means that for the believer, place is not just physical and geographical. Place is also spiritual and symbolic of God's presence and provision, like Adam in the Garden, Israel in the Promised land, the wilderness, or in exile. For Israel, it was always about the land. Some members still struggle to try to make sense of this event from a spiritual standpoint. So, the loss of the building likely created a moment of grief and sadness that had a significant impact on many of the members at that time and thereafter.

Despite Rocellia's determination, some church members experienced a sense of homelessness or placelessness. There was a shared grief by some members over the loss of the building. It wasn't just the building, but all that it represented and provided. It had been the place of worship and community. It was the place where many had come to know Christ. It was the place where members went to talk, to see friends and engage in meaningful fellowship. Some members needed time to deal with it emotionally and some never did, choosing to join other churches. In the end, some members were able to push through the transition and others addressed it by leaving Bethany altogether.

During this challenging period of transition, the administration of the church had become decentralized and activities were scattered in many locations. Yet, they never missed a quarter providing classes for the students. Classes were held briefly at the Consolidated Plaza in Baldwin Hills, at Victory Institutional

Baptist Church under Pastor Richard Williams and Liberty Baptist Church under Pastor Cotton. The Bible school was renamed from the Bethany Christian Training Institute to the Bethany Christian Bible College (BCBC) in 1992. Staff meetings, the monthly in-service teacher training meetings and other meetings were held at Pastor and Dorothy's home, Pleasant Hill Baptist Church and Mt. Gilead Baptist Church.[44] Sunday services were conducted at Audubon Junior High school. Communion and baptism services were conducted at Mt. Gilead Baptist church and the Evangelism department offices were moved to Pleasant Hill Baptist Church with Pastor Sylvester Washington. Eventually, the church built a temporary bungalow (called "the Module") at the original church site to conduct classes until it was moved across the street to its current site. Overall, the church remained in some level of transition for approximately twelve years after the earthquake.

In Pastor Johnson's Homegoing service, his grandson Vaughn mentioned the earthquake that destroyed the church building and that different groups of people would hold meetings at their home and attempted to offer advice on what to do to address the church's issues. Vaughn said that Pastor would "shoo them all down." The decline in membership continued and people would offer more advice and Pastor Johnson never seemed to accept their advice. Vaughn said eventually he and his big sister Blaze, now teenagers, were in the kitchen with his grandparents Dorothy and Rocellia and decided to ask why he didn't take some of their suggestions. Rocellia took that as an opportunity to teach. His response to them was, "I wouldn't care if I showed up to church on Sunday and wasn't nobody in there but me and Dorothy. She gonna play that piano, and I'm gonna preach my sermon to my wife and along the way the Lord is gone bless it." Vaughn concluded, "Sure enough, he stuck with that mind of thinking. His faith was solidified, and he put in the work that matched it and here we are."

Nevertheless, efforts to rebuild were immediate. Pastor Johnson had assembled a committee of members from the church to develop a plan to rebuild. They had already acquired the 3 ½ acres of property across the street from the church in 1994. There were plans to build a 17,000 square foot sanctuary, an 8,500 square foot multi-purpose space/gymnasium, a 2,100 square foot evangelism outreach center, a 23,000 square foot Bethany Christian Bible College, a 1,500 square foot Bethany Christian Counseling Center, a 500 square foot commercial kitchen with 2,500 square feet designated for executive office space and conference rooms.

Unfortunately, the church seemed to lack the collective expertise and leadership to develop an effective plan of action and struggled in their efforts. Bad decisions were made. There were also some financial misjudgments and misdealings on the architect' plans that did not meet building codes which caused the church to lose money and progress, Rod explained. It was about six years later when Pastor Johnson asked Rod to attend a meeting with his rebuild committee at Pleasant Hill Baptist Church. The attendees included a project team that was hired by the church. After that meeting, Rod was asked to oversee their efforts and soon assumed the role of the project manager. He was soon introduced to the church as the project manager, yet he had no experience in this area either. According to Ed, the business of the rebuilding project was managed by Rod and Pastor Johnson. They'd provide periodic updates to the congregation.

By this time the people had become frustrated, according to Rod. It was taking too long and Rod thought that some of the membership were beginning to stop listening to Pastor Johnson on this topic. Yet, Rod admitted that through all of this adversity, Rocellia "hung tough" and remained committed to the fact that he was going to trust God. Rod felt that because the church couldn't borrow any money, the church had totally collapsed from a business standpoint. Yet, as he spent more time with Pastor Johnson every day, he observed that there was no doubt "come hell or high water" that Pastor Johnson trusted God. Pastor Johnson held on publicly and there was no way to assess the weight of the personal toll that this would take on him.

The chief task was to acquire new funding, but that was not an option, so the church had to sell some of its property across the street. They entered negotiations with the Los Angeles Fire Department to purchase some of Bethany's land, but those negotiations eventually broke off when they couldn't reach an agreement on a sale price for the property. A few days after a meeting, the City sent the church a letter saying that they were no longer interested in purchasing the property. It was a "thanks but no thanks" situation. In the meantime, the whole church was waiting for updates from the meeting, from Pastor and from God. In a Coordination Board meeting to provide an update on the transaction, the room was packed with people there to get news. Rod had to explain that there was no deal. It was a somber meeting.

Two years later, Rod got a call from a city councilman stating that the City of L.A. was interested in purchasing some of the church's property again. Discussions resumed. Within a few days, the church sold a portion of their property. From that 2005 sale, they were able to sell some of the property to the Los Angeles City for the Fire Department, then lease some of the remaining land to build Stella Charter Middle School in 2018. This allowed the church to rebuild a modest church building and pay off its mortgage. In February 2020, there was a ribbon-cutting ceremony at the new school to celebrate its opening and the fulfillment of Pastor Johnson's vision of a school for the community. Through all of its adversity, some pastors may have reasoned through this type of experience that God was not with them. Yet, Pastor

Johnson remained faithful throughout the entire experience. He never wavered, stayed strong through all the problems, mistakes, setbacks and disbelief. He had demonstrated his faith in God and his ministry never stopped.

The Ground-Breaking Ceremony (1997)

On a hot sunny Sunday morning on June 30, 1997, the people of Bethany gathered across the street as Pastor had envisioned for their Groundbreaking ceremony. Many of the men were dressed in their suits, the women were in dresses, some wearing hats and others waving fans, as most of them stood in the dirt and gravel (and shade-less) lot that would eventually become their new church home. The buildings had been removed, but you could still see some of the lines that marked the prior parking spaces.

Pastor Johnson stood in a beige suit, white shirt and necktie with sweat shining on his forehead that didn't seem to bother him. His wife Dorothy, L.A. Kessee, Joe Lee, Ed Russell and many other guests sat behind him. His message was entitled, "One Point Address" from 2 Chronicles 7:14. He talked about the ancient temple of Jerusalem but focused on the healing of the land. After Rocellia spoke, Lee Arthur dedicated the ground with these words. He said,

> "Rejoice in the Lord. We rejoice that God has put into the hearts of His people to break this ground to the glory of His name. I now set it apart for the building in the church. Let us therefore, as we are assembled, to solemnly dedicate this site to its proper and sacred uses. To the glory of God the Father, who has called us by His grace, in honor of His Son who loved us and gave Himself for us, to the power of the Holy Spirit who illuminates and sanctifies us." Then the crowd said in unison, "We break this ground." "For the worship," Pastor Kessee continued, "For the worship of God

in prayer and praise, for the preaching of the Gospel, for the celebration from the Lord's Supper," again the crowd shouted, "We break this ground." Pastor Kessee continued again, "For the comfort of all who mourn, for strength for those that are tempted, for light for those that seek the way," the recitation is repeated again. Kessee continues again with frequent chants intermittently as he spoke, "for the hallowing of family life, for teaching and guiding the young, for the administration of Christian baptism to those who believe, for the conversion of sinners, for the promotion of righteousness, for the world outreach program of the church, in the unity of the faith, in the bond of Christian brotherhood in charity and goodwill toward all men everywhere, in gratitude to the labors of all who love and serve this church, converted to the labels of all who love and service church in loving remembrance of those who have finished their earthly course, in the hope of the blessed immortality through Jesus Christ our Lord." Again the crowd said collectively one final time, "We break this ground," then collectively stated the last words of the litany, which could not be understood clearly for this reporting.

In the celebration, Pastor's older brother E.C. was recognized among the dignitaries, because Mt. Gilead had been instrumental in supporting Bethany after the earthquake. E.C. needed some help to stand up from his seat, but he spoke with a strong voice to say that he had to attend the ground-breaking ceremony to bless his brother and Bethany. The church's architect saw fit to mention that they would dig sixty feet into the ground and that the church would stand. As they prepared for the digging ceremony, Lee Arthur called for his wife Charlee to stand with him for the ceremonial ground-breaking, L.C. Stewart could be heard calling for his wife Daisy, Thera Lee was called to stand with her husband Joe, along with Pastor Johnson and Dorothy and a few others, as they took their shovels to break the ground, as Pastor Johnson said: "In the name of the Father, the Son and the Holy Ghost."

Immediately after the crowd cheered for the blessing of the land and the excitement that their journey without a building was coming to an end. They continued to celebrate the occasion as various people and all the ministry groups were called forward to take turns shoveling dirt. Sister Shenault, an older woman and longtime Bethany member of the church that served as a deaconess, got a turn to shovel some dirt and she used the shovel that she brought from home. Rocellia also gave special recognition to Tiny Moore for being one of the four founding members of Bethany and for allowing the church to be organized in her living room. Rev. Dennis Broxton was pushed over in his electric wheelchair to the area and helped to take a turn with the shovel as the final person to do that on that sacred occasion.

The church marched into their new sanctuary on June 3, 2007, approximately twelve years after the earthquake and ten years after the groundbreaking.

Pastor Johnson had also begun to transition all of his leadership responsibilities. Lee Arthur Kessee became the Senior Pastor of the Bethany Baptist Church and president of the Bethany Christian Bible College. In 2009, Pastor Sylvester Washington became the Executive Director of the National Evangelism Movement. In preparation for this book, Pastor Kessee joked with Pastor Washington that Rocellia was such a good leader, that "Preacher was such a big personality, such a big leader that it took two of them to try to handle what he did by himself." He acknowledged that Preacher, as he referred to Rocellia, was one of a kind.

In 2007, Pastor Johnson also wrote a resolution that the church "will lease approximately 32,000 square feet of underdeveloped land to the non-profit public benefit corporation for the sole purpose of building an education facility." This non-profit corporation became the Baldwin Bethany Community Development Corporation which made way for two new important educational initiatives inspired by the vision and legacy of Pastor Johnson. There was a summer academic program and a charter school. A handwritten somewhat obscure note in his handwriting from a page in his calendar dated January 20, 2008, was found, and it speaks to his interest in building a charter school:

Preparing people for a better life and greater service

Education

Expanding and developing our school of Christian education

A charter school preparing so that they compete
in colleges and universities.

Launch Academy became the summer academic program created by the Baldwin Bethany Community Development Corporation to address the STEM (science, technology, engineering and math) educational needs within the community. Stella Middle school was built for grades 6-8 to fulfill Pastor's vision for a charter school.

In his lifetime, he'd received countless awards. Perhaps the final one came on April 25, 2015, for a lifetime of remarkable service Dr. Rocellia was recognized by the City of Los Angeles with the address of the Bethany Baptist Church of West Los Angeles, which is located at 4115 Martin Luther King Jr. Blvd. to be named as "Dr. Rocellia Johnson Place."

In all, there should be no question of how he felt about Bethany. Of course, Pastor Johnson loved Bethany. Greg Tyler agreed, "He was committed to that church [and] nothing else. Everything he did was about that ministry." Greg attended Bethany with his friend Brit and decided to join in 1980 and became a minister in 1995. To describe the extent of that love, Ed Russell said, "He loved his family, but he may have loved Bethany more." If you ever wanted to know how he felt about Bethany, his daughter Rosalyn found a magenta-colored sticky note with another obscure message in his Bible that provided a clue. It appeared to be a note to himself about an idea for a sermon. It turned out that Rocellia preached that particular sermon at Bethany at the 6 p.m. service on the first Sunday evening in December 2007. It was entitled, "The Church at Philippi." Here is an excerpt of that sermon from Philippians 2:1-11 in his words:

> The Lord has a message for us out of that passage of Scripture and I simply want to talk and share some things with you in talking about the church at Philippi. The church that was then at Philippi. The church at Philippi is a model church. The church at Philippi was a kind of church that preachers would dream about pastoring. Not at the beginning, but at a point in time, you could dream about it and wish that you were the pastor of the church that was then at Philippi. I like to think of the Bethany Baptist Church having something in common with the Philippian church...So here at Philippi, we find the church with a humble beginning. Matter of fact one way that it reminds me of the Bethany Baptist Church, it was organized by Paul the Apostle, along with three other people. That's where it started. One more man and one other woman. The four of them together by the grace of God and the directions of the Holy Spirit. They were blessed to lay the foundation to the Church of God that would become a model even for us in the year 2007, beginning in 1958 and up to this time. If you wanna be like somebody, forget about what Reverend so and so is doing down the streets. Forget

about how many that they have in the congregation, but if you want to please God be a model like this church of history that is known as the Philippian church.[45]

The Apostle Paul commended the church for the way it supported him. Its support was unique. It was the only church that supported the proclamation of the gospel and financially supported the ministry (Php. 4:15; 2 Cor. 8:1-5; 9:1-5). To Paul, the church at Philippi was a model church.

In this sermon, Pastor Johnson raised the specter of a comparison with the Philippian church and the Bethany Baptist Church. Ironically, Bethany was also the first to support the mandate of the gospel in churches around the country. In this sermon, Pastor Johnson highlighted three other similarities between the New Testament Philippian church and Bethany Baptist Church – Their humble beginnings. They were both started by four people and started at the home of a woman and weren't affected by "religiosity," as Pastor Johnson put it. There was another important takeaway to observe, which is that this comparison speaks of his pride for Bethany. It wasn't a perfect church, but with all its imperfections, he considered Bethany as a church without the kind of issues of other churches. It is a church that other pastors would wish for. Although he didn't come right out and say it, this likely meant that he was proud of Bethany and considered it a model church.

Many years earlier in an Annual Church meeting in 1985, he spoke about the growth that he'd observed in and amongst the church. For Rocellia church was about doing the work of Jesus Christ. In Bethany's 1985 Annual Church meeting that was conducted in early November, Pastor Johnson opened the first night of the meetings saying that he wanted to share some things with those in attendance that he considered to represent the state of affairs of the Bethany Baptist Church and he wanted to share those topics with his audience directly out of the Scripture, directly out of the word of God. In this particular meeting, Rocellia either mentions the names of many of the people that were in attendance or their voices can be recognized, like Ruben Hill, Lonnie Kimes, Rod Miles, Joe Lee, Sidney Beach, Patricia Payton, Mabel Anderson, Carl Daniels, Columbus Wallace, Dorothy Johnson and Emilie Duncan. His comments helped provide insight into his theology of the church. He took his scripture text for the meeting from Ephesians 4:11-16 to frame his comments about the church's growth and maturity to date. From that passage of Scripture, he chose the topic "We Are Growing." He intended to extract insights and instruction from those scriptures that might benefit his leaders. The Apostle Paul wrote,

> And he gave the apostles, the prophets, the evangelists, the pastors and teachers, to equip the saints for the work of ministry, for building up the body of Christ, until we all attain to the unity of the faith and of the knowledge of the Son of God, to mature manhood, to the measure of the stature of the fullness of Christ, so that we may no longer be children, tossed to and fro by the waves and carried about by every wind of doctrine, by human cunning, by craftiness in deceitful schemes. Rather, speaking the truth in love, we are to grow up in every way into him who is the head, into Christ, from whom the whole body, joined and held together by every joint with which it is equipped, when each part is working properly, makes the body grow so that it builds itself up in love (Eph. 4:11-16, ESV).

He began his opening remarks by saying, "I'm glad to report that I believe that we have had more growth perhaps in the last year then we have had in any period of time within the life and history of the Bethany Baptist Church." For his first point, he said, "It makes me feel good and renews my hope and my determination by recognizing that we have had some growth in the last twelve months." One place that he thought he saw evidence of growth was during the 24-Hour Gospel Marathon. He continued to say that they were growing out of having a church to responding to the mandate of the Lord Jesus Christ. About his text, he spoke of himself being "in the pastoral and teaching area of the church and that we [he and Bethany] have grown in the acceptance of the gift of the ministry." He said, "I believe the beginning with the ministry itself and with the body of Christ itself is that we have had some growth in the fact that ministry from the top to the bottom is a gift that comes from God and it would have to be some growth when people have come to the point that they accept that gift which God has given to all of us."[46]

For his second point he said, "Number two, we have grown in having a broader understanding of the work and the functions of the church as ordered by Jesus Christ," and restated this point for emphasis. He added that "as ordered by Christ and not ordered by the Department." He stated that "All down through the times, we have an understanding of the work and function of the church that *we designed*. We design programs. We design barbeques. We design musicals. We design this annual day. We design Ushers day. We design Father's Day and Children's Day and Mother's Day, but we're getting a broader understanding and responding to the church as ordered by the Lord and Savior Jesus Christ. "Consequently," he said, "we find more people involving themselves in the ministry rather than programs. We find folks more diligent and putting forth more efforts involving themselves in the things that we are ordered to do by the Word of God and not those things that we sat down in a room and cooked up and decided that it would be good for the church. So, we've had some growth in understanding the word and functions of the church as ordered by the Lord Jesus Christ," he concluded. He continued, "We have learned that sometimes the church is at its best when it's just to keep people around here really involved in the work of the ministry and [that] the work of the ministry is not necessarily taking place on Sunday morning. It's taking place when most of us are sleep or watching television."

His third point was that the members of the church were growing personally. He said,

> I see some growth from the Bethany Baptist Church from a personal point of view. I see folks not only playing the piano, but I see them serving God. I suppose not only playing the organ and directing the choir, but I see them in the witnessing program and in another programs ministering one to another and really responding to what thus says the Lord...We are accustomed to the fact that the piano player only plays the piano. The director only directs the choir, that the Superintendent only superintend. The only thing that the Deacon does is deacon and the only thing that the preacher will get involved in is preaching. So, we've seen some growth [because] we're breaking out of those straits. Then we're growing collectively in responding to our Christian responsibility. People are beginning to take whatever job that they're doing in church seriously. People are serious about teaching Sunday school. People are serious about teaching in the Bible Institute. People are serious about teaching in the Computer and Word processing business. People are serious about following up and following through and involving themselves in the prayer ministry. People are becoming serious about being witnesses for the Lord and Savior Jesus Christ and we see a great deal of growth where people are becoming serious about what they're doing. People are becoming serious about ushering. People are becoming serious about having devotion on Sunday morning, becoming serious about preaching, serious about praying and about trying to win the lost to Christ...[moving

on to his fourth point] We have grown in the unity of the faith. We're having more acceptance and more tolerance one for the other. We're growing out of being complacent of worrying only about your own department and are beginning to think about how the other persons are doing over here in their department.[47]

Pastor Johnson went on to make this point to explain the standard for measuring such growth. He said, "When we talk about growth we do have to admit that sometimes it depends on what measuring stick that you're using. If you use a measuring stick as to what somebody else is doing down the street, we're doing great, but when you use the divine measuring stick we're just getting by. So, sometimes we can get carried away by using the wrong measures. You know sometimes if we want to measure our individual Christian lives by the life of somebody else, we're great a Christian." He says we say to ourselves, "I don't smoke, dance, go nowhere or bother nobody. I go to church often, so I'm doing great" - if I wanna measure myself by some other weak Christian, but if I wanna measure myself against the standards of Jesus Christ, [then] all have sinned and come short of the glory of God. He offered these words of caution, "Don't get carried away measuring yourself as an individual nor the church collectively by our own man-made measuring stick." Rocellia closed his opening remarks for that night stating that he wanted his church to grow in the acceptance of being satisfied at being functional in the body of Christ. He established a local church based on his theology of the church. It was a church that strived to achieve God's mandate to teach and make disciples. It was a place that sought to remain open and available to meet the spiritual needs of needy people, to take the gospel and the work of ministry throughout the world. He named her Bethany Baptist Church of West Los Angeles. In the next couple of chapters, you'll be able to read about Bethany, her history and her people.

Pastor Johnson and Dorothy seated in the future sanctuary.

4

Bethanites: A Peculiar People

I n his first letter to the general church, the Apostle Peter says of God's people, "But you are a chosen generation, a royal priesthood, a holy nation, His own special people, that you may proclaim the praises of Him who called you out of darkness into His marvelous light" (1 Pet. 2:9, NKJV). In those words, Peter could have also used the same words to characterize the people of Bethany. The privilege of being a member of Rocellia's church made them peculiar, like him. They were people that belonged to God, but were formed for Pastor Johnson and by Pastor Johnson so that God could use them in the work that he assigned to Rocellia. They loved him, not out of rote because he was their pastor, but more because of what he helped them to achieve spiritually and the fellowship they cherished together. Bethanities responded to his directives and his rebukes in a way that was righteous out of respect to their pastor and their desire to serve and honor God. Almost to a person, despite what life may have offered during that time, they consider their years at Bethany as the best time in their lives. This made them distinct from other churches.

Pastor William Turner said, "He was social with his people, but he was also stern with his pastoring. They loved him for who he was. In the socialized element, he was Rocky. in the church, he was Pastor Rocellia." Turner continued that Rocellia never liked being called Doctor, Bishop even Reverend, but Pastor. "He was Pastor Rocellia. That's who he was. That's the way he built a legendary church. Souls were saved. Miniseries enhanced people's lives. The evangelistic movement that ultimately became nationally acclaimed, helped so many churches to grow, including his church New Revelation." He added, "his name and his work will always abound in the historical documents of people who wanna grow their church."

Most of the new members of Bethany arrived with wonderful stories of how they got there and why they stayed. Some will be introduced in this chapter and many others that you'll meet as they share their stories about Pastor Johnson. Thera Lee was one of those people. In December 1963, while on vacation in Los Angeles, she visited Bethany and decided to relocate to become a member of Bethany after hearing Pastor Johnson preach. She became a member in January 1964, where she met her future husband Reverend Joe Lee.

Ed was honorably discharged from the Army in the State of Washington and he and Minnie were on their way back home to Texas, but decided to spend a weekend in sunny Southern California. They enjoyed the weather so much that they called their parents in Texas informing them that they would be relocating to Los Angeles. Upon relocating they lived with Ed's uncle until they were able to find their first apartment. While living with their Uncle, they visited Mount Zion Baptist Church where E.V. Hill was the pastor. He found out about Bethany from his friend Louis Kirkendall. They'd hang out on Saturday nights, but Louis would have to leave early to make sure he was on-time to march in with the choir in the morning. Ed and Minnie had been invited to Bethany by his friend Louis many times and after visiting a couple of times, they decided to join. Ed eventually decided to join Bethany and Minnie joined later after the birth of their daughter Gina.

Ed said he was ultimately attracted to Bethany because Pastor Johnson had a down to earth style and reminded him of his pastor back home in Texas. He appreciated that it was a small church with a good choir and a pastor that preached with a down to earth style and presented the gospel with clarity. Ed Russell eventually joined the choir, became Assistant Superintendent of the Sunday School under the leadership of Carolyn Lewis, was a Trustee and eventually became Dean of the Bible College.

Daisy Stewart, another longtime member, joined little Bethany on the first Sunday in November 1970. She lived in the area and had to pass the church to go to the market at the suggestion of Annie Jefferson, who Daisy said, "kept bugging her about coming to Bethany." Daisy told the story of B. Ruth Allen. Ruth Allen was from Philadelphia. When she arrived in Los Angeles, she was living in downtown L.A. and attending a white church. One day, she said, "I wanted to go to a black church." One particular Sunday, when Ruth Allen was on her way to church, she saw a black woman at a bus stop with a big church hat on. She said to herself that the lady must be going to a black church, so when that lady got on the bus she got on the bus behind the lady. When the lady changed buses, she changed buses. Ruth Allen ended up following that lady all the way to little Bethany. When she arrived, Pastor Johnson asked her, "Who'd you come with?" B. Ruth Allen responded, "I don't know. I just followed this lady with a big hat. I knew she was coming to a black church." That lady with the big hat turned out to be Annie V. Dawson, the sister of Dan Dawson and one of the founding members of Bethany.

Of course, there were too many members that were devoted

and sacrificed for the causes of Bethany and Pastor Johnson to remember and mention here. Some of those members that were directly involved in the ministry of the church as officers, preachers, teachers and counselors have stories and contributions that are shared throughout this book. Others assumed lesser-known and less visible roles, yet whose contributions were born more out of their personality and gifts to Bethany. Regardless of their contributions, all of the Bethany members shared a spirit of friendship and community as brothers and sisters in Christ devoted to making and living out their lives as disciples of Jesus Christ.

They started with people like Vernice Moore who opened her home for her new fledgling church, the first couple married at the church, Ronald and Deloris McMillan, the first teenagers Mary Evans, Ruthie Peete and Annie Emerson, and the first baby, Rosalyn, born to Pastor and Dorothy Johnson.

At one time at big Bethany, Geri Landry read the announcements for the church at the 11 am service. This was well before the days of digital bulletins provided on a church's website. Geri would stand at a podium in the front of the church, just to the right of the preachers that were seated in the pulpit area and in front of the choir, which had the effect of a stage for her. Geri approached this role with flair and professionalism as if it was the morning news. She was always beautifully dressed in bright colors, often adorned with a church hat that matched her outfit. She spoke confidently, sharing her sense of humor and biting wit that turned the announcements into a Sunday event. Deloris McMillan succeeded Geri and offered a warm, meeker style that represented her personality.

There was also the crew that worked in the church's industrial style kitchen that was led by Vernice Moore and Robbie McGee (Nash). Tiny was a founding member of Bethany, but in the kitchen, she was known for her delicious cabbage and Robbie was known for her tasty peach cobbler. They'd work with a faithful dedicated group that included Mabel Anderson, Frankie Bollin, Evelyn "Aunt Bae" Cole, Sister Flowers, Louise Brown, Richard White, Eugene Tolliver, Daisy Stewart and Ellis Quarles. This group would cook delicious meals for the church like large-scale gatherings, repast meals after funerals and meals for the kids and volunteers at Vacation Bible School.

Daisy Stewart was another member with two unique gifts to Bethany. Even at the latter stages, Daisy can remember key historical moments in the past, although she didn't remember that she was in the first graduating class at Bethany. Other than that, she remembers events and encounters, things people said and stories that made her invaluable in the course of writing this book, like remembering the last name of a young preacher that left Bethany over thirty years ago or immediately recall of the first and last names of the people that used to work in the kitchen over forty years ago. Daisy is also a network hub of the Bethany community. She helped as a one-person network who often refers to the phone book that she has kept for decades, not the list in her cell phone. So, if you need to know or contact someone that had been at Bethany for any period or their children, Daisy either knows them or knows someone that can find them. It is this treasured gift that helps maintain the family and community of Bethany over the years.

There were men like Deacon Sullivan Lewis and Ruben Hill, two of the first deacons at little Bethany. Ruben became a trustee and Coordination Board member at big Bethany. Ruben eventually became the chairman of the trustee board with the move from little Bethany to big Bethany successfully completed under his leadership.

Columbus Wallace is another one of those special contributors.

He became a member at little Bethany. For years, he served as the Director of the Sunday School, taught a class on prayer and the book of James. In addition to those duties, Columbus was an avid man of prayer, which he'd offer at the 6 a.m. Wednesday prayer meetings. He was also an avid supporter of Pastor Johnson and Bethany. Yet, one of the things that makes Columbus special is that he was ready and willing to have Pastor Johnson's back when other members couldn't or wouldn't. For example, there were several occasions, which Rod Miles shared when Columbus demonstrated by his actions his love for his pastor and his church. There was one occasion when Columbus was willing to physically protect his pastor. There were two other occasions after the earthquake when the church didn't have the $15,000 to $25,000 to move the modular building from the old site across the street to its current location. In a trustee board meeting in which they were discussing the issue and the conversation was becoming more passionate, when Columbus heard the issue that was confronting Pastor Johnson and that he didn't have the money, Rod said that Columbus pulled Rocellia aside out of the meeting. When they returned Rocellia said, "I can write a check for $15,000. Who do I make the check out to?" Even after the new offices were set up there was no furniture, no computers and no refrigerator for people to have a cold drink or a place for them to keep their lunches. Columbus voluntarily bought several desks and furnishings for the office, three Macintosh desktop computers and a refrigerator so the church could become operational.

There was Ellis Quarles who served as a deacon and preacher. He was a warm, friendly and caring brother that loved his family and enjoyed dressing well. He worked with the men on Saturday. He worked early morning hours at the Post Office and served in the Army reserve which took him away for weekends out of the year, but he never let those responsibilities interfere with his Christian service. For example, on many first Sunday nights when the service would end around 9:30 p.m. and he had to leave for work in the morning around 4 a.m. for his morning shift, he always made time to stand around and fellowship with the men of the church while the parking lot cleared. Ellis also was a cook. He'd help in the church's kitchen and cook barbecue for the church picnic every year.

Willie Rowe was another brother that quietly devoted his service to Bethany. He was someone that wouldn't necessarily take the lead, but he was someone that you could count on to help and support you to do the work. Rowe also had the knack for being an encourager by speaking to people, checking in with them to see how they were doing and letting them know that he was thinking well for them. His son Brandon told a story about how Willie was making sandwiches to give away to people without homes. However, these sandwiches were not skimpy. Brandon said his Dad was making the kind of sandwiches that he would like to eat, on the good bread, piled high with meat, lettuce and tomatoes as you'd buy from the delicatessen. That's who Willie Rowe was.

There were the church secretaries like Jimmie Davis, Oscar Harvey and Cheryl Warren, the current secretary, that all embraced the role with a sense of worth and purpose that extended well beyond answering the phone and doing various administrative tasks.

Annie Jefferson was a powerhouse of a woman in a small frame and known for her grayish-white natural style hair. She worked in Child Development at the church, taught youth evangelism and worked in the church's nursery. Annie and her son Anthony joined little Bethany in the winter of 1963. Her primary contribution to Bethany may have been as the primary babysitter and potty trainer for the children of the church. It's impossible to count all the children that she kept. As such, Sister Jefferson may have established most of her ministry and legacy directly into the lives of the Bethany children; she was tough, but lovingly cared for the children. Her methods were effective for the times and would be questionable today, like giving castor oil for ailments, hot sauce on the fingers so kids won't suck their fingers. She'd have a separate potty for each child and she'd put them on it after every meal until they did their business. Victor said they'd eat good home-cooked meals, but Daisy's daughter Staci remembered that they occasionally ate some type of goulash for lunch that was a mixture of "some of everything."

Sister Jefferson was considered a great babysitter and the children that she cared for as kids are now adults, like Marcus Richardson, Karen Wright, Terri Emerson McNeal, Staci Stewart, Craig Gaines, Tanya Edwards, Keith Billingsley and his stepbrother Kenny Harvey, Kenny, Willie and Amanda Jackson and her daughter Tiffany, David Daniels, Victor and Charise Williams, Aaron and Alicia Tyler, Carl Daniels Jr., Marcel and his sister Monique Warren, Cynthia Williams and her sister Sylvia and her brother Chris, Terri Mains Breland and her sister April Ward, Tracie Williams, Stephanie and Samantha Berry, Robbie, Diedre and Vinita Hall and countless others.

Some of the things that made Bethany most unique was its ministry culture, its sense of community and its friendly nature. Bethanites were not the usual group of church friends, that would lose touch once they change church memberships. They'd remain Bethanites. Even if they saw a member at another church they'd greet each other as members of Bethany and ask about things related to Bethany. They identified themselves most by terms of ministry, knowing people for things like being the Evangelism counselors that visited their homes or members of certain classes or students of various teachers at Bethany. They represented a unique family of believers that was forever bound together by the church's ministry and their fidelity to Pastor Johnson and his teachings. Many of the members are Facebook friends after several decades and after they have joined other churches. Hazel Shipp recently mentioned the saying that says it all, "Once a Bethanite, always a Bethanite."

Even among members that have moved away decades ago, some stay in contact and still visit the church when they're in town. That point was affirmed during the preparation of this book. There are far too many examples to list them all here, but a few that came up that can be highlighted are Hazel and Janet Montgomery (relocated in 1995) and this author (relocated in 1990). Greg Tyler told the story of Janet who had been a member of Bethany and a loyal alumnus of Tuskegee University who had relocated to that region of the country years earlier. When Greg's granddaughter decided to attend Tuskegee and when Janet found out, she told Greg, "If she needs anything, call me and I'll be there." He said that when Janet visits for homecoming she always looks up to his grand-daughter, because of her relationship with Pastor Johnson and Bethany. The truth is that in many ways Bethany is still a church. It's just scattered because there's not a Bethanite that spent any time under the teaching of Pastor Johnson and his "Rocky-isms" that doesn't still consider himself or herself a Bethanite.

The things that made the members of Bethany a peculiar group of people were their fondness to worship and to learn together as Christians. Bethanites were rough riders. Hazel Shipp and her husband Emmitt were good examples. She told the story that she and Emmitt, both faithful members of Bethany, had decided to go on a nice relaxing vacation to Monterey, California, at the same time the church had planned a workshop in Monterey.

Monterey is famous for its golfing, coastline, beaches and sailing and local wineries. So Hazel and Emmitt probably had thoughts of taking a quick flight up from Los Angeles, staying at a relaxing hotel, doing some sailing, sipping some local wine and enjoying the scenery during the day, then attend the meetings during the evenings. When Pastor Johnson heard that they had planned to be in the area at the time of the Workshop, he asked them to ride with the team on that seven- or eight-hour drive in one of the two church vans up to Monterey. Despite their plans, as the rough riders that they were, Hazel and Emmitt got on that church van with the team and made the trek to Monterey. According to Hazel, it all worked out well. She and Emmitt changed their itinerary around the Workshop schedule. They enjoyed their trip and saw it as their opportunity to become involved in the Evangelism ministry.

The influence and directives of Pastor Johnson to the members of Bethany had formed its unique culture. Over the years they had been taught what some call "Rocky-isms." Rocky-isms were those unique Bethany-specific teachings of Pastor Johnson that made them unique from other congregations. Some of the more memorable Rocky-isms were – You don't leave church before the benediction. You don't walk when the invitation to accept Christ or join the church was being given. You were committed to attending multiple services on Sunday. Never miss a Communion service. Many of its members admit that they still adhere to these teachings today.

Pastor Johnson was known to be a tough leader. As a disciplinary method, Pastor Johnson would occasionally confront members indirectly about an issue publicly over the pulpit. He'd come out from his office and head directly for the pulpit to grab the microphone. He wouldn't mention the person by name, but they always knew who he was talking about. He chastised a young preacher for preaching too long and causing the early service to go overtime. He'd get on the person for praying a long altar prayer then leaving early. In any case, he was an equal opportunity discipliner. It didn't matter your title, role, or family status. Everyone was subject to these chastisements. He didn't hurt your feelings, but you'd definitely get the message. The members that heard these rebukes would also immediately learn not to make that same mistake, which was partly the point.

Bethany was not just a church. It was a family of believers. Bethanites were bound together at significant times in their individual lives where they were experiencing their spiritual formation together as a family and community. This transformational experience of the new birth, an outlook of evangelism and a commitment to discipleship created a shared vision and a shared work. This unique relationship created opportunities to build their lives together around the work of ministry. This made their bond so unusual because it connected with them beyond just being "church friends" to helping them forge lasting relationships based on their fellowship and faithfulness in the work of Christ, for which they had been taught to be mindful of God's Word through the ministry of Pastor Johnson. This made the Bethany experience – the classes, the Communion services, the Workshops, the Marathons – a "high time" in the lives of every former and current Bethany member that they will always cherish.

Auxiliaries of the Church

Bethany was all about ministry, but oddly Bethany used the word "auxiliaries" to refer to its many departments, boards and ministries. Auxiliaries is an odd, untraditional word that according to the Oxford Dictionary defines "a group of volunteers giving supplementary support to an organization or institution." In the history of Bethany that were several auxiliaries that are worth highlighting that Pastor would often mention, like the Counseling Center, the CEEA, the Men of the church, the Prayer Ministry and the Pastor's Aid (which organized the Annual Pastor's Tea), the music department, the men of Bethany and the preachers of the church. These groups will be used to further describe the people of Bethany and how they ministered together.

C.E.E.A.

Among the churches more prominent ministries that Pastor Johnson spoke of often was the Christian Endeavor for Educational Assistance (CEEA), Bethany's Counseling Center, the Pastor's Aid and the Coordination Board. Christian Endeavor for Educational Assistance (CEEA) was organized to "provide financial and administrative assistance, encouragement and guidance to students who were trying to better themselves through higher education." Some of its services included tutoring, counseling, employment and letters of recommendation.[48] Some of the notable recipients of the C.E.E.A. were Anthony Doyle, B. Ruth Allen, Sandra Mitchell, Lee Arthur Kessee, Erma, Roosevelt, Kenny and Willie, Gloria Burroughs, and Gina Russell, which both eventually earned doctorate degrees.

The Counseling Center

The offsite Counseling Center was fully staffed with certified counselors that offered various services to the church and community, which included substance abuse counseling, crisis intervention, stress management, marriage and family counseling and other services. Pastor Johnson was also willing to provide information about how other churches could provide similar services.[49]

The Prayer Ministry

Pastor Johnson saw the church's corporate prayer as an opportunity for ministry. Charlee said that after a few workshops in 1980, he asked her to become Bethany's first Prayer Coordinator. Charlee said she coordinated prayer activity for church, like coordinating prayer topics for altar calls, established in-service prayer meetings during the preaching, established prayer partners and prayer chains among the members, as well as partnering with other churches involved in the Movement to get them on one accord with certain prayer activities. Pastor's wife Dorothy replaced Charlee as the second Prayer Coordinator in October 1981. One of the enhancements that took place were that Prayer Workshops were conducted at churches to teach the importance and practice of prayer. She also led breakout sessions on prayer at the Workshops.

The Pastor's Aid

The Pastor's Aid was the auxiliary of Bethany that was responsible for caring for the needs of the pastor. They hosted a one of a kind event each fall called the "Pastor's Tea," which was originally started under the direction of Anne Lucas around 1965-1966. The Pastor's Tea was based on the theme of the Fruits of the Spirit from Galatians 5:22, which reads, "But the fruit of the Spirit is love, joy, peace, longsuffering, gentleness, goodness, faith, meekness, temperance: against such, there is no law." This was also an event that Pastor and Dorothy Johnson and their family looked forward to each year because it provided an opportunity for the church to honor their marriage with tributes of love, as well as an opportunity for them to fellowship with new members. One year, Pastor and Dorothy were presented with a framed portrait drawn by the author of this book.

The purpose of the Tea was to create an annual celebration and fellowship of the new members that had united with the church within that past calendar year that included songs, praise, prayer and an old-fashioned tea which involved home-cooked foods from each auxiliary, according to long time Pastor's Aid president Lula Hines. Lula described it as a time of rejoicing set aside to celebrate the harvest of the gospel during the fall season of harvest. She became a member of Bethany around 1985 as a result of the church's evangelism teaching. She graduated from the BCTI in 1991 and became President of the Pastor's Aid in 1993 and led that department for fourteen years.

On this fellowship night, auxiliary members were assigned a specific fruit that was symbolic of the fruits of the spirit. Apples represented "love" and were assigned to the Evangelism department and Prayer ministry. Plums represented "gentleness" and were assigned to the choirs. Pineapples signified "temperance" and were assigned to the ministerial staff and the men's ministry (the MOB). Bananas signified "longsuffering" and were assigned to the Sunday School and media departments. Oranges represented "meekness" and were assigned to the Youth and Children's departments. Berries represented "goodness" and were assigned to the Deaconesses and Deacons of the church. Peaches represented "joy" and were assigned to the Mission department and Nurse's Guild. Pears signified "peace" and were assigned to the Usher's Board. Grapes represented "faith" and were assigned to the Society of Adam's Ribs (SOARS), the church's women's fellowship. So, each auxiliary would have a table colorfully decorated with flowers, food, pies and cakes, etc. and a centerpiece based on their assigned fruit. In all, this was event was a warm, loving and friendly occasion that always created an atmosphere filled with the fruits of the Spirit.

The Men of Bethany

In that Annual Church meeting, Pastor Johnson commented, "The men who are called Deacons are involved in the work and service of the church. They're not involved in traditional deacon meetings."[50] The was evident every Saturday morning. Beginning around 1979-1980, around 9 a.m. on Saturday mornings a small group of men from the church, basically, deacons and aspiring deacons would meet at the church on Saturday mornings for fellowship and Bible study. They'd gather first thing in the morning each Saturday and leave around the time Children's choir practice would begin, as the building became busier with people arriving for the various activities.

The group was led by L. C. Stewart. L.C. became the chairman of the deacon board and in 1992 was ordained as the first assistant pastor in the history of the church. He led the Saturday morning Bible Study. The primary task for the Saturday gathering was to clean and organize the church for Sunday worship. Pews would be aligned by row. The carpet was vacuumed. The chairs in the choir stand would be neatly organized. The custodial duties would extend to vacuuming the carpet in the church foyer, cleaning the restrooms and classrooms and mopping the floors in the classrooms. The most special aspect of the gatherings was the fellowship. It became a community for many of the men that were not involved in other ministries of the church to develop life-long relationships, to serve as deacons and enter the ministry, such as Pastor Willie Davis (L.C.'s predecessor), L.C., Ellis Quarles, Greg Tyler, Jimmy Jones, Park Steen, this author. There were others, like Willie Rowe, Perry Stamps, Sidney Beach, John Madison, Charlie Daniels, Weaverton Terrell, Ronald McMillan, Andrew Wallace, Emmitt Shipp, Gary Williams, Amos Wallace, Reggie Edwards and Jay Wiggs and more that offered their support over the years.

Rod Miles said that after the 1994 earthquake, there were challenges with weekly meetings, operations, and meetings and many ministries and auxiliary meetings. Daisy mentioned that the Bible Study classes didn't stop. Some groups met at member's homes and some came to a halt due to a lack of a place to convene. According to Rod, the Men's Saturday group had already begun to experience a significant drop in attendance and after the earthquake, attendance declined further and eventually ceased meeting for the next three years. However, as the faithful servant that he was, the Assistant Pastor Reverend L. C. Stewart continued teaching every Saturday even when only one member showed up.

There were meetings held among some of the brethren like James Mitchell, Perry Stamps, Elbert Tuffs and Reginald Edwards and a decision was made to have a meeting to call on all the men of Bethany to come together, but they had to find a place to convene. Rod spoke with brother Willie Rowe, another faithful member of Bethany, about the meeting and intentions and Brother Rowe opened his home to host the meeting. Rowe's home was large enough to host the men and was close to the church. They scheduled the meeting for Saturday, April 5, 1997. Rod said that the turnout exceeded their expectations. He described it as a "mob" of men that met that one time. Therefore, the group was officially named the "MOB," the Men of Bethany.

Ironically, one day after he had resigned as Senior Pastor and he was preaching at Pleasant Hill Baptist Church, he made a statement during a service that he never really liked the name – the MOB. Yet, Pastor Johnson did not allow his personal preference to hinder the MOB name being used. Rod felt that it was also clear that day that he was grateful for the support of the MOB which stood in support of him and what he came to do – share God's word to all who would listen. He was truly an example of a good leader, recognizing what will benefit the body of Christ rather than leaning on his personal preferences.

Due to the overwhelming response to that meeting and Pastor Johnson's teaching during those trials, Rod said he was inspired to help organize the Men of Bethany, the MOB, which had been birthed during that meeting at the home of Brother Willie and Sister Doris Rowe. A steering committee for the group was formed and Brother L.C. Stewart was chosen to be their spiritual leader. The group reorganized again under Rod's leadership in 2009 and Jimmy Valentine assumed the leadership role in 2013.

The men chose Psalms 133:1 as their mission scripture because it reads, "Behold how good and how pleasant it is for brethren to dwell together in unity!" Their mission statement was, "Build a united men's ministry that develops and encourages men to be Christian leaders at home, in church and the community at large – winning souls for Christ." Their goal was to form a unique organization of men that stemmed from diverse gifts and talents in their different capacities so that they could serve the Lord and the local church at Bethany. Their organizing was an expression of their commitment to willingly submit themselves to edifying the church and each other.

The Preachers

In its history, Bethany has had dozens of preachers that either announced their calling there as a son of Rocellia or were journeyman preachers that joined and left. Some of the best records can account for at least forty ministers that either served under Pastor Johnson or announced their calling to the ministry under his pastoral leadership. Their names are listed at the back of this chapter. Overall there were almost forty preachers. Among this list of men, they all contributed to the ministry of Bethany in some way. However, there was a smaller group of these preachers whose contributions were significant to the life of Bethany, but not as well known. That's not to minimize the contributions of others, only to mention those men that helped shape Bethany either by their preaching, teaching, or by the contribution of their wisdom, character, or personality. Most of them are not remembered for their preaching oratory, not because they weren't good at preaching, but more because every preacher at Bethany was expected to be active in the other areas of ministry within the church, especially as Evangelism counselors and teachers. So, they were just as likely to be known for their teaching skills and the classes that they taught. The vast majority of these preachers spent more time teaching than they did preaching. It's important to remember these men of God that began their ministries at little Bethany.

L.C. Stewart and Greg Tyler were recognized as the only two Assistant Pastors in the history of the Bethany Baptist Church to date. They were among a long list of preachers that never held that title officially, like Reverend George Hall, Reverend Dennis Broxton, Oscar Harvey, Joe Lee, Bruce Emerson and Paul Peete that had dedicated their lives to the service of Bethany. Let's begin with the ministers from little Bethany, Kelly Bollin and George Hall.

Kelly Bollin was one of the founding members of Bethany. He was initially a deacon when Bethany was founded and later became a minister. Mary Evans said that he was a very good Bible teacher and a respectable preacher. His sermons were Spirit-filled, although he did not have a whoop. Mary described it more as a whine. According to her, Pastor Johnson depended on Kelly a lot. He taught Bible class. And helped keep the building clean. He also would go and pick members up and bring them to church and take them home. Many times, he'd make two or three trips to see to it that everyone got home. Mary said that he was Pastor Johnson's backbone.

According to Cecile, her father E.C. and George Hall were friends in Oklahoma. According to Mary Evans, Rev. George Hall came to Bethany after he left his church, Philadelphia Baptist Church, and was a great Bible teacher and Pastor Johnson's friend. Rev. Dennis Broxton came to Bethany from the Florence Mission which was a Bible Study that he and her brother Rev. J.P. Evans started on Florence Avenue and Harvard. When her brother took over, he turned that Bible study into a church named Florence Missionary Baptist Church.

Bruce Emerson remembered Rev. George Hall as a mentor that steered him away from beginner preacher and family mistakes. Bruce said, "Rev. Hall took me under his wing and gave me pointers about being a preacher." Bruce said that some of the lessons that Reverend Hall shared were for him to exercise "character qualities such as humility, honesty, and faithfulness." He told Bruce "not to preach for people's approval but God's approval and to learn the Bible, doctrine and principles because that's what you'll be preaching about." For his personal life, he advised Bruce, "do not neglect your wife and family. Don't let your calling cause your wife and kids to hate you due to neglect. Finally, always be yourself. Don't try to pretend to be something or someone that you're not." As a preacher, Bruce said, "He was your typical Baptist preacher. He was a storyteller. An inspirational singing preacher." He added "As a man, he was very likable, easy-going and charming."

Reverend Broxton accepted Christ as a member of Mt. Gilead, which was Pastor Johnson's home church, and also entered the ministry there. According to Pastor's niece Cecile, she was a member of Mt. Gilead when Broxton accepted his calling and preached his first sermon at Mt. Gilead. She remembered that he didn't finish his sermon because he seemed to struggle with anxiety as she described it. Yet, she felt that Hall and Broxton were good preachers because, like Rocellia, they were serious about the word of God. Broxton later moved his membership from Mt. Gilead to Bethany where he served as the Associate Pastor, teacher and counselor at Bethany. Broxton suffered a debilitating accident in 1976 that left him depending on a wheelchair to get around. Reverend Herman "Billy" Turner became a member of Bethany about six months after the move to big Bethany in

1971. He remembered seeing Pastor Johnson alone cleaning out some clogged sewage in the back of the building. Billy said he'd often visit Broxton after his accident and occasionally take him to church. According to Billy Turner, he never spoke of himself or his accident. He might talk about Pastor Johnson, Bethany, or the Bible, but never himself according to Billy. If you asked a question about himself or something personal, he'd change the topic. Billy said, "As soon as you walked in the door, he'd open the Bible and preach to you." He only heard Broxton preach once, which was at Bethany one Sunday that Billy had taken him to church.

A couple of interesting notes about these two men, Reverend Hall and Reverend Broxton, was that they were both members of Mt. Gilead before joining Bethany and each man was married to one of Rocellia's sisters. Hall was married to Pastor Johnson's baby sister Orenthia and Broxton was married to his sister Ada Mae.

Reverend Oscar Harvey joined little Bethany in 1960 and became its sixtieth member. He left Bethany to pastor a church in Ontario, California, but returned to Bethany a few years later to become an Associate Minister at Bethany. Like Joe Lee, he was somewhat of a Bible scholar, known for his deep theological mind. He enjoyed delving deeper into God's word and sharing what he learned. He preached deep messages that were often difficult for the common churchgoer to understand, which went over the heads of most church members. He taught a General Bible study class and *God's Plan of the Ages* from Louis Talbot's classic book by the same title. In his later years, Oscar worked as the Church Secretary and spent time researching and writing a book.

Ronelle Damon was a child when she became a member of little Bethany in 1963 with her father Reverend Ronald Stovall, who was one of the ministers at Bethany. Ronelle told the story that beginning when she was three years old until she was nine, she'd go to church with her father who was an associate minister at the church. Her mother Marie was not yet a member of Bethany. Nevertheless, she said her father had a crew of women at the church that took care of her. Ronelle said that Frankie Bollin would feed her. Wanda Benton and Rose Bronson dressed her and did her hair and she'd hang out with Ruthie Bollin-Peete and Barbara Wheatley.

The preachers at Bethany can be identified by two distinct groups. There was the early group from little Bethany like Kelly Bollin, George Hall, Ronald Stovall and Oscar Harvey. The latter group included Joe Lee, although he was a member since little Bethany, Willie Davis, Paul Peete and Bruce Emerson, which were ordained in the same ceremony in 1982. Incidentally, Paul and Bruce were invited to preach at a 24-Hour Gospel Marathon in Texarkana, Arkansas, that same year.

In addition to the preachers at Bethany, two other young ministers were adopted by Pastor Johnson – Reggie Williams and Kerwin Lee. Reggie was the stepson of Joe Lee and the son of Joe's wife Thera.Pastor Joseph Lee, the son of a pastor, had a warm sense of humor and was known for his oratory and deep thoughtfulness and reverence for studying and preaching God's word. In his time at Bethany, Joe sang in the men's chorus, taught Sunday School and served as a Deacon before he became a preacher in 1979. Reggie said that Joe's father, Pastor Moses Lee Sr., the pastor of St. Paul Baptist Church in St. Louis, Missouri, preached at Bethany on several occasions. Reggie said Lee Sr. was a really good preacher and singer that loved to tell stories.

According to his step-son Reggie Williams who was also a young preacher at the time, Joe considered Pastor Johnson to be the gold standard of preaching because of his boldness, his confidence, his effectiveness and the way he so powerfully presented the word of God. In addition to his devotion to the Bible and his deep theological and doctrinal presentations of Scripture from the Old Testament, Joe was known for two other things – one thing was his long, moving and fervent prayers. Joe had a gift of going to the throne of grace to speak to God for his people – always adoring God, confessing sin, expressing thanksgiving and prayerful petitions for others. The second thing was that it was always interesting when he spoke because he would say the word "begin-ding," instead of "beginning." Even if he read, "In the beginning," Joe would say, "In the begin-ding." It seemed funny because Joe Lee and Oscar Harvey were probably Bethany's most educated preachers. After all, they both studied at Los Angeles Bible Training School and Talbot School of Theology in La Mirada, California. So, it wasn't because he didn't know the difference. So, some members thought it was a funny word choice and would joke about it, but overall it was accepted as a Joe Lee preacher thing. Joe Lee eventually left Bethany to pastor the Community Baptist Church of Fontana for twelve years.

Interestingly Joe and Reggie entered the ministry only about a year apart. Reggie announced his calling to the ministry in 1979. He was living in San Diego while in college with plans to become a doctor. He was attending Mount Erie Baptist Church in San Diego when he experienced his urging from God to enter the ministry. Yet, he considered Bethany to be his home church and Pastor Johnson knew him well. He sang in the Pastor's children's choir, served on the youth usher board, and regularly attended Sunday School at little Bethany.

Reggie approached his new pastor at Mt. Erie and shared the testimony of his calling. The pastor challenged him to pray to confirm his calling three times. He eventually suggested that Reggie go back to his home church and talk to his pastor about preaching his first sermon where the people knew him best and would be more encouraging. So that's what he did. Joe arranged a meeting at Pastor Johnson's home for them to discuss the matter and within a few weeks, Reggie was scheduled to preach his first sermon on a first Sunday night at Bethany.

Reggie remembered the occasion that he was preaching his first sermon at Bethany. He thought things were going well, that the Lord was present using him until he got to the end of his message. He said that he expected to just stop talking and take his seat. Which if you are making a speech, would be the appropriate way to conclude. However, in the tradition of the black church and black preaching, the congregation is expecting a more dramatic close to a sermon. You have to ascend to the point of marching Jesus up the hill called Golgotha, whoop in a way to engage the organist, sing something, or do all of the above. All of which tend to escape the abilities of a first-time preacher. Reggie paused. He said he looked out at the congregation and could tell that everyone was expecting him to say more. It was probably a little awkward for both parties. He didn't panic but eventually began to speak the words that came to his mind and developed a rhythm, describing the Lord's crucifixion. The people applauded and he took his seat.

After he took his seat, Pastor Johnson stood up to extend the invitation. Reggie said that when Pastor Johnson stood up he took time to graciously explain Reggie's long pause. He pointed out that when Reggie paused that it wasn't because he didn't have anything else to say, but that he had given an account of Calvary according to Luke's gospel. Reggie admitted that he had no idea of that. Reggie said that Rocellia went on to link Luke the physician to the fact that since Reggie was in college to become a doctor that maybe the Lord was going to use him to minister to the body and the soul. Pastor Johnson's response that evening made it a special night that he has never forgotten and praised him for.

It was an occasion that Pastor Johnson used to affirm Reggie's calling and to mentor that young preacher. There were at least three other occasions when Rocellia's words blessed him. That was how Rocellia blessed you. He'd just say something that seemed so clear that it was like a revelation to you. One was the statement that Reggie heard from Rocellia that there were three types of minds – small minded people, who spend their time talking about people; average minded people who spend their time talking about current events; and great minded people who spend their time talking about ideas. After hearing that, Reggie decided to strive to be a great minded thinker. The second was that the Christian lifestyle is the highest class of living. The third memorable statement occurred in a conversation that he had with Reggie when he told him that God suffers a man to prove himself. Reggie said that he didn't elaborate on it, but he took it to mean that some aspects of the ministry would be difficult and that Reggie needed to endure those times, which he eventually found to be true and helpful to him. In all, Rocellia had given him an opportunity to preach his first sermon. He had given him his license and later ordained him as a minister to fully affirm his calling and ministry. Reggie is pursuing a Seminary degree and credits his relationships with Joe and Rocellia for providing a foundation for him in the gospel.

The other young mentee, Reverend Kerwin Lee, credits Rocellia with provided him with a pastoral model and mentor. Reverend Kerwin Lee is the Pastor of Berean Christian Church in Stone Mountain, Georgia. Lee said he believed that every minister needs both a model for ministry and a mentor in ministry. There is a notable difference between the two. A model is someone who can inspire you from a distance, while a mentor provides hands-on guidance and direction. He said that he was fortunate to decree and declare that Dr. Rocellia Johnson was both for him. He said Rocellia "modeled excellence on how churches can prioritize discipleship, evangelism and leadership development to their congregants and community. Likewise, he mentored me by spending countless hours, one on one, pouring into me when Ifirst started preaching and later on pastoring."

Kerwin's mother Thelma Lee had been a member of Bethany since the seventies. He was raised in Los Angeles and While in college in Alaska on a basketball scholarship, when he accepted his call to preach and began to prepare himself for full-time ministry. It was around this time in the early eighties that he began to visit Bethany where he met Pastor Johnson. He has earned a Doctor of Ministry degree since the founding Berean Christian Church in Stone Mountain, Georgia, which began in 1996, and according to Pastor Lee, it has grown to over 10,000 members in three locations.

Pastor Lee was an immediate favorite preacher of Pastor Johnson and Bethany because of his infectious humor, his contemporary insights and his biblically sound and practical three-point sermons. He was selected to deliver the eulogy for Pastor Johnson at his Homegoing Service in 2018. Pastor Lee joked about why he, among all the well-known and more senior pastors that were in attendance, was selected for such a momentous and esteemed task. Yet, he remarked that he was deeply humbled and honored by the assignment. He chose his scripture text from Acts 20:17-21, where Paul traveled from Miletus to Ephesus to meet with the church elders. He titled the eulogy, "Why We Should Celebrate the Life and Ministry of Rocellia Johnson." He spoke briefly about Paul's third missionary journey - his movement, his statements and the attachment to Paul while highlighting some similarities between Paul and Pastor Johnson. The framework of the sermon provided three reasons to celebrate Rocellia, which were his humility, his generosity and his inclusivity concerning the Gospel.

Regarding Pastor Johnson's humility, Lee preached that

Rocellia Did not "lose touch of who he was." "He did not walk like nobody, talk like nobody, sing like nobody, preach like nobody, dress like nobody," Lee explained. He said that as a pastor, Rocellia had always been generous with his resources, his pulpit, his teaching and his time. As an example of Rocellia's generosity of his time, Pastor Lee told the story that one day when he began to visit Bethany as a young minister, Pastor Johnson invited me to come down and sit with him to talk. Lee said that he thought the meeting would only last about twenty or thirty minutes, but they talked for four hours. He was surprised that a man of Rocellia's stature would have four hours to give him as a young preacher, but that was undoubtedly the reason they talked so long because he was a new preacher with sights on a life in pastoral ministry.

The third reason that Pastor Johnson should be celebrated, according to Pastor Lee, was because of his inclusivity to the gospel. He said, "Johnson's goal to get everybody to know the name of Jesus." He said of Rocellia, "He was concerned about those on Rodeo Boulevard, which was a street that traveled through the black neighborhood in Los Angeles and Rodeo Road, which was the street in Beverly Hills known for its wealth, affluence and celebrity. Hence, he said, "We have the Bethany Bible college and the Evangelism Movement because he was concerned about Salvation for everyone." Pastor Lee concluded his sermon by saying, "We not only celebrate him [Rocellia] today, but every day. We ought to take the time to celebrate him because our lives are better because of Pastor Rocellia Johnson."

"I'm the person I am…a better preacher, a better pastor because he [Rocellia] touched me," Lee proclaimed in the eulogy. He shared for this writing that "Much of my success as a Pastor is a result of all that Pastor Johnson had poured into me. Furthermore, some many other pastors and churches survived and thrived because of the principles provided to them by Dr. Johnson. While he has gone from labor to reward, his legacy is still strong among those he influenced greatly. I am so happy to be a part of that number!"

Among the other preachers of Bethany, Willie Davis Jr. became head of the deacon board, became a minister and pastor at Unity Christian Church. At Bethany, Willie was known for his fun nature and wonderful engaging sense of humor. Reverend Davis taught Evangelism 104 and the Short life of Christ amongst other courses. As the Pastor at Unity Christian Church, he gave a lot of the younger ministers from Bethany the opportunity to preach and develop their preaching skills because Unity was a very small friendly church that provided a forgiving audience and financial donation to those young preachers.

Paul Peete and Bruce Emerson took lead roles in the pulpit during the 1980s. Paul taught Evangelism 103 and the Book of Ephesians and was a faithful member. His voice could often be heard in the pulpit praying, reading the Scripture, or just encouraging the preacher. At Bethany, Paul was typically the lead minister in the pulpit and Communion service on first Sunday night, which meant that he'd often be responsible for leading the order of worship. If Paul was not present, Bruce would assume the lead duties. Bruce taught Basic Christian Doctrine, God's Plan of the Ages and Hermeneutics and also served in the Prayer Ministry. Bruce said of his experience as a minister under Pastor Johnson's leadership, "The beautiful thing about being a preacher under Pastor Johnson was his willingness to let us preach. He encouraged us when we needed it. He corrected in love when we made blunders. He didn't try to put us in a mold or certain style of preaching, but let us be used as God directed us. He was a wonderful mentor."

Reverend Brian Skinner shared a story of his arrival and growth at Bethany, which characterizes the work of the preachers and their contribution to his walk with Christ as a new Christian.

Skinner felt the fellowship of Bethany began with the church's secretary, Jimmie Davis, as she peeked out of the Pastor's office door, which was off to the side to warmly ask him, "Can I help you?" as he stood outside looking for the schedule for Sunday School. They proceeded to discuss the options for Sunday School for his children, while Jimmie encouraged classes for him as an adult. Because she reached out to his need for classes, Skinner considered her response as the fruit of Pastor Johnson's ministry of meeting people where they are, which was important because it was so welcoming and established a common grown and a relationship.

Skinner eventually joined Bethany around 1976 after several visits. Upon joining, he noted that a team of men was sent to visit him at his home, which included Rev. Bruce Emerson and Ed Berry, who was not a minister at that time. In a series of visits, they shared booklets to help him get started in personal Bible study, which was the beginning of his discipleship and lessons in evangelism. Skinner then made his way to a Bible class with Rev. Joe Lee, but he felt that Joe's teaching was too intellectual and too hard for him. He said, "I like him, but I can't handle this." He remembered that someone pulled him aside to suggest that he attend Rev. Willie Davis's class. Reverend Davis was the husband of Jimmie Davis who had graciously greeted Skinner at the door. He said Rev. Davis taught with great joy and that anything you wanted to know, he'd take the time to answer it, which made Skinner "feel at home with him" and drew Skinner into coming to Bible class. Later, someone suggested that he also attend a class in Genesis taught by Rev. George Hall, which he was teaching from Arthur Pink's book *Gleanings in Genesis*. It was in this class that "his eyes started getting opened to the word of God." Skinner said that Rev. Hall "was the best teacher and no one could teach like him." He had decided that he would attend another class and stayed there until Rev. Hall could not teach any longer due to illness.

Skinner said that during this time he was not yet involved in evangelism, but this teaching kept him coming back week after week to hear more of Pastor Johnson's preaching and teaching from Rev. Hall. When Rev. Hall became too ill to continue teaching, so someone suggested another class, a family class, that was taught by a knowledgeable and compassionate teacher named Sterling Irving that was also from the West Indies like him. He said this was the class that birthed his calling to family ministry. Skinner said that Reverend Harvey "took a liken to me." He said, "If you asked him [Oscar Harvey] one question, he's going to explain the whole Bible to you." This was largely true, but well worth the time. Skinner said he'd later visit the church in the afternoons to talk with Rev. Harvey about his newfound calling to the ministry. Skinner said, "These are the guys that Pastor Johnson had there." These men taught him the Word, helped him to understand his spiritual gifts and set him on a path to accepting his calling to the ministry and Christian family counseling.[51] Just as they had in Skinner's story, the preachers ministered in the classroom in ways that supported the work of Bethany and became extensions of Pastor Johnson.

For all the people that came through the doors and served the Lord, it was never about doing church. It was about being among a community of believers. Their collective values were shaped by their faith in Christ, their trust in his Word and a passion to be soul-winners for him. They had been admonished by their pastor to respect God's word and to have a sanctity for worship. Titles and the size of the church were unimportant. If there was anything that they took pride in it was leading someone to Christ or helping a person be assured of their salvation. All of these things made them a peculiar people dedicated to ministry, including the list of the church's ministers which you'll read next.

List of Bethany Ministers

Andre Rowell

Bill Burwell

Brian Skinner

Bruce Emerson

Carlton Emerson

Charles Molungalu

Coleman Zeno

David Garrett

Dennis Broxton

Dewayne Brown

Dewayne Deas

Edward Berry

Eddie Cole Sr.

Eddie Pierson

Ellis Quarles

Eugene Bollin

Frank Warren

Gary Bowles

George Hall

Greg Tyler

Harry A. Mitchell III

Herman "Billy" Turner

Hermon Tatum Sr.

Jimmy Jones

John Gates

John Bowden

Joseph Lee

Kelly Bollin

Kenneth Jackson

L.C. Stewart

Larry Hargrew

Larry Harold

Lee Harris

Louis Lloyd

Lonnie Kimes

Oscar Harvey

Park Steen

Paul Peete

Reginald Williams

Rex "Bo" Cortez

Rommy Turner

Ronald Stovall

Roosevelt Jackson

Steve Adams

Tyrone Gordon

Wade Johnson

Walter Speights

Willie Davis Jr.

Note: Some names may not have been available.

5

The Musical Hermeneutic

Traditional gospel music helps create an atmosphere for worship. It stirs the spirit and emotions of the congregation and helps move them to the sermon. Although Bethany celebrated the traditions of gospel music, the emphasis at Bethany was not just on the sounds of the voices and musicianship. The listeners were to do more than just hear the lyrics of a song. They were to hear God's words in those lyrics. Thus, the songs required a proper hermeneutic – a gospel message and a ministry message. The overarching goal was to solicit a response from the listener to the good news of Jesus Christ. It is this ministry of translating the gospel song into the presentation of the gospel message that helped the hearer respond to the gospel.

From the beginning, Bethany was acknowledged for its choir, before it was known for its teaching. They weren't just special for their great choir, but for how the music ministry had aligned with the teaching emphasis of the church. Unlike many other churches, the music ministry at Bethany was not separate from the primary ministry and mission of the church. Keith Williams explained that one of the problems (in some churches) is that preachers have today is that their musicians are not involved in ministry. There was a single ministry focus at Bethany and that was to share the gospel of Jesus Christ in Scripture, song and sermon. This emphasis required a commitment to music and evangelism. Bottom line – it didn't matter how well a song was sung, how well the congregation enjoyed it, if people shouted, or how popular the song was on the radio, if it did not communicate the message of the gospel or the Christian life, it wouldn't be on the choir's song list.

Ultimately, there was always an awareness of how a song could be interpreted. The lyrics were subject to scrutiny. Laura Cole said, "There was more music that we did not do because of the words. The songs might sound good, but were they scripturally sound and connected to the church's ministry?" This was important because Pastor Johnson was concerned about the words that his congregation would hear. This was confirmed with Laura Cole's recollection of one Sunday when the choir gave a beautiful rendition of Walter Hawkins song, "Changed," which was a song Laura led. A section of the lyrics is as follows:

I sit at my Savior's feet

To do what must be done

I'm gonna work and work

Until my Savior comes

She said afterward that Pastor told them, "Don't sing that song no' more. Y'all ain't changed." They didn't sing that song anymore. Another song that Pastor didn't want to repeat was "Take Me Back" by Andre Crouch. Pastor Johnson didn't like the idea that if you are struggling, feeling far away from God, to restore your relationship with him that anyone would need to go back to the place where they first believed. That may have sounded good in a song, but it didn't make sense.

Keith Williams and Cathy Henderson (Mitchell) arrived at Bethany with a wealth of musical talent and valuable experience from various churches. Keith was an accomplished musician and knowledgeable of the black church music culture. Cathy had sung in solo concerts and professionally and since then recorded with Byron Cage. They both recognized that the level of commitment to the music and Bible study that was required at Bethany made it new and unique. Cathy said that through her involvement in the Evangelism classes, she gained a new perspective for the message in many of the songs. As a result, Keith and Cathy were both challenged to grow spiritually in their faith and personal ministry. Keith said, "I'd say about six or seven months after I was there and got involved in evangelism, I began to understand the application of the word and realized that this ain't no game," Keith said. In all, they both felt that this made Bethany a one of a kind church.

Cathy remarked that the commitment among the choir and musicians was unique. "They were professional in their focused approach. They were concerned with how the music sounded and always showed up on time and they didn't leave once they were finished singing, as many choirs did elsewhere," she said.

Emilie Bowman (Duncan) joined Bethany in 1960 and upon Pastor Johnson's request started directing the choir for her first time. She said that Rocellia was serious about the choir from the beginning of his ministry. She said he once told her, "The choir is the biggest headache in the church." It wasn't their sound or ability to excite people, the size of the choir, or the song selection that mattered most to him. His choir needed to understand how to reach people, not with their gospel songs, but with the message of the gospel. According to Emilie, he understood better than most people that the issues that plagued the typical black church choir, like purchasing robes, the prima donna attitudes, not leaving church service until it was over, not selling tickets, etc.

Emilie admitted that she didn't realize how right he was until she attended a National Workshop, which helped her to fully view some of the choir issues that were occurring within local black churches.

Rocellia knew that to prevent these issues from occurring within his choir, he'd have to create a structure based on a sense of discipline and decorum. These efforts included ensuring that they would attend church regularly, enroll in Bible study and serve in other areas of the church's ministry, in addition to singing in the choir. So, he set out to systematically use the ministry of the choir to introduce and encourage choir members to pursue a deeper relationship with Christ through the Evangelism classes. Pastor Johnson was aided by the commitment and insistence of strong choir leadership that supported his directives for every choir member to enroll in Bible classes.

There were a couple of issues that Pastor Johnson would often speak against. One issue was that church choirs shouldn't sell tickets to musicals or any other church event. Just as he didn't charge for Evangelism Workshops, Pastor Johnson was also against the church selling chicken and barbecue dinners to raise money. His philosophy was that taking up an offering was acceptable, but was against the local church selling anything to raise money.

The other issue was for choir members to leave church early. On one occasion, Emilie remembered, one of the choir members walked out of the choir stand to leave church early. No one else was walking at the time so everyone noticed her. As the choir member was making her way down the aisle and out the doors of the sanctuary, Pastor Johnson made it a point to make sure that everyone in church knew that this choir member was leaving because she was going to work. For him, that was one of the few acceptable reasons to leave church early.

According to Emilie, Rocellia would also occasionally hold meetings, sometimes on Sunday mornings, with the choir on what he wanted from his choir. He'd attend choir rehearsals to listen and encourage the choir members to attend church regularly and to be on time. He also encouraged his choirs to attend Bible classes to learn God's word from scripture instead of song lyrics to help them learn what they were singing about. Eventually, the emphasis of music was incorporated into the Workshops via musicals and also began to share his methods with other pastors in his teaching in connection with evangelism. To accomplish this, the choirs needed to become better stewards of their gifts.

In a class that he was teaching at Bethany in 1998, Pastor Johnson explained his reasoning on the matter of decorum in the church. He said to the group,

> There's certain behavior that goes with being in the House of God. There is certain behavior that you can display after your walk out [of the sanctuary] other than what you can do when you're in there, like moving around, socializing and having conversations. There is a decorum that ought to be a part of our Christian character and a part of our worship when you are in the presence of God in worship. Amen.[52]

Rocellia's success with the choir may not have been more evident than during the 24-Hour Gospel Marathons, because they required each choir member to commit to the rehearsals, proper attire, singing schedule, service, and to do all of that as an act of ministry. Emilie said he'd meet with the choir to establish the needed decorum. After the Marathon, she said he met with them again to congratulate them for how they conducted themselves during the service.

Guest Appearances

Emilie said that when Bethany first launched they didn't have a musical staff, but as the word got out about this new church, they were able to assemble a choir. Prior to Dorothy's arrival, Bethany didn't have any musicians. Before Bethany had its own musicians, various musicians like Charles Turner, Kenneth Ulmer, Arthur Branch and Richard Williams played occasionally at worship services and church programs. According to a document on the history of Bethany history trivia, the first singing group at Bethany was called "Menturn Glee," which was directed by Charles Turner. They sang at Bethany's Second Anniversary service. The "Vesperettes" was another guest singing group at Bethany. They were a young adult singing group that included Brenda Williams and her friends Joyce Johnson, Delores Johnson and Barbara Gibson, that were members of Mt. Gilead at the time. Dorothy Johnson accompanied them on the piano. Emilie said they also had other outside groups to come in and sing.

A sixteen-year-old, Richard Williams said that was his first musical contact with Bethany was as a guest musician for the Young Adult choir musical in 1968. He's currently the Senior Pastor of Victory Institutional Baptist Church in Hawthorne, California. Coincidentally, Richard's parents had neighbors that were members of Mt. Gilead Baptist Church, before his experience at the musical at little Bethany. He had already considered Rocellia to be "cutting edge" and not as traditional as his older brother. He didn't become a member of Bethany, but in 1972 he returned to big Bethany to become a member of their musical staff to play for the Young Adult choir until 1977 when he returned to his former church to acknowledge his calling to the ministry.

In addition to the many guest musicians, the great gospel singer Mahalia Jackson considered the "Queen of Gospel Music," once visited little Bethany. Emile said that Ms. Jackson was sitting in the pews and at the end of the service Rocellia asked her to come forward. She spoke and sang a couple of songs, one of the songs was her hit "Precious Lord."[53] According to Emilie, "She tore it up," and it was like the church service started over again. They were so engulfed by a spirit of joy and jubilance of the voice of this renowned singer that time became unimportant. According to Emilie, that service didn't end until about three o'clock in the afternoon. Service started at 11 o'clock in the morning.

In the late seventies and eighties, Natalie Cole was a member of Bethany and when she was in attendance she would occasionally sing at the church. Almost every time Pastor Johnson saw her in the congregation, he'd usually call her forward to sing "Yes, Lord."

Little Bethany also had a large Men's chorus because it drew a large section of the men's membership from within the church. This is quite unusual in itself. Other than Dan Dawson, a lot of the men weren't known for their singing voices, like Joseph Lee, who was known for his preaching and teaching and Ed Russell who became the Dean of the Bible college and head of the Trustees.

Little Bethany Choirs: Adult Choir (Above); Mens Choir (Below)

An Abundance of Talent

Overall, throughout its history, Bethany was always blessed with talented musicians and a blend of voice and musical talent, beginning with Dorothy, Emilie and Reggie. Charlee Kessee admitted that even then she was captivated by Bethany's many choirs, especially the young adult choir, which was her peer group.

Dorothy's family said that she first displayed an interest in music when she was just three years old. As a surprise, her mother bought her a miniature baby grand piano to play. Emilie recalled that "Dorothy would play the piano and eat mustard from a jar," while she was pregnant with her daughter Rosalyn, which they thought was funny. When she finally joined Bethany, Dorothy played the piano and Charles Turner played the organ. Dorothy was the first official piano player for Bethany. She did not receive a salary for playing the piano at little Bethany. Dorothy would play at every service. Interestingly, no one has played the piano at Bethany regularly since her passing in 2008, which meant that Dorothy was the only pianist in the history of the Bethany Baptist Church to date. Her graceful voice and musicianship along with Emilie's commanding presence as the director of the choir created a great musical legacy for Bethany that has never been surpassed.

Richard said that he "couldn't say enough about a kind of symbiotic relationship that Dorothy, Emilie and Reggie had with Bethany's Executive choir," which was the adult choir, "along with me, James [Williams] and Dorothy with the Young Adult choir." They all had to work "hand in glove," as Richard put it, to ensure that their efforts were cohesive and seamless in their teamwork and coordination of the music and "keeping the voices together" for the congregation. Richard attributed most of this chemistry to Dorothy. Emilie explained that it helped that Rocellia was familiar with Dorothy and her singing and playing

Dorothy playing the piano in a church service
at Audubon Junior High School.

at home and Mt. Gilead. So, he knew the type of music he wanted from them. In the early years, they'd had to deal with arguments at choir rehearsal every Thursday night with a few choir members over "their song." Once those issues were addressed, things improved. New members continued to join, and they began to develop Bethany's music ministry.

The "Bethaniares" was another in-house singing group at Bethany that was a church favorite. Christine Wallace said that Pastor Johnson was asked to do a lot of preaching revivals around the country and he needed someone to sing for him on those occasions. So, he asked certain choir members if they'd be available to travel and sing for him on certain holidays and during the summer. According to that Bethany trivia document, the group originally included Emilie Bowman (Duncan), Dan Dawson, Delores Walker-Long, Brenda Williams and Dorothy Johnson. The group was later reorganized to include Gussie Gaines, Minnie Russell, Ella Cannon, Emilie and Dorothy, who sang and played the piano. Christine Wallace would fill in on occasion at local singing events and eventually replaced Ella. They eventually bought themselves some singing robes and named themselves the "Bethaniaires." Gussie had a beautiful, smooth alto-tenor voice that had become a favorite soloist church favorite. Christine said another one of their favorite songs was "The Lord Will Provide."

In a 1979 recorded audio that was provided by Emilie - Emilie, Minnie, Dorothy, Gussie and Ella sang their rendition of a song titled "Do You Know Him." Gussie and Ella shared the lead with Ella singing the high soprano part. They sang it slower pace, which highlighted the musicianship of Dorothy on the piano, Reggie on the organ and added their trademark angelic four-part — *Oh-oh-oh-oh-(ohhh), Oh-oh-oh-oh-(ohhhh), Ohhh* — harmony which made this a popular classic song that seemed unique to them.

Richard felt that they didn't focus so much on the instrumentation, as they did on the blend of their voices. Dorothy and Emilie were impeccable in their singing diction and harmony. The five women were intentional about their harmony, their diction and their annunciation. They did not sing as five soloists. They trained their voices to blend together to sing as a single voice that personified the music of Bethany's ministry.

Reggie Shaw was a professional musician that sold pianos and organs at Colton's Pianos and Organs in Carson, California. He sang and played the organ and occasionally directed some songs. He was an expert organist and had a smooth tenor singing voice. Richard said that before he joined the music staff at Bethany, he was already a classically trained musician that had been playing since he was seven years old. Yet, he said that when he arrived at Bethany, Reggie Shaw was the church's full-time organist, but he occasionally needed coverage on some Sunday's due to his work schedule. So, Richard described himself as an "intern" that learned from Reggie, because Reggie was an exceptional organist and as Richard put it, "He could make that organ talk."

During the late seventies and eighties, Bethany was blessed with another talented crop of choir directors and musicians, such as Michael Stone, Richard and his younger brother Keith Williams, Barbara Williams (Beach), Eddie and Laura Cole, Carlton Emerson with the Children's Choir and Rodney Potts with the Young Adult Choir. Michael Stone played the piano, organ and occasionally directed the choir. Some of the talented voices included Dorothy and Emilie, the Bethaniaires, the Vesperettes, the Men's Chorus, Reginald Shaw, Gussie Gaines, Christine Wallace, Ella Canon, Eddie and Laura Cole, Luella Bailey, Rex Cortez that was known as "Bo," Carl Daniels and Cathy Henderson Mitchell.

There was also a children's choir and a Young Adult choir that were equally talented. During the 80s, Bethany's Young Adult choir included Daniel Dawson Jr. and Rodney Potts as the musicians with Cherise Williams as the director and talented voices like Danise Dawson (Daniel's sister), and Cathy.

Laura and Eddie brought their music pedigrees with them to Bethany. Both Eddie and Laura were music professionals. They got married in December 1978 and moved to Los Angeles in June 1979. Laura was a music teacher with a beautifully trained opera singing voice and taught music. Eddie was from a famous musical family. His father Edward was a jazz musician who played with his famous brother, Nat King Cole. Like his father, Eddie had also become a skilled musician and director of his college band. He had gone on to tour with his cousin Natalie and perform with Ray Charles and Chaka Khan.[54] Eddie and Laura met in college as music majors, got married and moved to Los Angeles. Soon after arriving, he began to tour with his cousin Natalie.

Eddie's Aunt Evelyn and his cousin Natalie Cole were already members of Bethany at the time. So, when the young couple arrived in L.A., Aunt Bae told them they were going to church on Sunday and introduced them to Rocellia and Dorothy. Dorothy told them "rehearsal is on Thursday," and they were there. So, they joined Bethany that Sunday and were at choir rehearsal on Thursday night. Laura's orientation counselor when she joined that Sunday was Charlee Harper Kessee and the team leader for their evangelism visit at home was Johnny Anderson a long-time member and usher at Bethany. When asked about their initial impressions of Pastor Johnson, Eddie said that he was attracted to Pastor's Johnson's evangelical teaching. He explained the scriptures. Laura added that he wasn't the stereotypical preacher that non-churchgoers disliked or that they felt just wanted their money. Pastor Johnson was real, with down-home common-sense wisdom. Eddie said that he was a Christian when he arrived but hadn't become assured of his salvation until he attended an Evangelism 101 class.

Keith Williams, Richard's successor as Bethany's organist, explained that the music is a very integral part of evangelism as it pertains to Sunday worship because it was often the reason people came to church and inspired them to return. Many of the choir members were also Evangelism counselors and Bible teachers. On their assigned Sunday, they'd leave the choir stand in their choir robe to stand behind a new member that walked down to the front of the church and escort them to the office upstairs to get information and share the gospel. They might also meet the person again during a "follow-through" visit at the person's home.

There were two other qualities that were unique about the Bethany choirs. They didn't leave the choir stand once they were finished singing and they traveled well. When it was time to go to a visiting church for a 3:30 pm service, they'd show up and usually fill up the church's choir stand. Yet, they didn't try to put on a show. They were there as servants committed to ministry. In a 1985 Annual Church meeting, Pastor Johnson spoke about the devotion of his musicians and choir to the church's ministry.[55] He said to the various auxiliary (ministry) leaders in the room,

> You'd be surprised how many good churches in town that would like to have one musician that that they can depend on. When the tithers [of the church] are marching, the choir stand is practically empty. They are tithers. The musicians are just not musicians, they are servants. They teach. They sing. They direct. They play. They are involved in Sunday school. They are involved in service. They are involved in mission. They are involved in witnessing. And so, we just don't have a singing unit. We have some servants who are serving, and they give up their time singing. That's a wonderful group. That group is responsible for at least twenty-five percent of

the total income that comes into this church. And if you had to walk in here two or three days without that choir, it would be a sad sight. There's not another unit in this church that has the impact on the wallet that those people in that choir carry. Not just good singing. This office wouldn't function without the support of those folks coming out of the choir stand to meet people. You see'em hitting the streets to meet people. Some of our crack [dynamite] counselors are in the choir. [Attendees laughed at the use and juxtaposition of the words "crack" and "counselors]. If I could brag a little bit, I don't know another church on this side [of town] or nowhere in the black community that has a choir involved in service. The musicians in these churches, the preachers can't tell 'em nothing. They don't tell 'em nothing. If it ain't no rehearsal, they ain't there. Many of them, after they get through directing, they'll sit outside or go someplace until the [preacher] is ready to whoop. But our folks are involved. They are superintendents. They are trustees. They are prayers. They are all of that stuff.

It is this perspective that Pastor Johnson shared that made Bethany's musical ministry so unique. Keith said that once you get involved in that ministry you have to apply it. This was different from any other churches at that time. It wasn't just I like this song and I think it will go over well. At Bethany, it was always a little bit deeper. It was about how the singing complemented the ministry of God's word.

Keith remembered a time when Bethany visited a church for their Pastor's anniversary and there were other churches and their choirs. The piano at the church was out of tune and difficult to play on. One of the other musicians from another visiting church complained to Keith, "This piano made me look bad." After Bethany did a song and Keith played that same piano, that musician asked Keith, "How'd you make the piano sound like that?" Keith replied, "I don't know." His attitude was "if you can't play these keys, play some of the other keys." The point was to find keys to what worked and give God the glory. Keith explained, "It wasn't how you sound, it was who you're playing for." He credits this attitude to the teaching he received at Bethany and the need to be focused on the task.

In all, God sent talent to Bethany in the forms of musicians, singers and choir directors. Some of them became more familiar with Christ and others came to know him at and because of Bethany. Yet, they brought with them their vast array of musical talents, gifts and hearts for praise. As they began to avail themselves of the teaching, preaching and ministry of the church, they became servants. This helped them to apply their Christian service beyond the choir stand on Sunday to minister Monday through Saturday to share the gospel and to do the work of ministry.

6

First Sunday Night

Just like almost everything else he did, Pastor even took a unique approach to communion. He approached his first Sunday night Communion service or Lord's Supper as if they were conducting a meal like the New Testament disciples would've done it today. Of course, it was always done in the evening because that was supper time, according to Pastor Johnson. It was always a joyous and solemn and sacred occasion, which Bethany members treated with a sense of reverence. It was the service that you didn't miss. If you were preaching, it was always the best service to preach because you'd always have a full house.

Pastor Sylvester Washington said, "While we were attending Fuller, he sort of took to me and started to invite me to Bethany to preach during the Communion service." Washington said that Pastor Johnson and Bethany had one of the most well-attended Communion services that he had ever experienced. Bethany's service would start at 6 p.m. every first Sunday night of the month. Yet, he noticed that Pastor would remain in his office, which made Washington wonder why Pastor Johnson was not out in this service. Washington said that Rocellia had taught the church so well that they could conduct the service without him. He'd eventually make it out there at 7:30 or 8 p.m. when service started at 6.

If you didn't know better, you might get the impression that Pastor Johnson would remain in the office because communion wasn't a big deal. That wasn't true. Communion was the most important and most sacred service at Bethany and the atmosphere displayed that reality. All the lights would be dimmed as communion was being prepared. The ministers would leave the pulpit to prepare the table. Bethany never used the convenient little cups with the juice and wafer attached. It was the tradition that every first Sunday one of the deaconesses would bake the flour-less bread that was served at communion. At least a couple of the deacons would arrive at church at least a couple of hours to pour every glass of juice and place it in the silver dish.

Communion was an event. No one emphasized communion like Pastor Johnson. No one created an atmosphere or an experience like Pastor Johnson. Rod Miles explained it perfectly. He said, "Once you got to the level where you could appreciate what communion represented that's when it started having meaning. To see his dedication to Communion service, communion was another service. It wasn't part of the six o'clock service. It was its own service. It was a separate service and he had a whole 'nuther perspective of letting you know that it's time." To Rocellia, communion was not just a ceremony. It was important and extremely sacred because it focused on the person of Jesus Christ and his sacrifice for mankind. He looked at it this way:

> Once you understand that the gospel is a person. It's not a set of religious rules about do's and don'ts. It's not a series of suggested ideas that come from God and was written in the scriptures. But the gospel is a person. And once you

understand the in depth meaning of the gospel being a person it's going to upgrade your thinking and your response to the service that we call communion. But as long as you just sit there and see the gospel as a religious ritual you will never be able to separate communion from the Super Bowl. The Super Bowl will get you every time. Aaaa-men.[56]

When Pastor began to recite Isaiah 53 verbatim, the deacons would line up and move the table to allow the ministers to come from the pulpit down in front to serve communion. The deaconess would also come forward dressed all in white, with their heads covered, and white gloves to lift and hold the linen that covered the communion table. The ministers would position themselves on the left and right sides behind the table. The deacons would subsequently line up on both sides in equal numbers. One of the ministers on the right side of the table would be responsible for help breaking the bread and handing the silver communion trays to the deacons one at a time as they moved to their serving areas around the church.

It was very important to Pastor that those distinctions be made. They always wore dark suits and white gloves and served in tandem to their pre-determined areas of the sanctuary once for the bread, then again for the juice. During all of this, the choir would sing as the musicians played at a low volume. Emilie Duncan usually directed the choir, while Pastor Johnson's wife Dorothy Johnson was on the piano and either Keith Williams or Reginald Shaw would be on the organ. No one would speak or leave their seats. Again, it was considered a sacred time.

Pastor Johnson had made it a practice to recite all three-hundred and eighty-six words of Isaiah 53 verbatim as part of the Communion service. He'd read to help the congregation prepare their hearts and minds to partake of communion. Pastor Washington said that he was so impressed with the practice because he had never heard or seen that kind of thing done before. He said that without knowing all the importance, he adopted this practice of preceding their communion with the recitation of Isaiah 53. He said that at some point, "I remember complaining to Pastor Johnson about not getting the people to attend communion the way I felt that it should be. I told him that I didn't understand. He said, 'You're not interested.' I responded to him, 'Yes, I am interested, that's why I'm asking you about it.' 'No, you're not interested,' he smiled and repeated, 'You're not interested.' Then he offered clarification, when he said, 'The people are interested in what you're interested in. When you can show a little more interest.'" So, Washington said, "I had to find a way to teach the people my interests and concerns for it and it changed everything about it. It had to be important to me. If I couldn't show that to the congregation, it wouldn't be important to them." That helped explain the significance of communion to Pastor Johnson, why he put so much emphasis on it in the manner that he did. It was because it was important to him.

The entire communion ceremony would begin after the sermon was preached and the invitation to accept Christ had been extended. The ceremony alone could take at least forty-five minutes or longer. Yet, time didn't matter. There was a very deliberate process in which Pastor Johnson would take as much time as necessary to make sure that every person was in the proper spiritual position to receive communion.

Once communion had been served and the glasses had been collected, they then conducted "The Right Hand of Fellowship." This was the opportunity to welcome all new members into the Bethany family. Each person that had joined the church that month or that had not done it previously would come forward to receive a right-handed handshake from the Pastor, ministerial staff and the choir and the deacons that lined up along the window to shake hands with everyone in the congregation as they came around from the front of the church. The choir would end up in the center aisle with every person has returned to their seats now standing awaiting the benediction to conclude the service. Oddly enough, most of us would stand around the front of the church talking and saying goodbye while the parking lot cleared. In all, it was the most important service and we enjoyed it together as a family.

This ceremony provided the tone and imagery that helped the attendees to feel and experience the sacredness of the Lord's sacrifice in a way that made it meaningful and memorable. In that, it also created opportunities for their reconciliation. It was where they began to understand and appreciate the true meaning of communion and it became alive for them. Everything that was done, from the actual breaking of the bread to drinking juice, dimming the lights and playing the music quietly and the somber atmosphere made the experience powerful. Besides, Pastor's recital of Isaiah 53 offered dramatic oratory of the crucifixion. It was like you could picture it. This all helped make a service that people didn't want to miss. For members such as Cathy, she said, "This was the first time as I thought about the crucifixion and cried." She felt that the crucifixion was presented in a way that was deep, meaningful and widely considered one of her fondest memories of Bethany and Pastor Johnson.

After minutes of quiet reflection Pastor Johnson would say, "Somebody's not ready." He was never in a hurry or rush when it came to communion. Washington remembered that he may do that for another fifteen minutes to make sure everyone had the proper attitude before they took communion, which he thought was very unique. Washington said he'd been there several times when the church didn't get out until 10 p.m. and no one left. He admitted that he didn't know what to think because Pastor Johnson was so different from the other pastors that he had experienced. He just observed him.

There was one occasion when the bread wasn't prepared for Communion service. Someone had forgotten to make the bread. Rod had the honor of having to go tell Pastor Johnson. An hour before service, Rod went into his office and said, "Pastor, they didn't bring the bread. Do you want me to go across the street and get some crackers?" Rod thought, *"What did I say that for?"* Pastor Johnson was upset, but they didn't have communion that night. He was not going to substitute the bread for crackers. This happened one other time but this time it was during a gospel Marathon. Rod had learned his lesson from the time before. When he informed Pastor, Rod said Pastor chewed him out this time, asking him, "How come you ain't got that, Rod?" Rod tried to explain that he had never made the bread before. Someone eventually showed Rod how to make the bread. Rod went back to tell Pastor that it was done and when Pastor Johnson heard that Sister Dawson helped then he was okay.

The Lord's Supper is an important event in the life of the believer because it is supposed to make them remember His sacrifice. This fact was important to Rocellia and something he made clear at every Communion service. He would place a unique focus on two particular statements from the Apostle Paul. In 1 Corinthians 11, of communion, the Apostle Paul wrote:

> For I received from the Lord that which I also delivered to you: that the Lord Jesus on the same night in which He was betrayed took bread; and when He had given thanks, He broke it and said, "Take, eat; this is My body which is broken for you; do this in remembrance of Me." In the same manner, He also took the cup after supper, saying, "This cup is the new covenant in My blood. This do, as often as you drink it, in remembrance of Me." For as often as you eat this bread and drink this cup, you proclaim the Lord's death till He comes. Therefore, whoever eats this bread or drinks this

cup of the Lord in an unworthy manner will be guilty of the body and blood of the Lord. But let a man examine himself, and so let him eat of the bread and drink of the cup (1 Cor. 11:23-28, NKJV).

Those two significant statements were, "Take, eat; this is My body which is broken for you; do this in remembrance of Me" (v.25) and, "Therefore whoever eats this bread or drinks this cup of the Lord in an unworthy manner will be guilty of the body and blood of the Lord" (v.27). Rocellia took these two statements very seriously. He'd correct any that said the bread "represented" the Lord's body, because of Paul's words that it was the Lord's whole body that had been broken, not just a few bones.

Rocellia's moving citation of Isaiah 53, where the prophet Isaiah foretold of his suffering, helped him to illustrate the fact that the Lord's body was so badly tortured and beaten that it was hardly recognizable. Pastor Johnson wanted to make sure this was something his members understood and remembered. With that, he was equally concerned that they took communion in the right relationship and with the proper attitude about His death and resurrection and the presence of any personal sin in their lives. So, when he'd say, "Somebody's not ready," it's likely that he wanted to make two things very certain. First, that everyone remembered the tremendous sacrifice that Jesus paid for salvation for their sin. Secondly, there was also an awareness that this ceremony could not become just another tradition or ritual that's done without its appropriate sacredness and contemplation. Therefore, it was essential to him that everyone examine themselves, as Paul encouraged, to reflect deeply on their relationship with the Lord and any unconfessed sin in their lives.

Those first Sunday night services demonstrated Pastor's intentionality with Isaiah 53 and Christ's sacrifice. They made a deep impact on all that would be in attendance to help them to understand the sacredness and importance of the Last Supper and communion. This service also helped the congregation to be intentional about worship overall, which in some ways prepared them for the idea of a 24-Hour Gospel Marathon. The next chapter will describe that completely unconventional event and provide some of those memories.

7

The 24-Hour Gospel Marathon

"Who could ever conceive of anything like that?" Greg Tyler marveled about the idea of a 24-Hour Gospel Marathon. This was another one of those things that was based on Pastor Johnson's unusual relationship with God. The idea was both biblically sound and spiritually significant, but it also seemed to have a tinge of craziness because it was an idea that was so far out there that it was inconceivable. The 24-Hour Gospel Marathons were one of a kind events that illustrated Rocellia's sense of how God's church should approach worship to God, which was as an around the clock event for the glory of God. Yet, it was so organized and well received.

The idea seemed to fit the expression that he would say often to his members. He'd say, "It's the Lord's day all day" to express what he felt was the proper attitude toward worship and church attendance for every Christian. Needless to say, this expression also characterized the long services that were held at Bethany and the expectation that his members would attend each of the three Sunday services at the church, including the occasional 3:30 p.m. services when the church would fellowship with other churches.

The 24-Hour Gospel Marathons were held annually on the weekend of the first Sunday night in October non-stop from 9 p.m. Saturday to 9 p.m. Sunday evening. The first sermon was usually scheduled to begin around 10 p.m. on that Saturday night, then Midnight, 2 a.m., 5, 7, 9, 11 a.m., 1:30 p.m., 3 p.m., and concluded at the 6 p.m. Communion service. Some of the preachers over the years were Pastor Sylvester Washington who preached at every Marathon, along with other well-known pastors like Kenneth Ulmer, E.V. Hill, James Morton from Atlanta, T.M. Chambers, Donald Gardner, William Turner and Bethany's current Pastor L.A. Kessee, who is known around the country for his preaching, and countless others.

The members of Bethany immediately embraced the unique and unusual requirements of the Marathon. Most members would commit to attending the full 24-hours, serving in their auxiliaries, but always on-time to hear each preacher, even during those twilight hours which were always the hardest times to stay awake. When it was concluding after the Communion service there was always a crowd. Visitors would attend, but they would typically leave and come back rather than commit to the entire twenty-four hours.

Again, the idea of a 24-hour worship service seemed to fit the expression that he would say often to his members: "It's the Lord's day all day." Huns Lee, son of Joe and Thera Lee, who grew up at Bethany, mentioned how on those Sundays when Pastor Johnson preached, the church wouldn't get out until around 1:30 or 2 p.m. That meant that for most members they had been at Church since 9:30 a.m. for Sunday School and wouldn't get home until 6:30 or 7 p.m. from the afternoon service. Pastor Johnson would say, "You don't have time to go home. Just grab something to eat and be back on time."

The challenge was that by the time you got out of the church through the slow-moving crowd, said your greetings and goodbyes and made your way to your car, another thirty minutes may have passed. By the time you were able to leave you only had maybe an hour before you had to either head back or be on your way to the other church. Regardless, Bethanites would grab something to eat as Pastor had directed and be there on time. The Hamburger City fast-food stand, located across the street, was a popular and convenient favorite, especially during Marathon weekends.

Of all the Marathons that Bethany hosted, the 1988 Marathon was especially memorable. The theme for this Marathon was "Rescue the Perishing." The *L. A. Times* had a reporter there to chronicle the 1988 Marathon. The *L. A. Times* wrote in their 1988 article to commemorate the tenth Marathon,

> Now in its 10th year, the Marathon was conceived by Bethany's pastor, the Rev. Rocellia Johnson, as a sort of Olympics of prayer, a 7-Eleven approach to fighting sin, a battle of the preachers, an ultimate revival meeting. As Johnson figured it, too many non-churchgoers have too often used the excuse that they could not find time to attend services. Others said they were just plain turned off to the frequent demands for donations. Johnson's solution: a free, non-stop 24-hour gospel [worship] service.[57]

They added a quote from Gerri Landry, the church's announcer,

> We don't take any offerings," explained Bethany spokeswoman Gerri Landry. "And over 24 hours, no one has an excuse not to come. If they work the day shift or the night shift, whenever they're ready we'll still be open . . . even when the bars have closed for the night." In addition to fiery sermons, worshipers are regularly treated to gospel performances by an 80-member church choir, a prayer

version of the "wave," personal spiritual counselors, a bacon-and-egg breakfast, a brisket and mashed potatoes lunch and overnight care for toddlers and teenagers.

Gospel Wins Over Satan in 24-Hour Marathon

By PAUL FELDMAN
Times Staff Writer

It's standing room only as Rev. T.M. Chambers, above, gets into high gear at 10th annual Gospel Marathon. As the children's choir drifts off to the Land of Nod, Vivian Eldredge joins prayers, songs.

A copy of the Los Angeles Times article that included
a photo of T.M. Chambers climbing the pews.

The preaching roster for that 1988 Marathon was T.M. Chambers at midnight, Lloyd C. Blue, Kenneth Ulmer, A. L. Lewster, Luscious Pope, Austin Williams, R.T. George, Sylvester Washington, William Turner and James Morton. The *L.A. Times* article highlighted Chambers, who took the pulpit at Midnight to a packed church. They described him leaping into the first row of the pews, as if to be climbing, and quoted him saying, "S'cuse me, I've got to move upstairs."

24-Hour Gospel Marathons were greeted with great enthusiasm and were a great success. The *L.A. Times* reported that more than 300 Bethany members pledged to remain for the entire 24 hours, with many people wearing buttons that read, "I am committed to stay." One long term member told the *Times*, "I wouldn't miss this for anything – if I was in traction, I'd make them wheel me in," enthused one long-time congregant, Norma Washington, as she sipped a cup of tea while awaiting the next minister and sermon. One of the nurse-aids, Betty Johnson, told the *L.A. Times* that there was "a contingent of nine nurses, decked out in gleaming white uniforms that were available if anyone needs first aid or faints, or if there is another earthquake."

Pastor Johnson would say that he wanted to reach the people at the Page Four bar across the street. He also wanted to reach the people that were on the street that needed Christ. The *L.A. Times* quoted him as saying,

> "We can get high, we can get real high," declared Johnson, opening the services before an overflow crowd of almost 1,000. "It doesn't cost a dime and you won't come down on Monday. We're going to prove to Los Angeles that Saturday night does not belong to Michelob. Saturday night does not belong to the devil, to sin and to drug dealers."

Pastor Johnson was effective in this hope. The *L.A. Times* reported that, "Also among the all-night worshipers were several reformed drug abusers who received their first exposure to Bethany by stumbling in during previous Marathons. "I used to use cocaine, dope, anything I could get my hands on," recalled Monique Taylor, a former professional singer garbed in a red and tan Bethany choir robe. "But I decided to try the Marathon two years ago. The next thing I knew, I was taking a Bible class and then I joined the choir." Another woman confessed, "I was out at a party, but instead of going home, I'm staying here all night," explained Alberta Tanner, who arrived at 1:30 a.m. decked out in a short, black cocktail dress. "Everyone parties, everyone has a good time, but this is one time each year where you can cut it short and go and spend the night at church with the Lord."

Vicky Kelley, a longtime member that joined the church in 1974, recalled that in 1987, the prior year, the church experienced one of the sixteen aftershocks from the Whitter earthquake, which shook the church and interrupted the service. The actual earthquake had occurred three days earlier.

Early that Sunday morning, the wall of stained-glass windows could be heard making a rattling, tinkling sound and the lights above the pews swayed slightly. Not everyone left, but many people went into a panic – screaming, shouting and running out of the church. The shaking happened when it was dark, sometime between midnight and dawn. In the *L.A. Times* article, Pastor Johnson was quoted as saying that after the quake, "People really began to pray." He added this story, "We even had a fellow who had ducked out and gone home. He was pulling into his driveway when the earthquake hit – he turned sure around and came back."[58]

Through the course of the night, it was clear that the earthquake was on the minds of many of the attendees. There were several mentions of the earthquake during the night by Natalie Cole,

Reverend Gardner and Pastor Johnson. Natalie Cole gave a brief testimony at what she mentioned was her first full-time marathon, before she sang a rendition of "It's Real," which she said she learned from her cousin. Natalie also recalled that it was one of the first gospel songs that she learned when she came to the Lord.[59] In one of the refrains of the song, she mentioned the earthquake in the song. As she sang the words "This is real," she said, "Think about that earthquake the other day, I want you to know that I prayed, I prayed to God in earnest. Oh, I prayed, oh I prayed to God in earnest – not caring what folks said." Then, Rocellia stood to make what he described as some "serious remarks" before the choir sang again and Donald Gardner stood to preach. At the end of his remarks, as the musicians began to play their instruments to sing "Thank You Lord," he asked the congregation, "How many people wanna see a little shakin'? Anybody here wanna see it shake? If it shakes, you better reach up to God."

After the choir sang, following the sermon of T.M. Chambers, Donald Gardner asked the congregation to turn to someone and say, "I'm glaaaad," as he proceeded into a pre-sermon whoop just before he led the congregation in singing, "I know the Lord will make a way." He resumed his whoop with more "Yes, He wills" and "Ain't He alrights." He continued to hum and groan as he said he was waiting on the Holy Spirit for his help. After giving honor to God and acknowledging Pastor Johnson and the other ministers, he said "The other morning God sent us a telegram…and He is still in control." He was likely referring to the earthquakes. He took his Scripture text from Matthew 24:2-7 which was about the sign of the coming of the end. He read the verses in his own dramatic reading, emphasizing all the things that the text says, "must be," while Pastor Johnson and others encouraged him on. Jesus said to his disciples that one of those signs would be earthquakes. In his prayer leading to the invitation, he said that "the Lord had shown me the ground opening up and closing back up again." He added, "If it's well with your soul if this building falls ain't nobody worried about it."

Ironically, with all the mentions about the earthquake that occurred days earlier, around 7:42 a.m., the church building began to shake. When the trimmers stopped, people ran out of the church and were still emotionally shaken when the services resumed.

Yet, it had become a matter of urban legend because it cannot be recalled exactly who was preaching at the time of the shocks and what occurred. Some people that were in attendance say it was Reverend Donald Gardner and others say it was Reverend T.M. Chambers. Chambers preached at midnight and Gardner followed him at 3 a.m. The story is that the preacher left the pulpit before finishing his sermon and hurried out of the church with the others and it's not exactly clear if or when he returned. The quake occurred well after Gardner would've left. So, it can't be confirmed that either preacher was speaking during the quake. The truth is that Gardner had to leave immediately after he finished preaching as announced by Pastor Johnson.

There was something special about the idea of being at church for twenty-four straight hours without going home or going to sleep (if you could help it), that made this event a little crazy and glorious at the same time. Initially, there was an awkwardness of trying to keep your eyes open, your head from lowering as you try to stay awake to listen to the sermon at two and four o'clock in the morning on a Saturday night. Each year the attendees learned when to go get a cup of coffee or to go outside for air.

The toughest hours of the Marathons were between 2-5 a.m. If you could get through those hours you had a chance to complete the entire 24 hours. At first, it was awkward and a little embarrassing trying not to fall asleep in church. Yet, you could look around and see people falling to sleep with their heads back, mouths open, even snoring. There was a level of empathy that was developed, and people helped each other endure. Everyone shared the same challenge, so if someone noticed a person in a visible position, like upfront where the deacons sat, the choir stand, or the pulpit, people would tap the person on the shoulder and encourage them to go outside to refresh. Others would simply go to sleep and usually someone would wake them, then take their place. After you've been through your first Gospel Marathon, you'd just get up, walk out, wipe your face or you'd go eat some cookies and get some punch or go take a nap, then go back in when you were ready to continue. When it was over, Pastor Johnson would always tell his members to be sure to go to work on Monday to be blessed.

The 24-Hour Gospel Marathon was a unique event that required a unique leader. Lee Arthur said, "You gotta be a special breed, a special personality to motivate participation" of members to attend and provide 24-hour support because you couldn't depend on visitors or people from other churches to show up and provide support. He added, "Nobody could've done that, but him. Number one, he was the only one that the fellows I knew would preach for at an event like that for nothing" and show up at those hours.

Pastor Sylvester Washington was one of a few preachers that preached at every one of the 24-Hour Gospel Marathons that Bethany conducted. He asked somewhat in amazement, "First of all, who's gonna have a 24-hour service? Nobody believed it could happen or would happen? It did and the news of it was buzzing all over the place." He saw another Pastor try it a couple of times, but he failed because the preachers wouldn't show up. As much as he credits Pastor Johnson, he said he has to give the Bethany members credit for being there. They showed up. The choir didn't leave.

Rev. E.V. Hill speaking at a Gospel Marathon at Bethany. Seated behind him from left to right: Pastors Charlie Green, T.M. Chambers, Rocellia Johnson and Lee Arthur Kessee.

Pastor William Turner, who had preached at several Marathons said, that Rocellia "stepped out the box again to organize a 24-Hour non-stop preaching Marathon." He remembered at the first Marathon when he was invited to preach that he was "scared to death," because he was scheduled to preach at 3 a.m. and he "knew that nobody would be there." He said that when he walked into the church "there were wall to wall people." He said, "Wow!" He recognized that Bethany had demonstrated obedience because Rocellia had demonstrated obedience to God.

According to Lee Arthur, it was considered an honor to be asked to preach at a Marathon. It was something special to be a part of that special event. Lee Arthur told the story of when E.V. Hill preached at the first 24-Hour Gospel Marathon. E.V. Hill was a prominent preacher across the country, a friend of Dr. King and pastor of the largest African American church in the country at one point.[60] Hill knew L.A. Kessee and said to him in amazement, "Who is this guy Johnson? Where has he been? How come I don't know him?" Lee Arthur responded, "Doc, he's been here all the time. He's not a guy who blows his own horn. He's not a guy who is out among the guys talking about what he has and boasting and bragging about the kind of ministry he's got going on." He added, "Hill said, 'I pride myself on knowing anybody that's anybody and here's a man right here in my town, right down the hill from my house and I didn't know him until I got invited to preach here. When I mentioned that I was invited to preach in this Marathon to some guys, they said, 'Wow' and told me, 'You don't wanna miss that.'" Again, this was a major event and no one else could've achieved the size, scope and success of this event except Rocellia. As Lee Arthur concluded, "You have to be a major personality to do something that major."

8

A Teaching Covenant

B ack in 1958 when Rocellia prayed to God for the acquisition of the church building that would become little Bethany, he made a promise to teach that established a covenant between him and God. The term "covenant" presupposes two or more parties who come together to make a contract, agreeing on promises, stipulations, privileges, and responsibilities.[61] In covenants between two people, the responsibilities are shared equally between the two parties. However, in the agreement between God and man, God bears the greater burden. He wouldn't just owe Rocellia the building. In their agreement, God was responsible for the building, the assembly of the people, making sure His word goes forth and that it does its intended work in the lives of the people. In other words, as Rocellia faithfully taught, it was God's job to bless His word. This was the agreement that he would honor throughout his ministry. Rocellia and his team established the Evangelism classes, created systematic Biblical instruction, organized the Bethany Christian Bible Training institute, provided teacher training sessions and helped other pastors to adopt a teaching emphasis as the fruit of his vow to God.

For Rocellia, that sacred agreement was that if God gave him the building then Rocellia would teach God's word. God would fulfill His promise by giving the building and Rocellia would honor his part of the agreement by teaching God's word. He was faithfully devoted to keeping his promise to God. There was never a meeting, gathering, sermon, class where teaching was not required. In fact, he wrote into the bylaws of the church that every Tuesday night there would be a Bible study. So Rocellia was committed to teaching because of the mandate to "teach all nations" from Matthew 28:19. It was his vow that made it his lifelong passion.

His promise to God, "I will surely teach your word," announced his commitment to teaching God's word and made Biblical instruction the central thread of his ministry. Beginning at little Bethany, Pastor Johnson began to build the foundation for teaching. At big Bethany, he established the structure for Christian Education, equipped the organization and established the curriculum. All of this work blossomed into the National Evangelism Movement and the Bethany Christian Bible College, which still exists today. Pastor Johnson's emphasis on teaching the Word of God systematically on weeknights at the time was unconventional within the black church. And in honoring this vow, he introduced many pastors to the importance of formal, systematic instruction of the Scriptures.

In the Black church tradition, Bible studies were relegated to Sunday School or mid-week meetings, with the books of the Bible as the focus. Pastor Johnson recognized these aspects of the teaching tradition within the church but understood that these traditions were insufficient to meet the requirement of God's call for His church. So, while Rocellia didn't invent teaching at church, his approach to expanding teaching could be viewed as another of his innovations.

The vision of Bethany's ministry as a church began with the teaching of evangelism. In an early Coordination Board Meeting, auxiliary leaders were encouraged to catch the vision as leaders to be disciples and witnesses for Jesus Christ. The report says, "We have heard the message and the voice of our Pastor for the past twenty years and the only way we can catch the vision is through understanding, learning, studying God's word, getting involved, submitting ourselves totally to Christ, committing ourselves to evangelism, which will constitute faith in action."[62]

The Big ideas

One of Rocellia's innovations was to expand the teaching. Rocellia saw the need to expand the teaching to classes on evangelism and classes from the various books of the Bible. Key to the efforts of making disciples were the Christian Bible Training (CBT) courses. CBT classes were filled with new believers and new members that came to the church through the follow-through evangelism of the church, which will be discussed in the following chapter. These various classes were different from traditional Sunday School instruction because they provided discipleship training. These were round-table groups, like small groups, that worked through their workbooks to help the person to gain an understanding and some level of maturity of the Christian walk.

Bethany had already developed an expansive Sunday School department that provided up to thirty-six classes for all age groups. Teaching at Bethany exploded from Sunday School and a single weekly Tuesday night Bible study to momentous evangelism classes to spark a dynamic Sunday Christian Bible Training (CBT) curriculum of about ten small group classes and a robust list of at least another twenty-seven classes to the Bethany Christian Bible Training Institute (BCTI) that has impacted a city and churches everywhere. This represented an expansion from dozens of students per week to several hundred students per week.

Ed Russell told the story that Pastor Johnson attended a conference on evangelism and came back to form the Evangelism Department with a class of five students. It's widely considered that the evangelism conference was related to Dr. James Kennedy or his ministry, but that cannot be verified at this late date. The intent was to create a course of study to equip church leadership, Sunday School teachers, Evangelism trainers and general Bible study teachers. Nevertheless, because of the interest, the class grew. Charlee Kessee mentioned that she was motivated to be one of the next people to attend the class.

According to Margaret, the first classes were focused on systematic Bible teaching that they called it "curriculum planning." Margaret was friends with a member of little Bethany named Hazel White that she called "Jo." Margaret was working the graveyard shift at the Post Office and couldn't attend church regularly. She told her friend Hazel that she had prayed to God that if He got her off the graveyard shift that she would be able to church more regularly. Hazel told her that it was a little church, but she liked it and thought Margaret may like it, so she invited Margaret to visit Bethany. Margaret eventually joined Bethany and became an instrumental part of Rocellia's team as he established the church's Bible and Evangelism classes, CBT and the Counseling Center. She also co-taught several of those Bible and Evangelism classes with Pastor Johnson. Over the years, she had developed a special closeness, almost familial relationship, with Pastor Johnson, Dorothy and Rosalyn. She felt they had taken her under their wings.

Margaret Williams said that Pastor Johnson's *God's Plan of the Ages* course that he taught at little Bethany provided some of the groundwork for his systematic teaching and evangelism training. She said that Oscar Harvey, Columbus Wallace and Rev.

John L. Gates taught one of the first classes together that was instrumental in developing which was a systematic approach to evangelism. Margaret said that Rocellia eventually took over that systematic teaching effort and developed the first Evangelism 101 class. Margaret also said those first five students of the Evangelism class were Carolyn Lewis, Rev. Walter Speights, Monica Ingram, Roberta Tate and herself.

This effort led to the formulation of the Evangelism classes, an expansion of Bible classes, including the Christian Bible Training (CBT) classes, which eventually would become the Bethany Christian Training Institute (BCTI) and later renamed Bethany Christian Bible College (BCBC) in 1992. These evangelism classes became the evangelism classes called Evangelism 101 through 105 and eventually Evangelism 106, which became the foundation for the teaching ministry. Some of the other classes included the Books of Genesis, Romans, Ephesians, Gospel of John, James, God's Plan for the Ages and more. There were also classes in Data and Word Processing and Job Training in the 1980s which was very forward-thinking for a church in those days. The school offered a certificated program with an annual graduation ceremony for all students. As the news of the classes spread around the city, people from churches around the city attended the classes.

In an Evangelism team meeting in November 1982, the team further discussed the idea of "expanding the teaching ministry." Yet, there were concerns raised in the room around the CBT classes and their potential impact on Sunday School classes and what's best for a student's growth and service.[63] In those discussions, Pastor Johnson acknowledged that Sunday School is the mainstream teaching source within the local church and that most people get their basic Bible teaching from Sunday School. Yet, the consensus was that student's that completed CBT may be best discipled by proceeding to either a Basic Christianity type or other Bible study classes without missing Sunday School learning or negatively impacting the Sunday School's efforts. The ultimate aim was to make the Word of God available. Pastor Johnson explained this in one sermon,

> I believe we have come to believe and feel the Bible is inadequate and not sufficient to do the job that God assigned it to do. There's a lot of church folk that feel that we need another treatise aside from the Bible. That we need something else. That there is something God left out. God's word was good enough to create and design the universe. God was wise enough to make a man and to breathe into his nostrils the breath of life and man became a living soul. He was wise enough to put the sun out there and the moon out there and decorate the heavens with stars.[64]

His point was that if God was wise enough to do all those things, he was certainly wise enough to put what was necessary in the Bible to get us from glory to glory. Pastor Johnson wanted to establish a rigorous level of systematic instruction that he hoped would eventually allow for accreditation to a four-year college. So, he implemented a curriculum that provided a strong biblical foundation, exams, homework, grades, teacher feedback, lesson plans, a student government and teacher training. Yet, this Bible instruction needed to be available to every Christian from the college graduate to others and it needed to be free of charge. Thus, the slogan, "a school designed with you in mind."

Team Teaching

The concept or method of "team teaching," usually a woman and man team, was later introduced. At a Teacher's Training Workshop in 1989, Brenda Williams led a class on "team teaching." Brenda became a member of little Bethany in the late 1960s from Mt. Gilead. She was a talented artist that could've attended a prestigious art college in Los Angeles, but pursued a career in teaching as her calling instead. She had earned a master's degree in Education. So, Brenda was the creative traveling team member that would take photographs and prepare the transparencies used for teaching presentations. She used her artistic talents to create the original fisherman's logo that is still being used today and developed the curriculum for the Evangelism 103 class.

In the training workshop, she explained that the concept and strategy of "team teaching" were based on the premise that more than one teacher was better. Brenda said that team teaching wasn't just two people teaching in the same room or taking turns teaching, because two people teaching in the same room does not mean that they're on the same team. According to Brenda, team teaching involved two teachers sharing the roles and duties of planning, preparing, evaluating and instructing a class together. She said, "Pastor added that 'Team teachers ought to complement each other.'" To emphasize the need for team teaching, in that same meeting with Brenda, Pastor Johnson said,

> Sometimes we can be doing things very well and what we're doing is alright within itself. When you have one teacher one class receiving this kind of information and somebody else receiving another kind of information, even though it may be good, but if it is not synchronized…we will wind up sending out conflicting signals.[65]

Teacher Training

Teacher training meetings called "in-service" were conducted monthly and quarterly at Bethany to instruct the teachers in effective teaching methods to ensure successful learning outcomes. These sessions were required of all teachers to ensure that they attended the meetings, understood the instruction and used them in their preparation and execution in their teaching.

Teacher Training Workshops, like the one in Phoenix in 1998, were also held in various cities around the country for teachers involved in the Movement to continue to train those teachers in teaching methods. Attendance was required.

At a Teacher Training Workshop for Evangelism in Phoenix, Pastor Johnson said that you cannot have too many techniques for teaching. "When you find yourself running out of methods and techniques," he said, "then it's time to busy yourself doing some reading, doing some research and those kinds of things to keep your axes sharp." He added,

> Teaching in the church constitutes a very unique setting. In the church you have a setting that is unique to the church itself. It is different than you find in many of the other institutions simply because in institutional type settings you're primarily dealing with people who are primarily on the same level of learning, but within the church itself we have all kinds of personalities and we have people who are on different levels and different wavelengths of learning. It becomes the responsibility of the teacher and of the church to minister effectively to the entire body of Christ. There are some folks there who did not finish grade school, etc., etc. You may have master's degrees and PHDs in your class, but it becomes necessary to minister effectively to all those people because if you are a baptized born-again believer in Jesus Christ you are a member of the body of Christ.[66]

Pastor Johnson's emphasis on teaching techniques was not just about the Bible. It introduced and taught a systematic approach to instruction and a formal methodology to provide effective teaching methods that equipped both the teacher and the student to use their gifts and fulfill their callings. Thus, the mission was to provide teaching that exceeded Sunday School and weekly Bible study to a variety of other courses and to churches around the globe. At the core was the instruction of evangelism, which shaped education to go and teach and make disciples. He'd brag about all of the ways that his people were serving and being educated, like the Computer Center that benefitted the youth and people preparing for employment.

Before attending a Workshop, Pastor Ray Brown said that he was only teaching a new member's class and general Bible study at his church and had become frustrated looking for good study material to use. Brown spoke about the strategy to expand teaching, saying, "It would help this church move to the next level. Now," he joked, "we've got so many classes going on I can't even keep up."

The Institute

At its core, the school began with Evangelism classes, which soon evolved into more Bible classes. The expansion of the classes evolved into the formation of a Bible college. According to Ed Russell, Pastor Johnson formed a five-person committee to formulate a plan for what would become the Bethany Christian Training Institute (BCTI). Those five people were Ed Russell, the Director of the C.E.E.A., Margaret Green for curriculum, Columbus Wallace, the Superintendent of the Sunday School, Bill Burwell as Christian Education Director and Dan Dawson. They sought to achieve accreditation and to offer college-level instruction. However, their goal was not to create an institution within the church, but to create a place of systematic instruction where God's people could come to learn God's word free of charge.

To achieve a high-quality instruction that met the educational needs of his congregation, Rocellia engaged professional educators from among the congregation like Bill Burwell, Brenda Williams, and Ed and Minnie Russell. He also engaged professionals like

Shelia Tolan for a job readiness skills class, Martha Coleman in art and graphic design, Wade Johnson, Karen Butler and Barbara Mitchell in Information Technology/Data Processing and others for their respective professional knowledge and skills. By doing this, not only did he build a great teaching program, but he also effectively found ways for all of his members to exercise their callings and vocations for the work of ministry. In fact, this was an underrecognized aspect of his overall ministry.

This is significant because throughout its history Bethany has been blessed with talented people in every type of work that willingly used their gifts and talents to fulfill their vocations in Bethany's ministry in ways that helped Pastor Johnson and Bethany to fulfill its calling as a local church. In fact, Pastor Johnson was adept at leveraging the gifts and vocations of his members. It also fit his strategy of expanded teaching because it allowed him to effectively equip and leverage the entire membership of Bethany for the work of ministry. At a Teachers Training Workshop, he said,

> My style of ministry is that I like to harness the expertise and the resources of the church. I like to do the kind of things to make your talent available to the service of the Lord…The evangelism process makes it possible to tap and make use of those resources that the Holy Spirit brings into church. It is possible to make every member of the body of Christ functional in that body.[67]

This approach gave way to the diversity of the church's leadership and Evangelism team members, which allowed each of these people to express their vocations (secular and sacred), gifts, talents and experiences into the work of ministry. This was also significant because it allowed them to fully approach their work in ministry the way that God had created and called them. Pastor Johnson touched on a related topic when he made his comments at one of Bethany's Annual Church meetings.[68]

Shelia was a former Registrar for the school. Shelia joined Bethany in 1985 at the suggestion of her mother, who heard about Bethany's evangelism ministry from Seaside workshops. Shelia eventually joined Bethany for many of the same reasons – the choir, communion and being impressed by the teaching of Rocellia. Overall, she worked with the school as a faculty member and Registrar for at least twenty-four years.

The program at the BCTI provided a traditional higher education with a faculty-led by professional experience. Course outlines and lesson plans were required. Every class required a course outline and a weekly lesson plan. There was homework, mid-terms, final exams and grades. Students formed a student government with officers that addressed the needs of the students and acted as a liaison for the school. In a Teacher's workshop somewhere, he was teaching to a different group of potential teachers of Evangelism, and he offered some comments that helped explain his philosophy for tests and teacher evaluations in church. He cited evaluation, which he said was another term for examination, along with preparation and presentation as important areas for effective teaching.

The BCTI curriculum included certifications in Data Processing and Information Services which helped provide students with technological training for basic computer training, word processing, data entry and basic programming skills for job readiness and career advancement. This was incredible, to be offered free of charge in the late 1980s. Pastor Johnson said,

> Even in the church, if preparation, presentation and evaluation are not taking place, then when it comes to teaching you're half-steppin'…So the examination is just asking a question to see if you understood and have learned the [correct] answer. So, you never know if a person learned or not until

you have asked them some questions.

And you can learn by failing an examination if it's a good examination. Taking an examination, you can at least learn that you were wrong…How many times have you gone to school, sat down and wrote a twenty-page paper, that you spent three days on it, you researched it, you've written it well, you have all your stuff in order and it's laid out just like you want it and you can just see a great big "A plus," but when you get it back…Had nobody critiqued that paper and give it back to ya' you would've walked out always thinking that you had it nailed down. In fact, you learned by somebody who knew [that] corrected you…People have to understand that they can learn by failing. I'm not ashamed to say this – I went to college and flunked a whole semester. I made a "D" in one class. It was a shock. It was tough to go back to college again, but out of that failing experience, down the road, I'm sure that I really learned more than some of the folk walking out of there making A's and B's. I failed the examination, but I wasn't dumb about everything. I just missed the exam.

Jesus often used evaluation after teaching. One incident that always comes to my mind is the episode in the life of Jesus when he was down at what we call in theological circles the birthplace of systematic theology the place they call Caesarea Philippi. I was just using those terms because preachers like to hear 'em sometime…It began with Jesus giving his disciples an examination. Understanding that an examination is asking a question in whatever form to see if you know the answer. His examination was to the disciples, "Who do men say that I the Son of Man am?"…They said, that's easy. Some say Moses, some say Elijah, some say Jeremiah, some say John the Baptist and some say you're one of the prophets. Jesus said fine. You gotta "A" right there. The next part of the question was, "Who do you say that I am?" Peter said, "Thou art the Christ, the Son of the Living God.[69]

Upon completion of the program, the students were awarded a formal graduation and diploma. Students wore caps and gowns. The faculty looked professorial as they were adorned in their academic regalia with their robes and hoods displaying their own educational accomplishments. There were commencement speakers, class valedictorians and diplomas for the graduates.

The First Graduation

Ed Russell, the Dean of the school, said that the first graduation was on June 29, 1986, with seven women graduates, which were Dorothy Chambliss, Mary Evans, Wanda Frierson, Evelyn Robinson, Hazel Shipp, Daisy Stewart and Rhonda Wilson. The ceremony also included eleven graduates from Bethel Baptist Church where Reginald Pope was the pastor and seven youth graduates. According to Ed, this was the smallest graduating class and the largest was the class of 2005 which had fifty graduates. Rhonda Wilson was the first valedictorian and Dr. Bill Burwell was the commencement speaker for the first graduation. In her speech as class valedictorian, Rhonda graciously acknowledged that she had learned to "share God's word in her everyday life." She also encouraged others that have already made a commitment to study God's word to "continue to study with sincerity and diligence."[70]

Shelia said, "The graduations were ceremonial celebrations! Filled with all the pomp and circumstances it was an experience that many of the students had never had." According to Shelia, it took weeks of preparation, but it was worth it to see the students and their families celebrate their accomplishment." Mary Evans is a long-time member of Bethany's Adult Usher board and was the class salutatorian, one of those seven graduates. She said that she was so excited to be a part of that first graduation. She became a member of the BCTI faculty in 1988. To date, there is an estimate of about 730 total graduates since the school's inception, not including the graduates from elsewhere around the country.

Again, all of this was available at no cost to the student. Pastor Johnson was very conscious of the financial concerns of potential students. He was determined to make sure there were no financial barriers that would become excuses or prevent students from attending these classes. So, the classes were offered at no cost to the student. The slogan was "A school designed with you in mind." This is still the school's policy today.

The emphasis on teaching had always been founded on and integrated with the work of evangelism to frame a curriculum for soul-winning and discipleship. The two were never separate because they were both essential to the mission and ministry from Matthew 28:19 that admonished evangelism and teaching and Ephesians 4:11 that focused on the equipping of the saints for the work of ministry. In the next chapter, you can see the broader role of the Evangelism classes, how they prepared the students for the ministry of sharing the gospel. It will also share the impact of evangelism upon pastors and churches around the country. All of this work was born out of his covenant to teach God's word.

9

The Gospel of Evangelism

I t was clear that evangelism was the most significant aspect
of his ministry. Pastor Johnson and his team developed a
methodology of evangelism and discipleship that fit the black
church and the black pastor and shared it with churches around
the country. He understood evangelism and discipleship to be
central to the mission of the Christian church. The focus of this
ministry was ultimately on teaching God's people to be witnesses
and fishers of men. This chapter will share the development and
growth of this ministry, provide a conceptual look at how he was
able to develop a methodology that resonated with other pastors,
the Evangelism classes that were developed and the phenomenon
of the Workshop, all of which characterized Bethany as a sending
church.

Evangelism was at the core of his calling and his ministry. With
the help of a great team and an obedient church, he developed and
proclaimed methodologies to equip his members and churches
around the country to respond to the mandate in Matthew 28:18-
20. He led the effort to organize within his church a department
with a single effort to win souls. He set up classes for them to
learn evangelism to become witnesses. He organized a team to

travel with him to share the gospel of evangelism with pastors and churches nationwide to effectively share the gospel and make disciples, which eventually formed a movement.

To begin, Rocellia keenly understood that the gospel was the truth of Christ proclaimed to the world. There is a dual quality of the mission to proclaim the gospel that he strongly accepted. He knew that the work of evangelism existed in two parts – the message and its proclamation. He built a ministry approach around these two pillars and grounded in the mandate to make disciples. Rocellia recognized that part of the problem within the church that affects teaching and the work of discipleship is how Christians interpret the word of God in the work of ministry. Thus, he also understood that teaching the word of God was required and the central thrust of evangelical efforts.

The challenge for the teachers was not just teaching a Bible class. It was in helping them and their students to understand the mandate and to effectively confront the tension between sinful man and a holy, righteous, but merciful God. So Rocellia made sure that people understood that the work of evangelism and discipleship involved restoring that most sacred relationship. The gospel plays a central role in healing this breach. Pastor Johnson said,

> To help first of all in ministry and to the spiritual, so that's where the evangelism process starts in ministering to the spiritual because before you do anything else it becomes necessary to win a person to Christ. You are in endeavoring to restore lost man back to a right relationship and a right standing with God…And how you restore that broken relationship is by the gospel because it is the gospel that is the power of God unto salvation to everyone that believe. God left nothing on this green earth to bring lost folk to a saving knowledge of Jesus Christ but the gospel. That's why

it's essential to know what the gospel is.[71]

In 1975, Pastor Johnson officially organized the Evangelism Department at Bethany, although Carolyn Lewis had already been appointed as the first Evangelism Coordinator. According to Ed Russell, this was after he attended a conference on Evangelism, which likely was at Dr. James Kennedy's *Evangelism Explosion*. It's not clear when this occurred, but it was likely within the early 70s before 1975. Kennedy's ministry began in 1962 and was incorporated in 1972. Charlee admitted that she didn't know about the conference, but that she knew that he had begun reading the *Evangelism Explosion* book by Dr. D. James Kennedy from Coral Ridge Presbyterian Church in Florida.[72] Charlee said, "We saw film after film each week on Dr. Kennedy speaking. We saw films of Dr. Kennedy speaking about how he started in evangelism." She said, "So Pastor was reading all this, and he was showing us all these films, films on role play, all of this."

It's important to understand that Pastor Johnson did not devote his life's work to evangelism because he attended a conference and saw some videos. It could only have been a move of God that urged him not just to this work, but to so completely devote his mind, heart, being and resources to it. Rocellia had been sent by God at that particular time in history and for that particular community to do the work of evangelism. In fact, it wasn't likely that he spoke of this calling in a way that was distinct from teaching, preaching or being a pastor. This calling to share the gospel and make disciples was approached as a basic responsibility of faithful ministry that was intrinsic and congruent with the nature of God's call upon him and in each of the offices he held. Thus, the fruits of his calling were evident in every aspect of his vocation. This allowed him to live and serve the Lord in a manner worthy of that calling, just as Paul encouraged in Ephesians 4:1. He could respond so faithfully because he understood that there are many things that God would want his people to do, but according to Matthew 28:18 doing the work of evangelism and discipleship was imperative. Rocellia understood that and approached this task with the importance and urgency that the Lord requires.

An Evangelism Department

In the course of responding to this ministerial mandate, there were several milestones that shaped this period in the life of the Bethany Baptist Church, which made it distinct in focus from little Bethany. Little Bethany was defined by its organization, growth and teaching emphasis and Big Bethany would be defined by its development of the Evangelism ministry and its national outreach, which later became known as the National Evangelism Movement.

Several pivotal events launched this department into that national ministry. These milestones were the organization of the Evangelism department and the assignment of Carolyn Lewis as the first Evangelism Coordinator in 1975. Carolyn was the daughter of Sullivan Lewis, an early member of Bethany and one of Bethany's first deacons. The first Evangelism class was organized and taught in 1978. In 1979, a group of evangelism classes were taught at the church and made available to the community. That same year, the first workshop was held by Pastor Lusk of Bethel Baptist Church in Seaside, California. A few years later, Deloris "Dee" Berry replaced Carolyn Lewis as the Evangelism Coordinator and took on a national scope of responsibility.

Dee Berry had been raised in the church from childhood, but considered herself a babe in Christ because she had no real understanding of the Bible. She relocated to Los Angeles in 1974 and joined Bethany in 1977 upon the invitation of her longtime friend Sister Irene Thomas. She described her early days as a "whirlwind experience." She remembered that John 3:16 was the first Bible verse that she learned. As she continued to attend and started meeting people, she became more comfortable and began to "figure things out" and gradually begin to understand Pastor's sermons, which helped her realize that she was lost and led her to faith in Christ. She became a student of the Tuesday night Bible class that was led by Pastor Johnson and learned about Christ's work to provide her salvation. This started her journey as a child of God. She continued to learn and grow in her faith. It also inspired her quest for ministry. As a student of Pastor Johnson, she soon began to recognize the Holy Spirit moving on her heart compelling her to a life in ministry, which after a long period of discussions with Pastor Johnson and working around the church she became the second Evangelism Coordinator.

As the Evangelism ministry was developed, it was launched by the leadership of Pastor Johnson and the force that was known as Sister Carolyn Lewis. Carolyn had been the Superintendent of the Sunday School and president of the Coordination Board before Pastor Johnson assigned her as the church's first Evangelism Coordinator. She was a strong, often no-nonsense, loyal, committed, Spirit-filled, yet kind and loving person. Her primary tasks were to organize the home visitations of new members, coordinate Evangelism teams and their schedules and to maintain the necessary contact paperwork and information. Carolyn was perfect for this new role because her personality and determination fit the need to provide a strong sense of coordination to make sure the team members were on time for their scheduled appointment at the church and at the respective homes of the people they were to visit.

Charlee Kessee recalled that when she was a team visit leader, Carolyn would set up the home visits for the various Evangelism teams, then call them until she reached them to make sure they arrived at the church on time for prayer and review the paperwork to make sure they were on-time at the new member's residence. Being too tired or late for the scheduled visit was unacceptable. Charlee said, "She would call me, and she would hound me. She would say, 'Now when you get off work,' and I could be in San Bernardino working that day, 'You come straight home, you come straight to the church…because you have a visit and you need to be here by such and such time for prayer, so you guys can leave and get there.'" Charlee admitted that Carolyn was a powerful person. Pastor Johnson had a knack for drawing people to the church and surrounding himself with people who were as serious about God as he was.

Carolyn was responsible for scheduling and coordinating home visits, but she wouldn't wait to schedule a team visit. She'd do her own fieldwork. She was known to commandeer one of the two church vans to make unannounced, unscheduled appointments with new members. It was nothing to see Carolyn roll up in that dark green van to stop by to see how you're doing. Barbara Mitchell, a new member of Bethany at that time, said that several times Carolyn would see her walking down the street and seemingly from out of nowhere Carolyn would pull over in the church van and ask her, "You coming to church?" Even if she hadn't thought about church or hadn't planned to go, she was afraid to tell Carolyn no, so she'd always reply, "I'll be there." Barbara thought Carolyn was a wonderful lady and credits her persistent style with leading her to Bethany and becoming a Christian disciple. Carolyn embodied the importance and urgency of evangelism.

Debbie Augborne-Allen also served in the role of coordinator working in the Evangelism Department. Debbie became a member in 1975 at the invitation of her neighbor Carita Watkins that was a member of Bethany. Debbie joined Bethany a few days after Carita had led her to Christ in her home. Debbie said that she loved the work and those were some of the best days of her life. She helped create procedures, scheduling visits with new members and organizing teams for home visits. She worked in that office for a couple of years around 1977-79 maybe overlapping with Carolyn, but before Dee. According to Dee, Debbie helped set up and coordinate the new department, helping lay the foundation for what would become a national ministry.

Coleman Zeno and Oscar Harvey, both preachers, had also worked faithfully as Evangelism coordinators for a period of time.

Dee remembers some of those early days as the department and ministry were being organized. According to Dee, the blueprint was Dr. Kennedy's book. She also remembered reading his book and watching films about his approach to evangelism. She also remembered that there were a lot of questions and trepidation among new and current members as they rolled out the program. It was such a new and different approach for church and people met it with some initial apprehension and anxiety. Dee said some people asked, "Why are you trying to change us?" New Members were unsure of why the people from the church needed to come over to their house. She said, "Some saw it as an invasion of privacy while others welcomed it."

Dee admitted that there were some challenges initially. So as membership grew, so did the teams. She said there were lots of obstacles from within and without. There were disagreements. There were also lots of late-night meetings to figure out what to do next. It took lots of prayer, strategizing and pastoral leadership required to make it all come together. The approach began to form. The message was better articulated and rolled out with a better understanding and reception. They also had to deal with developing the appropriate etiquette when visiting a person's home. Should they eat the cookies or accept a drink if offered?

All of this was important to make the proper approach for the sake of the gospel. It was important to be friendly and not offend the hosts, but after all, these weren't purely social visits. The model was improved upon as time went on.

As the efforts were taking shape, there was another realization that came forward. Dee said, "Over time we discovered people who had been in church for twenty, thirty, forty, fifty years and had no personal relationship with Christ. Just like me, going to church and having no understanding about anything just because that's what good people do. I have seen it with my own eyes, people sitting in church fifty years with no real understanding of why. There was a need to share the gospel of salvation. People had just been joining the church and following rituals."

Charlee told the story of a lady that was a good example of being in church all her life, doing church, being religious but never being assured of her salvation. Charlee observed this lady at a Workshop in Palmdale, California, in 1980 or 1981 at what Charlee described as a "fiery church." She said that on the opening night session which was coincidentally called the "Firing up session," that there was one particular lady that Charlee said was fired up. Charlee said that this lady was one of the loudest voices in the audience. She'd loudly shout "Amen." She'd talk back to Pastor Johnson as he spoke, repeating his words, which was the custom in a traditional Baptist church setting. Charlee said that when Pastor Johnson would pace back and forth as he spoke, occasionally pointing his figure randomly at someone as if he was speaking directly to them, this lady would talk back even more. When the breakout sessions began, Charlee noticed that this lady was in her session. Charlee said that one of the things they wanted to know was, who in the group was assured of their salvation (according to the Scriptures). Charlee learned that for all her energy and enthusiasm, this lady didn't know if she was saved. She was a product of a conventional church and the person that needed this ministry.

Margaret remembered the story of the wife of a local pastor from Oklahoma, that was not involved with the Workshop or Movement, but happened to be visiting the city and had decided to attend the event with some friends. The lady stood up and asked the church to pray for her because she was very stressed and was considering suicide. Pastor Theopolis Peoples, the host pastor, asked Margaret to go speak with the woman. Margaret left her coat, purse and money inside to hurry to speak with the lady. On an empty bus, Margaret counseled her and the woman accepted Christ and she helped her to be assured of her salvation based on the scriptures. Afterwards, they went to get some coffee and when they saw Pastor Johnson, the woman told him, "I just accepted Christ!" The lady had admitted to Margaret that she had been attending church for years, but had never been introduced to Christ. Margaret said that she was still concerned with the lady's wellbeing that she had the lady stay with her in her room with her roommate to keep an eye on her. Margaret also followed up with her for a solid year. Two years later, the lady and her husband drove to a Workshop in Detroit from Canada, where they had moved, just to see Margaret.

This story captured the primary goal of the Evangelism ministry, which was to bring the lost to the saving knowledge of Jesus Christ. To do this, people needed to be trained with approaches on how to effectively present the gospel and the plan of salvation.[73] For this, pastor Johnson leveraged the teachings of Dr. James Kennedy's *Evangelism Explosion*. Pastor Johnson's innovations were most evident in the way he took the framework of Kennedy to structure the Evangelism classes, the team etiquette of the home visits and developed the dynamic concept of the Evangelism Workshops. Each of those initiatives was uniquely designed for the context of the congregations that Rocellia was trying to reach.

The Visits

Among the various approaches to evangelize, Bethany adopted the method known as "follow-through evangelism.[74] The follow-through method provided a means of evangelical outreach to people that joined the church, helped establish relationships and provided spiritual guidance with new members and prevented the church from losing contact with people that came forward. As Pastor Brown learned, "It shuts the back door in or closes the back door," which helps people connect with the church and helps churches connect with the people properly upfront. It was a one-on-one method of witnessing that helped a church to witness to its members and to help them become disciples of Christ.

Within the Evangelism ministry at Bethany, there were the Evangelism classes and evangelism counselors who handled the intake process when people came forward to join the church. The counselors were responsible to meet new members and share the "Four Spiritual Laws" and the qualifying questions if needed. The next step in the process was to schedule visits by one of the local evangelism teams. These would usually be a team of three that was responsible for a series of meetings with a new member, preferably at their home or at the church.

These visits would usually occur on a weeknight evening. This team would meet the new member and any family members that were present. The team might lead a group conversation or conduct one-on-one conversations, as appropriate. Those conversations would include a series of workbooks to help introduce the person to the Bible and salvation.

According to Debbie, on the night of their scheduled visits to new members, which was usually after work, the various teams would stop in the Evangelism office to pick up their contact information about the family and the pre-selected tracks and materials that would have been assembled and made available to them to review and discuss before their visits. The packets were assembled according to the age appropriateness for visits that involved children and there was enough for other family members that may sit in. The teams would gather for a group prayer before leaving for their respective visits and provide an update upon their return. Debbie added that all of this was done to ensure that the gospel was going forth and to let each new member we came in contact with to be assured that God loves them and so did we. "We were there to partner with them along their spiritual journeys because did not want anyone to fall away," she summarized so well.

There were also important protocols established to ensure a sense of decorum. Business attire was required and women wore dresses, which was prudent in those days. Initially, once in the home, the team would meet with the entire household. In subsequent visits, men would meet with men and women would meet with women, to ensure that there were no potential concerns. Ultimately the goals were twofold – to share the gospel and to establish relationships.

This aspect of the Evangelism ministry at Bethany became the key practice for the church's growth because it helped the church to meet and engage with every new member. Pastor Brown said Dr. Johnson would say, "We give them the right hand of fellowship and we have nothing for them. That was true, we give them the right hand of fellowship and we tell them to go straight to work, without ensuring that they are properly trained and equipped to serve."

There were three phases to this effort that helped launch the discipleship of that new member. First, the goal was to know if the person had a relationship with Christ and be assured of their salvation. In either case, the counselor would ask the two qualifying questions from the *Evangelism Explosion*, which are,

"If you were to die tonight, God forbid, do you think you'd go to heaven? Why or why not?" and "If you were to stand before God at heaven's gate and He asked why He should let you in, what would you say?"[75]

The second major step was to conduct a series of three visits at the person's home. These visits would be conducted by a team of three trained counselors that would help embrace that family and introduce them to three Bible study workbooks chosen to help them to embark on their own personal Bible study, which began the work of discipleship. In the follow-up meetings, the team members would break into one-on-one sessions to talk through the workbooks. The third phase would be to help the new members join a Christian Basic Training (CBT) classes on Sunday mornings, which they continue up to a year based on their maturity, then proceed to other classes.

The follow-through method provided a means for discipleship that extended to the household of new members. The way it worked was that when people joined the church, they'd be greeted by a trained evangelism counselor, men for men and women for women. Specially trained counselors would greet children and youth. Upon the person joining the church, they would proceed to sit down with that person to meet them, gather basic information and set up additional follow-up meetings at the person's home, preferably within the next week or so. That counselor would be a point of contact for that new member of the church Evangelism department.

The Evangelism Classes

From his learning about one-on-one and follow through evangelism, Pastor Johnson and his team developed a complete curriculum that allowed students to be introduced to evangelism, Scripture memorization, role play and understanding cults and false doctrines. This course of training consisted of six ten-week classes. The initial Evangelism classes were Evangelism 101, 102, 103, 104, 105. Evangelism 106 through 108 were added later.

Evangelism 101 was an introduction to evangelism. This was the class that Pastor Johnson taught and the class he recommended that every pastor teach. This course was designed to introduce the individual believer to the basic biblical principles of Evangelism. Evangelism 102 is designed to explore, comprehend and memorize the "seed plot" scriptures from *Evangelism Explosion*. Evangelism 103 was the "on the job training course" where students were taught the gospel plan in conversational form through role-play in preparation for evangelism counseling and home visitations. Evangelism 104 was a practicum course designed to develop practical evangelism skills. Evangelism 105 was designed to explore and confront false doctrines. Evangelism 106 had been added later to add teaching on counseling techniques to address spiritual, psychological and family and group counseling needs. It was eventually broken into three courses, 106, 107 and 108.[76]

When the program began and classes were being developed and rolled out, teachers would have to be reassigned from session to session to build out the program. Charlee said that she was originally assigned to teach Evangelism 102. When that class was completed, she was asked by Pastor Johnson to teach Evangelism 103, after the current teacher, Margaret was also reassigned, then she was asked to develop a curriculum for Evangelism 104 and to teach that new class. According to Charlee, she taught three different classes within consecutive quarters.

In 1989 there was a Teacher Training Workshop held in Phoenix, Arizona. According to Greg Tyler, Pastor Henry Barnwell of First New Life Baptist Church was one of the regional directors and the Director of Training for the Movement in Phoenix played an instrumental role in the success of the Teachers Training event and Evangelism Workshops that were conducted in his city. Here's some of what Pastor Johnson taught about teaching evangelism at that event,

> Instinctively by nature people do not really buy anything, they are sold [something]…So going to one whole process we are trying to do we are trying to sell the evangelism process by giving people an overview and taking them through the entire training process. Beginning with 101, having them to know that these classes are done in ten weeks of training in each of those areas and when they get back to their home church in their home base in that they will be spending basically sixty weeks going through and learning the process concerning those things then we sold them in a workshop.[77]

In a class that he was teaching to potential teachers of Evangelism, he outlined two of his four goals in teaching Evangelism 101. The other two goals were not captured on the audio. He said,

> In teaching 101 you're attempting to reach four goals. The main thing you're trying to do in that class is that the students will become aware as to what the Bible teaches about the basic biblical principles of evangelism. Not that they're going to be theologians. Not that they're gonna become Bible scholars, but that they would become aware as to what the Bible teaches about the basic principles of evangelism. Underscore the word "basic." The reason I ask you to underscore the word "basic" is there for the purpose of keeping you from turning that class into a class of systematic theology. Now, I'm not saying that you don't teach systematic theology in the church. Every church ought to have a class

in teaching systematic theology…So we're saying don't turn this class [into a class in systematic theology]. If you wanna teach some systematic theology, develop another class…

…Goal number two in teaching 101 is to endeavor to elevate the participants, the students to an appreciative level of discipleship. That's the end that you are teaching to. Don't go in there with the erroneous idea that you're going to make full disciples out of church-going folks in ten weeks. When it comes to discipleship you're not talking about ten weeks, you're not talking about twenty weeks, you're not talking about eighty weeks. When it comes to being a full disciple you're talking about a lifetime…So what you're trying to do is elevate the student to an appreciative level of discipleship.

Let me go back to recap the first one – Becoming aware as to what the Bible teaches about the basic biblical principles of evangelism. Not what I heard, not what they said, not what I thought, not what they're practicing across town – what the Bible says. And the only way they're gonna know what the Bible says you're gonna have to turn and take them through the Bible through that process and they'll discover that the Bible says it…Other words, you're going to make them know the difference between going to church and being a follower of Christ…You gonna make them aware that ushering every Sunday on the door and following Christ is not necessarily one and the same. You're gonna have them understand that singing lead in the choir, playing the instrument or directing the choir and following Christ or imitating Christ is not one and the same.

When it comes to discipleship, you can teach Sunday School. Let me go a little further. You can even preach on Sunday morning and not be a follower of Christ. There's no conclusive evidence that you're following Christ because you delivered a good message. In other words, you can do all of those things, you can perform all of those religious chores and not be a follower of Christ. The power and the joy of Christianity is not performing religious chores, but it's in following Christ. So, people will refuse to grow or they will not grow, especially when they think they are doing something right. When it comes to following Christ, you don't have to go around trying to invent your own definition. You don't have to thumb through the Bible and wonder and speculate and assume as to what's involved when it comes to being a disciple. You don't have to guess at that, you do not have to assume, because Jesus laid down the prerequisites himself for being a disciple, a follower – Jesus laid'em down…Because Jesus said something like this – "If any man" – He meant preacher man, deacon man, superintendent man, usher man, church-going man, if any man. When the Lord said any man he meant unlearned man, white man, black man, red man, yellow man, rich man, poor man, wo-man, tall man, short man, fat man, skinny man – any man. Jesus said if any man decides to follow me, the first thing that he's gonna have to do is to deny himself.

When you get your students in that class on that first night, they're gonna have to understand that right then and there, they're gonna have to practice discipleship. You gonna have to change your whole lifestyle. You gonna have to work all day, get off from that job, grab you a Big Mac and keep on steppin' to the church house. You gonna go home and turn that television, that one-eyed monster, off, get down on your knees and pray and spend some midnight oil preparing' to learn…Let me tell you this. Singing in the choir, ushering, coming to church dressed to kill, [wearing those] big hats, folks can't even see around'em, sitting on soft seats, air-conditioned just right, listening to good singing and good preaching have nothing in common with cross-bearing. Amen. Amen. That has nothing in common with cross-bearing. The mistake we have made, we have told folk from the pulpit as to how great they are as servants and folks have learned to call the kind of mess that we carry on in church – service.[78]

Regarding Evangelism 106, he said,

When you come to the 106 process is the area of evangelism that tends to sow the entire package together and bind it up in a nice little neat package. [Evangelism] 106 is designed to help us to become more effective as a helping person. So, in the evangelism process you are being trained to become a helping person that is being equipped to help other persons.[79]

These Evangelism courses were typically taught on Monday night, which was untraditional. Weekly Bible study classes were typically taught on Tuesday or Wednesday nights. Charlee explained that Rocellia chose Monday nights for the Evangelism classes specifically because he wanted to make attending those classes a priority for the week in a way that required a sacrifice. There was also the recognition that people would have to choose God's word and how to be a witness over Monday Night Football. So, every time a student enrolled, they had already made a sacrifice toward being a disciple.

The Team

Pastor Johnson had selected a small group of people from the church and other churches to travel with him around the country to conduct Evangelism Workshops. There are various accounts as to how Rocellia organized the Evangelism team. This book will not endeavor to explain his rationale or provide an explanation of how the team was organized. The goal here will be to attempt to describe how the team functioned.

One way to understand how Rocellia chose his team members is to look at how Jesus selected his disciples. Jesus provided an answer in John 15:16. Jesus told his disciples, "You did not choose me, but I chose you and appointed you that you should go and bear fruit and that your fruit should abide, so that whatever you ask the Father in my name, he may give it to you." This verse does not explain the particular criteria that Jesus used or what he saw in these men that were valuable to His mission. It could have been their heart, their gifts, personalities, or potential that fit his need. Whatever it was, it was based on his sole discretion. This explanation helps you understand how Pastor Johnson selected his team members. Maybe it was their gifts, their personality or availability, but whatever it is, he selected them at God's discretion. According to Charlee, "We just wanted to be obedient."

From that Workshop in Detroit that he had attended, Pastor Ray Brown saw a core group of people that Dr. Johnson surrounded himself with which gave him access to some of the greatest minds that were surrounding him. Brown felt that Pastor Johnson was accompanied by "some of the best, sharpest minds teaching in that Workshop," which he recognized would appeal to his education and professional team. He said that "the level of intellectual prowess of Bethany's Evangelism team excited them because they felt like they were being taught classes that should have accreditation in Christianity." So, this meant to Pastor Brown that he had access to some of the pastors and the relationships to ask questions and help shape him, as a young pastor during that time.

There was not a specific team for every Workshop. The Evangelism team consisted of a variety of people over the years beginning with the core leadership group that traveled with

Pastor Johnson and had responsibilities for planning, preparation of documentation and leading breakout sessions. There was another group without specific leadership responsibilities that occasionally traveled and assisted wherever needed. The other group consisted of pastors, like Pastors Washington, Kessee, Heath and Haynes that would travel with the team, had various duties, but played an important role in breakout sessions, either as teachers for specific classes or with one of the pastor groups as a peer resource or example of how the process worked. The team also played a more insular role in providing a resource and sounding board to Rocellia offering him feedback, consultation and affirmation on the day's events.

One of the main things that made the Workshops so unique was that there not led by the clergy. They were not ministers, nor were they the most experienced in ministry or the most knowledgeable of the Bible. In many ways there were ordinary Christians that made themselves available for this unique work. They adopted his attitude and philosophies of ministry. Pastor Johnson had orchestrated a diverse team from every department of the church that provided leadership to pastors and churches around the country. From pastors, teachers, church deacons, ushers, trustees and ministers and women, Pastor Johnson leveraged people with the requisite devotion, commitment and availability to work on his team. He also was astute at welcoming non-church workers that offered particular assets in business, education and the law that could contribute to the Movement. They were allowed to offer their expertise and were given a voice that Pastor respected and trusted. Ultimately, Rocellia built a team around a shared calling to the mandate of evangelism. Regardless of their individual contributions every team member was able to serve the Lord within their calling and vocation.

The late-night meetings and travels provided intimate communication and comradery that helped them to learn to work seamlessly together. These intimate meetings contributed to synergy, collaboration and skilled teamwork that was observed in how Pastor Johnson and the team worked so well together. Pastor Heath mentioned, "Those who knew Pastor Johnson, he was a night person. So, after we've done all of this [work at a Workshop] all day long he'd want to go out and eat and we spend private time together and before he closed the night his main thought was did they get it. He was so concerned that people got the essence of who Christ was and how to navigate through life with the evangelical approach. That no matter what happened during the day his main approach was did they get it. He would spend hours talking about how the evangelical movement could stir the heart of a person to the point that they didn't just hear it, but they got it and they wanted to move on with that perspective in mind."

Margaret said that Pastor Johnson was protective as they traveled. She remembered occasions in some cities that he wouldn't let them venture out in the evenings because it might be too dangerous. They'd be limited to visiting and socializing from room to room inside the hotel. Margaret said he'd tell them, that a lot was going on in those cities and that he was responsible for them.

Some of the team members were able to recall their favorite Workshops. Dee said her most favorite workshops were Trinidad, hosted by Rev Brian Skinner and his wife Christabelle. According to Dee, Rev. Johnson, Dorothy Johnson, Reggie Shaw, Jessie Williams, James and Vivian Mitchell, Hazel Shipp, Evelyn Grayson and herself traveled to attend. She said that getting passports, tickets, finding affordable housing was a challenge and that many Hindus were converted. Greg Tyler remembered St. Louis because it was so cold, and he enjoyed the hotel and amenities in Detroit. Margaret remembered the Workshop in St. Louis, Missouri in 1990, not because of the cold temperature, but because of a unique and that somewhat distressing encounter with that pastor's wife that came forward for prayer. Charlee considered the Workshop at Solid Rock Baptist Church in Port Arthur, Texas, as her favorite Workshop because the church's Pastor Lee Arthur Kessee, at that time, proposed to marry her and she began making wedding plans on the trip home.

In the early days, the team would travel by one of the church's two vans. Eventually, they would be able to travel by air. Just as there were favorite Workshops, there were countless episodes and experiences over the years. For example, Pastor Heath recalled one somewhat humorous situation with Rocellia about travel. Heath said, "We traveled a lot and I remember one time he [Rev. Johnson] called, he called me one night and said Heath we're going to Tennessee in the morning. American Airlines at 9:00 o'clock and he hung up." The challenge for Heath was that he was still working and had an employer to account for. "Fortunately," Pastor Heath said, "my job allowed me to go because it was receptive to this man on a mission." All of these memories and experiences revealed the man and built comradery that forged a team.

The Context

The evangelism program that Pastor Johnson developed was from the teaching of Dr. James Kennedy. Dr. Kennedy was a white pastor at a large conservative evangelical congregation in Coral Gables, Florida. In 1970, he wrote a book called *Evangelism Explosion*.[80] Pastor Johnson was astute enough to take the core of Dr. Kennedy's framework and develop an approach and curriculum. Pastor Johnson applied this information specifically to the local black churches around the country. In the minute notes from one of the Evangelism Team meetings, "Pastor Johnson stated they the team needed to take a closer look at the reality in the Black church, to be aware of the challenges that they may have to confront."[81] Rocellia was aware of the cultural aspects of the black church and developed his approaches to acknowledge and address any potential barriers, most notably among those black church traditions.

Pastor Washington noted that many of the pastors and churches had evangelism efforts within their churches, but did not have the systems and structures to offer a sixty- to eighty-week course of the curriculum. They also didn't see doing something like this nor did they view themselves as teaching pastors, so they would have to embrace the idea of developing a Christian Education department and approach to ministry. This is where Rocellia became a vessel to those ministries.

Pastor Johnson was able to adapt the model of evangelism to the forms and expression of the black church culture so that the mandate of the gospel was not seen as a foreign language or foreign concept. This meant that Pastor had the wherewithal to develop a ministry that could meet the needs of those churches. The proper name for this is "contextualization."

Contextualization is an important aspect of evangelism. Context speaks to being able to relate to a particular idea, fact or circumstance. It is the idea of being able to be *relatable and translatable* to the message of the gospel and applying it to a particular situation and circumstance of the local black church at that time. This was necessary and significant because the black church has always operated within its own unique culture and traditions. Being contextual helped the Evangelism team speak directly to that culture with a message and approach that could be understood and adopted by the pastors and churches of that community.

It helped that most of these preachers were familiar with the concept of context and contextualization because "context" was required for an accurate interpretation and communication of Scripture in order to understand the original meaning based on the original writing of the biblical text to help provide a better and more accurate meaning of the passage. It also speaks to the various situations and circumstances of life that God was calling them to serve and minister within. This made it relate to their calling and vocation from God, which is based on their particular context or "part of the vineyard," as Pastor Johnson would put it.

Nevertheless, being contextual was not just the type of language that Pastor Johnson would use. He would speak of the concept of contextualization as, "Meeting people where they are." As Pastor Heath shared, "Pastor was always concerned with did they get it." "Did they catch the vision?" was always his concern. This concern didn't just apply to if they heard the message, but more importantly, were they able to comprehend it and apply it to their situations. As a result, the strategy, approach and tenor of the Workshops that Pastor Johnson and the team employed seemed to deliver the message of the Movement within the specific context of the local black pastor and the local black church. This helped those pastors and congregations to see the mandate as a call from God to be applied to the churches they led.

This issue of context meant that Pastor Johnson had established a set of circumstances for the black pastor and black church that was related to their community in a way that would allow it to be translated to their people. He shared the social location that bound them together racially, culturally, ethnically, socially, theologically and spiritually. This meant that Pastor Johnson had already worked through many of the issues that he was teaching the pastors. Pastor Johnson was able to speak directly to the issues and concerns that the Pastors were having in their churches. He had taught the teachers and made teaching assignments, established the curriculum, established church policy, and taught Evangelism in ways that fit the church cultures no matter where they were around the country.

Pastor Ray Brown said when he began pastoring Resurrection Church, he had already begun to understand how necessary it was for churches to have discipleship and evangelism strategies in their church, but he could never really find one that fit the African American experience and church culture that allowed for a systematic process of sharing the gospel within the black church context. "A young man joined our church and had said, 'Man, listen, if you're interested in the evangelism process there's this guy named Dr. Rocellia Johnson who I met in Virginia.'" The man told Brown about the workshop in Detroit and suggested that he attend. Pastor Brown attended that Workshop, which he described as being one of the biggest at that time. That Detroit Workshop was held at the Cobo Hall and Hotel in downtown Detroit in 1992.

Brown said he took a team of people that he called his "Core Impact team," which came from a church with a membership of about two hundred people at that time. He said, "the experience blew their minds." He said that they were so impressed that when they got back, they invited Dr. Johnson to their church to do a miniature (preliminary) Workshop that summer. Pastor Brown said they haven't looked back since. Immediately, he said they began to see the growth. "Not only did people from our church attend classes," he said "but people outside of our church attended classes. Next thing I knew, we went from two hundred to five hundred to one thousand and we needed to purchase a new facility. Within ten years, our church doubled or tripled in new growth." He attributed a lot of that growth to the evangelism process introduced by Pastor Johnson.

Pastor Ray Brown mentioned that the evangelism process was structured in such a way that it allowed him to develop other processes in his church, such as new members orientation, etc. He even sent teachers from his church to participate in a Teacher's Training Workshop in Arizona. So, we were just sold on Dr. Rocellia Johnson and the evangelism process. What he loved and appreciated about Rocellia was his accessibility. Brown said, "You could call him on the phone and talk to him. He flew down on his own dime. He'd pour into you. He would encourage you. And the thing he would always do for me was, 'Brown, how did it go Brown?' (here Pastor Brown imitated Rocellia's raspy, but warm voice). "Every time there was something [done] he would always evaluate himself through you. He wanted to know what you thought." He said it was those kinds of things that endeared him to Pastor Johnson. It wasn't just his relationship with Pastor Johnson that made this so valuable. It had become a community where he made new friends and renewed old friendships. For him, it was a no brainer. Pastor Brown said that he saw this process as a way of developing a healthy church without trying to go through this process of buying a bunch of church rote books that had one size fits all. It meant to him that he could develop the material for his church in a way that will fit their church and Afrocentric cultures.

Understanding the context of the black pastor and the black church undoubtedly helped Pastor Johnson to develop the proper methods and strategies for the Workshops. These methods involved respecting the role of the black pastor and addressing his particular concerns within his congregation and community. This included providing them with the appropriate education, peer group and resources to be successful. First, Pastor Johnson presented this as a mandate for their particular church. He engaged other pastors as spokesmen, advocates and coaches. Third, he created training sessions specifically for the first-time pastor and returning pastors to coach them within their unique context. Lastly, he anticipated and addressed some of their concerns in the beginning made the team available to help teach classes and did not charge any money for these contributions.

The Workshop

The word "phenomenon" describes an occurrence that is impressive, extraordinary and remarkable. It is a word that aptly describes the Evangelism Workshops. They were a ministerial, evangelistic phenomenon. It's gospel focus, the team component, the elements that shaped the event and the unique qualities all worked to make it an extraordinary and remarkable event, which began in Seaside, California. The visit in 1979 to Seaside in northern California was the first official Evangelism Workshop and the launch of the National Evangelism Movement, according to a historical document.[82]

Please note. There were multiple trips to Seaside and two different accounts of that first inaugural Workshop.[83] Rather than attempt to dispute or referee either account after forty-one years when facts have been lost and memories have blurred, both versions will be provided. Charlee and Margaret said that near the end of 1979 (perhaps November), Pastor Johnson chose Charlee Harper (Kessee), Margaret Green (Williams), Ed Berry, Bill and Sherrill Burwell, who already lived in northern California at the time, to travel with him to conduct an Evangelism Workshop for his friend Pastor Lusk in Seaside, California. Debbie Augborne-Allen may have also attended.

Pastor Washington shared the story that Pastor Lusk of the Bethel Missionary Baptist Church called Pastor Johnson because he was burnt out, according to Washington, and was having trouble presenting a program for his church and needed Rocellia's help. Pastor Johnson organized a team of people from Bethany to drive up in one of the church vans to help Pastor Lusk.

Pastor Washington said that they didn't yet know what to talk about on their way to Seaside, but they used the seven-hour drive from L.A. to figure it out. When they arrived, Pastor Johnson and some others walked through the church. It was a nice facility. However, Pastor Johnson noticed the classrooms and said, "Hmm, ain't nothing going on in these rooms…It's too clean." The classrooms were not being used for teaching. Later, he provided a rough draft of what Evangelism 101 would become. He lectured on the lack of use of the facility and no teaching. Pastor Johnson made them aware that they did have something to do and did have the facilities to do So, but they weren't using them. Washington said, "So, the story is that from that visit to Seaside, Evangelism 101 class was born, and the National Evangelism Movement was underway."[84]

After that first Workshop, Dan Dawson said that Pastor Johnson and Bethany began to be known for their work helping churches develop teaching and evangelism training. According to Dan Dawson, Pastor Johnson eventually decided to establish a way to take this information to other churches. Dan told the story that after the Seaside workshop, they were sitting in the van and Pastor Johnson mentioned that he was going to Texarkana, Texas, to help there too. Dan said that didn't seem sensible to him, so he asked Pastor, "Why go that far for one church?" Dan didn't know that that one workshop could include twelve or thirteen other churches. He acknowledged Rocellia had recognized a need to help churches around the country. It wasn't just teaching evangelism. Churches needed help with developing a systematic teaching effort that would equip the saints for the work of the ministry and to effectively share the gospel.

Margaret and Charlee both shared memories from the second Workshop in Oakland, California, which showed that things weren't challenge free in the beginning. What made that Workshop unique was that the pastor wanted it, but his trustees and deacons did not. In fact, according to Charlee and Margaret,

they staged a boycott. According to Charlee, the team included
Ed Berry, Margaret Williams, Debbie Thomas (Augborne-Allen),
Pastor Johnson, Bill and Sherrill and herself. Upon their arrival,
the Pastor was somewhat discouraged. However, Pastor Johnson
spoke with him and picked up a broom and his six-member team
followed suit to prepare the church for the event that evening.
The pastor became was encouraged by their response.

As was the custom, the team would stay to attend Sunday
worship at the church before they departed. On this Sunday
morning, the boycott continued, so there were probably only five of
the church's members in the choir, but there was no choir director
or musicians. According to Margaret, Sherrill Burwell directed
the choir and the team joined in and sang acapella during the
service. Pastor Johnson preached. Despite the adversity, Charlee
and Margaret remembered it as a great worship experience and a
successful Workshop. Charlee said that they heard later that the
church eventually grew by leaps and bounds and that God had
moved.

In general, Workshops were thoughtfully, dutifully and
strategically prepared for and executed. Workshops were much
more dynamic than a meeting or conference. Workshops offered
a format and methodology that helped the events to be organic.
They allowed for an exchange of questions and information, to
demonstrate techniques and methods. They fostered relationships
with the team, leveraged peer forums and modeled various
learning options. A recognition of the need to share information
and best practices, a format to ask questions in a session or
create conversation and to provide affirmations of what works,
enthusiasm for the effort and communication that help was
available—all this was built into the gatherings.

When it came to those planning meetings with the Evangelism
team, in the early days, there were a lot of ideas, strategies

and plans being discussed by the people in the room. Pastor Washington noted that Rocellia could sit at the table with others around him and "allow their opinions and decisions to be involved in a way in developing a topic." According to Washington, Dee and Brenda are two great examples. Rocellia trusted Dee's input and he trusted Brenda's knowledge and ability to develop a youth evangelism effort. "Somehow he could take the different ideas and opinions and tweak it to make it what it became," said Washington. He concluded that Rocellia would continue to work with an issue until the right agreement was reached to get to the right approach.

In November 1982 in one of the Evangelism team meetings, the initial purpose of the meeting was to plan for the next workshop. Also, during that meeting, there were discussions about efforts to organize this into a national ministry.[85] Discussions included the need to establish an Executive Director, which would be Pastor Johnson, and an organization, which included three regional directors. This was announced at the Workshop held at Bethany in 1986. By 1991, the number of regional directors had increased to eight. An official name for this organization was also determined. Some of the names being considered were "Christians on the Move for Christ," "Servants for Christ," "Witness Business," and others. "The Movement" was the name chosen.[86] Many years later, Pastor Johnson said, "I remember when we started talking about this ministry as a movement. That was not just a name that we heard somewhere, but when we saw things moving. When we observed things being different in the church community we called it the Movement."[87]

Features of a Workshop

A Workshop was a collaboration of several elements, which gave it unique qualities. There was a roll call, a song, a cheer, an opening night message that's goal was to introduce the purpose for the week and make sure they all returned on the next several nights and there were the breakout sessions that allowed every group to be addressed. Lastly and equally important was that the Workshops were basically free. It all began with an effective and exhaustive planning effort. Each of these features helped shape the experience of a Workshop that made it memorable and effective.

First, each Workshop was initiated with extensive planning and document production. The Evangelism team would meet to discuss and plan for an upcoming Workshop many months in advance. There would be discussions of objectives, scheduling, logistics and concerns. Days before, documents were being updated or created and produced. The sound of the office copier could be heard printing documents and stacking them together. The conference table would be filled with stacks of papers to be collated together while the office staff and a few volunteers were busy putting documents together.

Prepping for the workshops was daunting. Dee Berry recalled all the typing, proofing documents, copying, packing, shipping or loading U-Haul trailers, packing the van. Airport and hotel accommodations and check-in for 8-12 people, scheduling meetings to coordinate all they had to accomplish. It was all-hands-on-deck. People came, young and old, to participate. People like Willie Jackson, Paul Goins, Faye and Gerald Pointer, Pat Tyler, Debbie Lee, Delores McMillan and her daughter Ronza, Coleman Zeno, Karl Johnson and Victor Williams. Everyone was helping. It was a glorious time, but not without its challenges and with the help of God, they got the job done.

The "roll call" was important. Greg Tyler, who was an Evangelism teacher and team member since 1985, spoke of the enthusiasm that was created by the "Roll Call." It was used initially to identify attendees and as a time to present their donations. It evolved into an event within itself. When asked why he thought the message connected so well with these churches and pastors, Greg Tyler said, "It's something that they had never heard. It made sense and ignited something that they have been looking for. Their members recognized the need, importance of it and once they got exposed to it they wanted more." Greg's assessment was affirmed by the stories of Pastor Brown and Pastor Stewart. Greg felt that the excitement of "roll call" was one of the things that helped the event to resonate with the attendees. It was fun and different. The churches would be called by name and they'd come forward with an offering. Eventually, the various churches began to get more creative. Each church would begin to add its own flair. They'd create cheers. Some would wear custom t-shirts to make their group standout.

Greg said that several churches made a big deal of this, like Cornerstone Baptist Church from Oakland, and some of the churches in Texas and St. Louis because they'd usually bring large groups. Greg said, "All of this created a lot of excitement and the people loved it." He added that Pastor Sylvester Washington did a great job as the hype man for the "roll call" by adding his own flair. According to Greg, "He was a natural." He'd start casually, calling out names, maybe call on the pastor or a church. Then some of the churches would "put on a show," as Greg put it, doing acts or performances with their long cheers as they made their donations. Washington would play along and have fun with it all. If there was more than one church from that city, he'd call out the city, then all the churches from that city would jump up in excitement, cheering, as they came forward. It was like they had just won a big prize. When a specific church was called out from among that group, they'd step forward and cheer more. Pastor Washington would continue to play along, artfully building enthusiasm throughout the audience. The entire part of the event could take at least two hours.

They adopted a theme song. The unofficial theme song of the Movement was "I Want to Be a Follower of Christ."[88] It would be sung often during those events as an expression of praise and devotion to the Lord. It serves as the anthem because it identified each person with the Movement and its cause of evangelism.

The "Fired Up!" cheer was a special, almost covert rallying call for people to express their enthusiasm for the Movement and the gospel. Preachers and members would shout it occasionally to signify their enthusiasm and commitment to the Evangelism Movement and the hearers would shout "Fired up!" in response. Reverend Skinner said that this phrase meant so much to him that the men at the prison where he often served called him "the fired-up man" because of his constant enthusiasm for the gospel. However, you'd only truly embrace and know of its meaning once you'd attended a Workshop. The phrase came about as the battle cry for the Movement at the National Workshop in Oklahoma City in 1984. According to Dee, the cheer came about when Pastor Johnson exuberantly asked the attendees if they were "Fired up!" This gave birth to a "Fired Up!" rallying cry.

On the opening night of every Workshop, Pastor Johnson would address the audience. Pastor Washington said the team would often not know what he was going to speak about, although he'd often speak from Ephesians 4:11. His primary aims were simple. His job was to educate them on the importance of discipleship and to inspire them to come back another night. Pastor Sylvester Washington remembered when Pastor Johnson suggested that they conduct a Workshop at Washington's church Pleasant Hill. Washington said that he was initially afraid to invite him because he was concerned that he might not be able to get enough people to attend all the nights. He said Rocellia told him, "You get 'em there the first night and it's my responsibility to keep 'em coming back." The Workshop was a success and around sixty students enrolled in the first Evangelism class at Pleasant Hill. There was a significance and accountability about that opening night that Rocellia understood and embraced. So, he had a few important, but simple goals for that night to inform and inspire in a way that people would return.

In addition to the distribution of information to particular groups, roll calls, songs and cheers, the breakout sessions provided a unique function. They served as functional small groups where intimate questions about the application could be asked and answered. Relationships would be developed, and attendees could be mentored. It provided a network of people experienced with newcomers and also established a sense of community. Some of the breakout sessions have included first-time laity, returning laity, teachers, pastors, pastors' and ministers' wives, youth by age groups and sign language. Many of the session leaders were laity and often women. Some of the Bible class breakouts included the Gospel of John, the Book of Acts and the Book of Romans. Brown said, "They had it designed so you could get a taste of each aspect of what they were teaching. I went to the pastor's classes. He added, "The pastor's class gave me that whole, it broke down the whole process. One of the things that they kept saying over and over was that this is not a program, this is a process."

This didn't draw much notoriety, but it was also customary for the team to worship and continue the fellowship with the host church on the connecting Sunday. Pastor Washington said he would often be asked to deliver those sermons. This was significant because it recognized tradition and demonstrated a fellowship with that pastor and church.

As important as any other features of the Workshops was the fact that they were basically free. Rocellia understood that cost could be a barrier for some churches to participate or afford to have

Pastor Johnson preaching at a National Evangelism Workshop.

groups from their church to attend. They'd take time to receive an offering to help offset expenses, but there was no official cost to attend. The offerings would rarely be enough to cover the entire costs for a team of 10-12 people for travel, hotels and food for a 4-6-day trip. To eliminate the potential issue, Pastor Johnson and Bethany assumed the entire financial burden of the Workshop. He'd never turn anyone away that needed his help. Washington said he'd say, "Folk who can afford us, don't want us and the folk who want us and need us can't afford us." He added that the ministry was primarily undergirded by Bethany as a result of Pastor Johnson's leadership and teaching.

Pastor William Turner told the story of how Rocellia brought his team of seven or eight people to his church in Pasadena. He commented to Rocellia that he didn't have the kind of money it takes to run this Evangelism Movement. He said Rocellia responded, "Preacher, it don't cost you nothing." Turner said that he couldn't understand how Rocellia and Bethany could conduct an Evangelism Movement for a week with that many staff members. That was radical. He said, "Many churches across this nation benefitted from the Evangelism Movement. Thousands of pastors have grown their churches because of Bethany's ministry and his church was one of the many that grew by leaps and bounds."

Not charging for the Workshops not only allowed some churches to attend, but it also allowed them to bring unlimited numbers of members from their church, like Pastor Brown and Pastor Stewart did, which significantly benefitted the pastor, increased its effectiveness and outreach to the participating churches, and helped ensure the overall effectiveness of the Workshop. He'd fund the primary costs of the event, which included the travel for the team of 10-12 or more people. The Evangelism team members served on a volunteer basis without any compensation. Yet, some of them would often pay their travel to attend. In addition, since the Workshops were a source of information and resources, some of the churches needed help with teachers to teach classes, the initial classes, until other teachers were equipped and assigned. So occasionally teachers would volunteer at various churches to help them start their program at no cost to the church.

Qualities of the Workshop

The Workshop has grown to embrace six important and distinct qualities, which is that it's organic, innovative, dynamic, engaging, relational and missional. These qualities and its features like the roll call and the breakout sessions, inherently work together to create a phenomenal experience for its attendees that results in groups of motivated disciples that produce faithful outcomes.

The Workshop was organic because from its conception of the original Evangelism team, the first workshops and its methodology, the Workshop was a living event developed by a diverse group of uniquely talented people that offered their knowledge and gifts to the mission. It was dynamic because while the meeting itself is planned and structured, it's not static. It displays energy and force of the Great Commission's directive to go that motivates the hearers to respond faithfully to the works of evangelism and discipleship. Its dynamism is also characterized in that the methods had changed and evolved over the years to ensure that the approach remains effective and relevant. There was no way to attend a Workshop without meeting people and making new friends, to be informed, enriched and inspired. It was engaging because it was designed by Pastor Johnson and the Evangelism team to build participation, to grow a community and to secure its involvement around this particular work of ministry in their local churches and communities.

The Workshops were another one of Rocellia's ministry innovations. Pastor William Turner added that Rocellia was also radical when he organized the Evangelism Movement, and his church, New Revelation Missionary Baptist Church, was one of the first churches to conduct a Workshop. As a co-host of the 1991 Workshop in Los Angeles, Pastor Richard Williams recalled how innovative he thought the National Evangelism Workshop was at that time. As a pastor of only three years, he also remembered how kind Pastor Johnson was to include him as "one of the collaborators," as he put it, for the annual Workshop. He said, "That national gathering helped me to further refine the focus of my pastorate and ministry toward a practical and effective approach to both church and evangelism." He also thought it was rather amazing that in a few years when Bethany was damaged in the 1994 earthquake, that the Evangelism classes were relocated to his church in Hawthorne from 1994-1996.

Pastor Brown was also especially appreciative of this innovation. He grew up in the 1970s and had become tired of the traditional church because he thought things were outdated as they approached the 1990s. He began to notice a disconnect in other local churches, other pastors and the conventions because of church tradition. He said, "The local church could come to the convention and participate with your finances, but you could take nothing back. I just thought it was a waste of my time and all my money to go to a convention and there's nothing I can bring to my church from the convention. It was different in the earlier years, but now it is not a criticism of the convention. It's just something that happens in Christianity, churches, conventions, they don't change with the times rapidly or easily." So, the first thing that Brown said he saw in Dr. Johnson, was that he was continually adapting to the times. His thing was to throw out tradition and to set up things in your churches and even in your preaching and all that meet practical needs.

The Workshop was relational because it connected pastors and churches, helped them to forge friendships and relationships that created a sense of community of learning, worship and service dedicated to equipping God's people for the ministry, especially related to evangelism and discipleship.

Pastor Johnson described Bethany as a "missionary" church, although that was never included in the church's name. In December 1978, Bethany and Rocellia had commissioned Phyliss Leftwich to foreign missionary service in Cameroon, West Africa. Sister Leftwich had been a member of Bethany since 1960 and involved in missionary service since 1961. She was also a registered nurse and had been a co-teacher with Rocellia in BE 101 in the late seventies and early eighties.

Regarding the church's department of missions, Pastor Johnson clarified that Bethany's Mission Department was involved in the total mission of the church. He said, "Mission was not a department called "mission." Mission represented the whole thrust of God's mission throughout the business of the church reaching across the country and beyond."[89]

All the qualities of the Workshop described worked together to make the Workshop a missional event. The word "missional" can be used to characterize the Workshop which has become a popular approach to evangelism and involves embracing an attitude, practices and actions of a missionary to outreach to the lost with the message of the gospel. Many churches today use that as the term to refer to their approach to evangelism. Rocellia said,

> You see we are spending a lot of time in prayer trying to get God to bring the world to church. Some of you out there are praying for God to bring some of your lost family members, your lost relatives, some of your lost neighbors and friends to church. That's backwards. God cannot honor that request because He is already mandated that it's not His job to go get him. That's yo' job.[90]

Pastor Johnson recognized that the church has a mission. However, missionality was not a part of Rocellia's vernacular, but he intuitively understood mission and what it meant to be missional. Therefore, the Workshop is a missional event because it is a meeting of a community of God's people that are devoted to that mission.

Pastor Brown mentioned that Pastor Johnson wanted to challenge you. Brown said, "He wanted to get something out of you. He would always say 'There's more in you than you realize.' That was his thing that he loved people young and old even at this his twilight years. So many young people loved him. And to be honest with you I would love to have that kind of legacy where people can say that he impacted my life, he changed my life." As his members began to take classes, Brown said they tell him, "Pastor I've been in church all my life, I never knew these things, didn't know that church was this hard. Didn't know I had to take a test or whatever. I've never been challenged like this before." "That was Dr. Johnson's thing, man," he laughed.

Pastor Brown said that as his members began to take seriously the agenda for the church from Acts 1:8 and the mandate of the church from Matthew 28 the way God designed the church to function and to grow, they narrowed their scope, which meant some of the stuff they were doing at church they should not have been doing, which he said sounded like a quote from Dr. Johnson, as he switched into his Rocellia voice.

Pastor Reginald Pope described this challenge as a "fight or flight" moment. In that initial one-on-one meeting with Pastor Johnson, Pastor Pope admitted that in that conversation he felt that he was confronted with a "fight or flight" situation. Rocellia said things like, "having some of the people at the church all the time, is better than all of the people at one time when people called they need to know that you're available and not get a phone message and that the church was more effective sometimes when it's scattered than it was together. He recognized that Pastor Johnson "came in with a good preaching and teaching program and was Scripture-based and he knew that it was what the church should be doing." He admitted that Pastor had challenged him in all those areas, but Pope accepted the challenge and went for it. He took thirty-six members to a local Workshop in Los Angeles at New Mt. Calvary Missionary Baptist Church when Rev. Lonnie Dawson was the Pastor. After attending the Workshop, his people were so excited that it was a job for him to hold them back until they could get started. They started conducting Evangelism classes and added staff, as needed.

To the larger point, typically, churches could get really comfortable with some of the things that go on in the church and gauge a level of success from it but didn't always recognize the urgency of the mandate and the challenge of carrying the cross. So, you know we find things that we can be comfortable with and I think that was one of the things was that Pastor Johnson was not worried about keeping you comfortable. He also wouldn't go out of his way from preventing you to be uncomfortable. Pope explained that Pastor would do that and create those "fight or flight" moments. He understood that change would require being uncomfortable.

At the Homegoing Service of Pastor Johnson, Dr. Warren Stewart, the pastor of First Institutional Baptist Church (FIBC) of Phoenix Arizona, said he makes a tribute to Pastor Rocellia Johnson every day in his morning prayer to thank the Lord for April 12, 1982, which was the opening night of the Evangelism Workshop at the Mount Calvary Missionary Baptist Church in Tucson, Arizona, and the night that he met Rocellia. Stewart said that as Pastor Johnson was leading his opening remarks from Jeremiah 1:9-10, which says, "Now I have put my words in your mouth see today I point you over nations and kingdoms to pluck up and to pull down To destroy and to overthrow build and plant," Pastor Stewart didn't understand why he'd choose such a Scripture text to speak about evangelism, so he asked Pastor Johnson and he said Rocellia replied, "Son, you have to tear up the fallow ground, the hard ground from tradition. You gotta break that up before you can put the new seed in." Stewart said he never forgot that statement and from that night his church "moved from being a traditional black Baptist Church to an evangelizing fellowship." His church experienced tremendous growth as a result of evangelism. He added that because of the words that Pastor Johnson also said that night on April 12, 1982, each year on every Sunday closest to April 12th, his church celebrates their Annual Evangelism and Discipleship Day recalling that day 1982.

Pastor Stewart shared how FIBC had been a leader in the community since 1905, but almost all of their ministries, all of the preparations during the week, choir rehearsals, usher meetings and everything else was geared towards having great Sunday morning worship experiences. However, their activities were not focused on going outside the church to present the gospel of Jesus Christ through evangelism. He credits attending the Workshop in Tucson, Arizona, at the Mount Calvary Missionary Baptist Church at the invitation of the church's host pastor and his Bishop College classmate, Reverend Theodus Ellsworth Gant II. According to Stewart, Gant was also a strong supporter of Pastor Johnson.

Pastor Stewart remembered that the Workshop began on a Monday evening, which happened to be his day off, yet he drove from Phoenix to Tucson to attend, but only on that opening night. He admitted that at that time, he didn't know Pastor Johnson and basically attended the event upon Gant's urging.

He remembered Pastor Johnson saying, "You cannot turn a traditional church into an evangelistic church without breaking up the hard, fallow ground of tradition and focus on Sunday morning." Pastor Stewart understood this immediately and considered it a revelation to him. This meant to him that FIBC "was going about ministry the wrong way and had not prioritized the Great Commission in Matthew 28:18-20. They had been "keeping house and having a nice worship service." Pastor Stewart gathered thirteen members from FIBC by van to attend the Workshop at Bethany in Los Angeles the following year in 1983.

Pastor Stewart and his team were "Fired up!" Evangelism and discipleship had become their number one priority. They became cheerleaders for evangelism at their church. Pastor Stewart and his team returned to FIBC and began to break up that fallow ground. They changed the terminology from secular terms, such as deacon and trustee boards to ministry terms, like deacon ministry, trustee ministry and usher ministry to rid themselves of the traditional terminology to express their focus on ministry. All of the activities shifted from Sunday morning church to how could they win people to Christ and once they were won, how could they be disciples. More importantly, Pastor Stewart started teaching the six recommended Evangelism classes at FIBC.

Upon the completion of a Workshop, pastors were encouraged to begin by teaching Evangelism classes. Typically, the pastors would either get help from Bethany or recruit members from their church to teach the other courses. Each class was ten weeks long. Pastor Stewart returned with his manual of all the classes and began teaching. He taught all six courses, which equaled sixty weeks (thirteen months) of instruction straight through with no breaks in between. It wasn't until he attended the next Workshop the following year when he mentioned how tired he was from teaching that he learned from Rocellia that he was supposed to take a break in the summer months. He said Rocellia fell out laughing.

Pastor Stewart said that because of Pastor Johnson's ministry, his church has experienced exponential growth as a result of this focus on evangelism and discipleship. They have at least one hundred and forty-seven sons and daughters in the ministry since then. They have moved from one building to a three-building campus worth $9,000,000, $7,000,000 of which was paid in cash because, Pastor Stewart said, "Doctor Johnson also said that night on April 12, 1982, that if you put evangelism first the money will come." Every year they'd celebrate an annual Evangelism and Discipleship Day recalling that day April 12, 1982, when he met Pastor Rocellia Johnson. They close every worship service with the song, "I want to be a follower of Christ." This transformation from church tradition to an evangelistic focus perfectly illustrated the message and capsulized the work of Rocellia Johnson.

A Movement

Three years after that first Workshop in Seaside, Bethany hosted the first National Evangelism Workshop. Pastor Johnson and the Evangelism team planned and continued to organize and refine the format of the Workshop. They gathered more members of the team. Some joined and some left. More churches had gotten involved, more classes were being rolled out and more graduates were being produced. Most importantly, more people were embracing the mandate and more people were coming into the saving knowledge of Jesus Christ because of their efforts. This interest in the Workshops ignited around the country created a movement. By 1980, it was reported that over seventy churches had heard the message of evangelism from Pastor Johnson and his team and almost two-hundred people had become active in the Movement.[91]

That first-ever National Evangelism Workshop was conducted at the Bethany Baptist Church of West Los Angeles in January

1982, the same year the NFL's Oakland Raiders moved to the city of Los Angeles. There were 450 people in attendance, representing at least 45 different churches and almost 70 pastors and ministers.[92] Charlee Kessee remembered her trip from Port Arthur with her husband Pastor Lee Arthur Kessee from Solid Rock Baptist Church and the two members of their church, Birdie Oderbert and Patricia Simmons, that were excited to visit Bethany and meet people from around the country.

In addition to the National Workshop, in early May 1981 and 1982, Bethany hosted a "Christian Education, Mission and Evangelism Week." These events were organized more formally like a revival or Pastor's anniversary week. The week was filled with the attendance of at least fourteen local guest churches and pastors each present on a specified night, a master of ceremonies and themes of Christian education, mission and evangelism for each night.

Charlee thought those events in 1981 and 1982 may have been organized for Pastor Johnson's anniversary week, which seems likely. She explained that Pastor Johnson often took an untraditional approach to his anniversaries by giving them an evangelistic title and theme, like the one year that his anniversary theme was "Rescue the Perishing." Pastor Johnson and his wife Dorothy were recognized in the program for their sacrifice and service. The week was filled with the attendance of at least fourteen local guest churches and pastors each present on a specified night, a master of ceremonies and themes of Christian education, mission and evangelism for each night. In all, it was a tremendous event with an unconventional focus for a week of church meetings.

Bethany hosted National Workshops in 1982, 1983, 1986 and 1989 with Bethel Baptist Church and Pleasant Hill Baptist Church as co-host churches other Los Angeles based Workshops in 1989, 1991, 1994, 1997, 1998, 2005, 2006 and 2013. Bethany also led the efforts for the Workshops in Las Vegas and Reno. Mt. Gilead Baptist Church also hosted two local Workshops in Los Angeles in the early 1980s. In total, there have been thirty-six National Evangelism Workshops that have reached over 160 churches and thousands of Christians across the country to date.[93] The only year when no National Workshop was conducted was 2019, following Rocellia's passing in 2018.

In the following years, there were National Workshops conducted around the country in cities,[94] such as Oklahoma City in 1984 hosted by Tabernacle Baptist Church, with 273 registered attendees with nine co-host churches and again in 2009 when Prospect Baptist Church was the host church with Dr. Lee Cooper Jr. as the pastor. The fourth National was held in Phoenix, Arizona in 1985 at First New Life Baptist Church under Pastor Barnwell with fifty-two churches, three hundred people from thirteen states in attendance. The sixth National Evangelism Workshop was at Silver Spring, Maryland in 1987 co-hosted by Mt. Joy Baptist Church and Round Oak Baptist Church. According to Daisy Stewart, it was at this Workshop that the Minister's Wives group was organized to help the pastor's and minister's wives to support each other, fellowship and study together. This was the first east coast Workshop and the first-time daytime sessions were conducted at a hotel.[95] The seventh National Workshop was held at Cornerstone Baptist Church and ten other churches in Oakland, California in 1988. This was the first regional Workshop for Bay area churches. Eighty-seven people came forward and fifty-five were baptized.[96] There was a Workshop in St. Louis in 1990 hosted by Progressive Baptist Church and 1999.[97] In 1995, the location was Detroit, Michigan in 1992 at the Cobo Hall (now named the TCF Convention Center).

A second and third Phoenix Workshops were conducted in 1993 when E.K. Bailey attended and again in 2003 and hosted by Pastor Warren Stewart at First Institutional Baptist Church. Pastor Stewart and his church hosted the twelfth annual National Evangelism Workshop in 1993 when E.K. Bailey was the keynote speaker.[98] At that event, Pastor L.A. Kessee introduced the speaker that he'd known since their days at Bishop College. Pastor Johnson sat next to Reverend Bailey in a soft and comfortable looking leather chair that reclined slightly as they leaned back.

When Bailey finally stood up to the microphone to speak, he expressed appreciation to Pastor Johnson and acknowledged that moment to speak at that event as what Bailey called a "signal honor." The preacher also acknowledged his friend Lee Arthur, speaking briefly about their longtime friendship, Pastor Barnwell as the host pastor and other ministers that he recognized from Bishop College. The title of his sermon was "Empowering the African-American Male" to talk about the plight and the predicament of the Black man in America. The text he chose for this sermon was Matthew 28:18-20, in which he explained that Jesus has given His people the authority, activity, ability and availability to go, baptize and teach - not to sell chicken dinners, but to make disciples. As usual, by the time he took his seat, the packed audience stood in cheers and applause to what they had heard.

The fourteenth annual Workshop was conducted in Philadelphia, Pennsylvania in 1995 at Jones Memorial Baptist Church under Pastor Paul Lee. San Antonio (Schertz), Texas was the site in 1996 where Pastor Ray Brown and Resurrection Church was the host church. In 1999, the National Workshop was held in Baldwin, Missouri and co-hosted by First Missionary Baptist Church under Pastor Richard Rollin. Chattanooga, Tennessee was the city in 2007 hosted by Second Missionary Baptist Church. Reno, Nevada in 2009. Las Vegas, Nevada was the city in 2000, 2001, 2002, 2004 and every year after 2010, except 2013.[99]

Initially, Workshops were conducted at various local churches around the country with other churches invited to attend. Before conducting a full Workshop, Pastor Johnson and the team would conduct preliminary Workshops called "Prelims" to introduce the concept and approach to local pastors and regional Workshops that focused on churches within a geographical region of the country. By 1991, regional and preliminary Workshops were held in Tulsa, Oklahoma, East St. Louis, Illinois, Jacksonville, Florida, Omaha, Nebraska and Los Angeles, Merced, Pasadena and Riverside, California.[100] Many churches would also travel to continue to attend year after year to continue to learn and to gather and gain additional insights as they continued to develop their own programs. Eventually, the Workshops were held nationally at a mutual location like Los Angeles or Las Vegas after 2010.

Other local Workshops had been conducted in Texarkana and Port Arthur, Texas; El Dorado, Arkansas Oakland, Santa Ana at St. James Baptist Church under Pastor Richard Kessee, Riverside, Palmdale and Pasadena, California at New Revelation Baptist Church under Pastor William Turner; Hartford, Connecticut; Tucson, Arizona and Las Vegas, Nevada, New Mexico. Doors were also opened in Omaha, Nebraska, Topeka, Kansas, Savanah, Georgia and elsewhere.[101] According to Dee, there was also Workshops held in Des Moines, Iowa.

The International Workshops

There were also two international Workshop locations. One was at Halifax Nova Scotia, Canada in July 1988 for Emmanuel Baptist Church with Pastor Willard P. Clayton, where a racially diverse group of people met in the multi-purpose gymnasium-auditorium at the Hammonds Plains Consolidated School with basketball hoops hanging from on the walls above. The team stood on the floor in front of the stage as they took turns speaking to the group of attendees. There were two Workshops conducted in Trinidad at the Bethany Baptist Church of Chaguanas, in Trinidad in the West Indies.

Rev. Brian Skinner had returned home to Trinidad in 1985 after many years as a member of Bethany. There had always been talk of a potential Workshop in Trinidad as Rev. Skinner planned to return home. Yet, the stories of the two Trinidad Workshops have never been publicly reported. In around 1992 or 1993, the first of the two Workshops were conducted in Trinidad. Skinner had organized a small church named Bethany Baptist Church of Trinidad and Tobago to be a part of this church fellowship. It was through this church that the Workshops were organized to reach to the steering committee of churches interested in evangelism. Yet, this Workshop was not just organized within a single church like a typical Workshop. It was with a group of churches in his particular Baptist Union and they had limited time to present.[102] The goal was to reach out to the many churches to teach them the methods and importance of presenting the gospel in an organized, systematic way to be effective soul winners. So, the focus of the team was threefold – to present the "seed plot" scriptures of the gospel plan, to teach them how to use them and to share some material to explain the follow-through method.[103]

In response to the efforts of Pastor Johnson and the Evangelism team, Skinner said the people were open to this information, but also guarded because it was different for them and they had a hesitancy to the American Baptist pastors. More than other Workshops, Skinner said that the pastors and churches that attended considered the materials that were handed out by the team to be extremely valuable. Everyone wanted a packet, but there was not enough for everyone. So, because of the desire for more information, another Workshop was conducted the following year to continue the work. There were plans to send money to buy a bus for the children to get to and from church, as well as to the doctor and so on. Unfortunately, the 1994 earthquake prevented future efforts. Nevertheless, Pastor Johnson was pleased that the people asked him to return and that he and the team were able to effectively present an outline of the gospel plan and the follow-through approach to evangelism. For him, Skinner said that he felt a tremendous amount of pride to see the mutual affinity and admiration between the two groups of Black people from different countries and cultures sharing their faith in Christ.

According to Brian Skinner, on one of his visits back to Los Angeles from Trinidad after Bethany's building had been destroyed, Pastor Johnson said to him, "Brother Skinner, you know a lot of people talkin' about if Bethany will make it, but we'll get back up." Then, according to Skinner, Pastor Johnson admitted, "I was kinda glad because I was trying to come up with some way to get them to that property [across the street]." He told Skinner, "I didn't know how to say [or do] it, but God did it for me."

Pastor Johnson and the team were in Trinidad for a week. During the evenings they would have church services and one of the pastors on the Evangelism team would preach. When they weren't in meetings, they were able to spend time in recreation enjoying the island. They enjoyed a festive dinner with some home cooking, a cultural meal with curry and goat where they ate with banana leaves. They visited the tropical Robinson Crusoe Island, named after Daniel Defoe's 1719 classic novel about a castaway on a deserted island. There was also a Rastafarian father and his musical family that played music for them, some of whose musical rhythms Bethany took back with them. They were also able to go fishing on a couple islands. They went to Tobago's Dillon Bay and Buccoo Reef which was a beautiful place for sightseeing because it had a 10-acre coral reef where the crystal water was so clear that you could see all the various colors of fish swimming together below. They went fishing on a boat, which was always one of Rocellia's favorite pastimes. Remarkably,

Skinner said that Pastor Johnson took off his necktie, but fished with his suit on. He remembered Pastor Johnson saying, "This is good, Skinner!" "He did not stop being Pastor Johnson," Skinner laughed as he told the story.

An Organization

In 2002, this effort was incorporated as the National Evangelism Movement. Pastor Johnson had already been named Executive Director of the National Evangelism Movement around 1985 and Sylvester Washington was later named Co-Executive Director in 1999. In 1986, at the National Workshop, which was held at Bethany, eight Regional Directors were assigned to provide an organizational structure that established pastors and churches in various regions of the country to provide a point of contact and support to churches in those respective areas of the country.[104] The leadership of the organization was transitioned from Rocellia to Pastor Washington in 2009 at the Oklahoma City Workshop.

As much as the National Evangelism Movement was providence by God, other factors helped shape its formulation. Once the local church Workshops reached a frequency, it became prudent to centralize the meetings in one location and conduct the event annually. It was also not possible for many of the local churches to host the event because they didn't have the resources to administer and coordinate such a large complicated national event. However, it was too expensive for Los Angeles and Bethany to be the annual host with its high hotel, meal and transportations costs. Full graduation commencement ceremonies were also conducted during National Evangelism Workshops.

A Mission Fulfilled

Dr. Rocellia Johnson formally retired as the Senior Pastor of the Bethany Baptist Church of West Los Angeles in 2009. For that special occasion, a retirement dinner was held at the Millennium Biltmore Hotel in downtown Los Angeles on December 18th, one day after Rocellia's eighty-seventh birthday.

Upon arrival, Rocellia's mood was great even though he was suffering from severe back pains all day, remembered his daughter Rosalyn. She had even taken him to the doctor earlier that day to get a shot to help alleviate some of the pain in his back. Rosalyn said, "I'll never forget that he could barely walk, sit, or stand that night." Yet, "like he had done so many times before," Rosalyn said, "He did his best to grin and bear it, trying to smile and greet everyone as he normally did." She said he was extremely happy when he walked into the hotel to see the beautifully decorated setting and to see everyone dress in their formal attire. He also noticed that the committee had worked so hard to coordinate to make his retirement party one of the most memorable and unforgettable occasions in Bethany's history.

The event was aptly called "A Tribute to a Living Legend." It was a formal black-tie event with Ed and Minnie Russell serving as chairpersons for a committee of seventeen other people named within the program. Several pastors traveled from around the country to attend, like Pastor Warren Stewart from Phoenix, Pastor Canon from Oakland, Pastor Kerwin Lee from Stone Mountain and Pastor Ray Brown from San Antonio. The menu consisted of filet mignon or salmon and fresh winter vegetables with fruit Florentine, New York cheesecake and crème Brule as dessert options. The program chronicled the many ministerial accomplishments of Bethany under the leadership of Pastor Johnson, such as the development of the Evangelism department, the Bethany Christian Bible College and the strong teaching ministry of the church, the many Evangelism Workshops, especially those in Canada and Trinidad. As they enjoyed an evening of distinction, they took time to reflect on his life of service as they dined, offered tributes and celebrated his extraordinary life in ministry.

For over 50 years Rocellia Johnson served God as the Pastor of the Bethany Baptist Church of West Los Angeles. In his time as pastor, he served faithfully and passionately for the sake of the gospel. Rocellia was a dynamic pastor that was a good shepherd able to lead his people from a small little church to a large building with classrooms that he filled with eager students. He preached as a truth-teller which created a bond between him and his listener. He was also an effective teacher because he helped his people to learn to become disciples. He did all of these things with a unique and untraditional flair.

Long before his retirement, Rocellia had said to a group in a class he was teaching at Bethany in 1998, "I don't intend to leave the Bethany Baptist Church in a state where you're gonna drift back into the mode of doing nothing but having church… .I'm going to promote the necessity of ministry."[105] True to his word, he ensured that experienced and leadership knowledgeable of Bethany and his policies were in place to provide stability to the church after his departure and to continue Bethany's work in Christian ministry. Rocellia was also very interested in the development of a charter school. An agreement to build a charter school was reached in 2017, eight years after his retirement, but he was never able to view the construction, which had begun the same month of his passing in September 2018. Yet, according to Rod and Rosalyn, the building of the school was important to him because it was to help fulfill his vision for education and ministry for the community.

The Bethany Baptist Church, the Stella Middle Charter Academy along with the Bethany Christian Bible College and the Baldwin Bethany Community Development Corporation all share the church's campus. In their agreement with the school, at Rod's insistence, provisions were made to ensure that some of the resources of the charter school would be available to Bethany for its educational ministry. A plaque that included a bust of Rocellia Johnson was placed on the exterior of the school facing the church to honor that vision.

In recognition of his years of faithful and remarkable service to the community, six years after his retirement in the spring of 2015, Rocellia Johnson was honored by the city of Los Angeles with a street named after him. The street near the entrance of Bethany at 4115 Martin Luther King Boulevard, which is the address of the church, was renamed as "Dr. Rocellia Johnson Place" in his honor. The celebration was well attended by his family, Bethany members, well-wishers and city politicians. The assemblymen and councilmen gave speeches and read declarations and honors on behalf of the city.

– Pastor Johnson accompanied by his daughter Rosalyn and his great-granddaughters. (Photo courtesy of Janices Brown).

In what might have been one of the last times preaching at a National Workshop, Rocellia said that he was happy with his ministry. He had been retired for four years and had only preached sparingly during that time. You could hear in his voice that he had aged, but his mind was as sharp as ever and he could still preach like he always had. He said, "When it comes to enjoying the ministry, I will measure arms with anybody. I believe that it's difficult to find even a good preacher who has enjoyed ministry more than I have. I don't have no bad days to look back at and say – I wished." So, he said that he was happy that night.[106] So, have all the people that have been blessed to know him, to hear him and to work with him.

Beginning with his decision to acquire little Bethany in that neighborhood, naming his successor decades early, to the move into big Bethany for the classrooms, to the idea of a 24 hour non-stop worship service as outreach, the sacredness of first Sunday communion service to the phenomenon of the workshop as a method for training in evangelism and equip pastors all demonstrated his unique abilities and an innovative and untraditional approach to ministry that makes him worthy to be remembered and modeled had also made him considered a radical.

The innovations of the Evangelism Workshop and the Bethany Christian Bible Institute allowed him to orchestrate an approach to ministry that didn't abolish tradition but built on it and in doing that he was able to expand the teaching paradigm within the local church and bless other pastors and churches through those endeavors. The idea of a systematic approach to teaching and teacher training was revolutionary for a local Black church at that time. His work in evangelism was based on the mandate to teach and to make disciples and should be remembered.

Epilogue:
The Necessity of Legacy

I n 1998, when Pastor Johnson said that he was going to promote "the necessity of ministry," he recognized that Christian ministry was essential and indispensable to the Christian life. To emphasize the point, when he teaching a series on understanding God in creation, he said to the members that were attending the class,

> The only point I wanted to make is the necessity of ministry. Don't ya'll let nobody take you backwards! I've taught you too long. I've shed too much sweat and blood. I've went out too long to leave here going home [to glory] and you're sitting up on that piece of land [across the street] just rockin.' ...The church of God is in the earth to serve a purpose. If somebody don't get out there to serve that purpose, stand up and say something! Say I told you to say it. Don't wait until I die. It's gonna be some teaching. It's gonna to be some education. It's gonna to be some ministry. It's gonna be doing something over and beyond having church.[107]

He made that simple, but profound and maybe prophetic, statement to help the students in that room understand that to be blessed and to minister requires more than just having church.

He contended that some blessings from God require work to receive and that we may be missing a blessing if we are having church that is devoid of ministry. He added, "Having church is just not enough to keep people strong and growing in the Lord. Church is about ministry. It's about serving God."[108] This statement characterized his life's work – to do ministry. Yet, it also recognizes that this work is not about him. It is a necessity because the work that he began is about God's mission, Christ's mandate and the faithfulness of Christ's church, which establishes a necessity for legacy.

During the writing of this book, a very sad reality was revealed. In the course of researching some of the great men and women that contributed to various churches, to Bethany and also the Movement, there seems to be a general tendency to speak to the current, which unfortunately seems to involve forgetting the past. Pastors leave ministries and churches that they have devoted their lives to with a retirement service farewell, maybe a plaque and a financial gift. Yet, there is often no mention of their work in a tangible way that provides a generational impact or that teaches new members about their sacrifices. Their stories can't be discovered through a Google search and their former church's website doesn't tell their story or mention their names. The work of these pastors should have a lasting application past those that were able to experience it first hand. So, as this story of Rocellia and Bethany has concluded, whether you were a member of Bethany or from another church, you are encouraged to remember those men and women that lived faithfully and to honor the work of ministry in their lives and work. Don't forget them! To Bethany and the churches within the National Evangelism Movement, more specifically, remember what you've been taught and remember the work that you have begun.

The necessity for legacy exists because things change. People get older. Society evolves. Churches appoint new pastors and change their ministry approach. The new pastor, no matter who he is, feels inspired to try new things and lead differently. Holding on to what the church has learned and who she has been has become more difficult as time has passed. Hearts still beat for the days of Pastor's Teas, meals served from the kitchen, Marathons and Workshops hosted at Bethany. Those events, the memories of saints gone on to be among that great crowd of witnesses, the relationships and life moments have become sacred and kept secure in the many hearts that remember. Bethany must continue his work to continue to be Bethany.

When God worked through Rocellia it was not for the unique and individual style that was to begin and end with him. Rocellia was God's vessel for change within His church, which was not to end with his departure. The pastor called to a church like Bethany doesn't have an opportunity, like he might have at other churches, to start over. He or she inherits a mission of evangelism and discipleship and a legacy of leadership and innovation that must be continued. This is the unique corporate call that remains upon Bethany. No matter their whereabouts, ex-members of Bethany remain in a sense of community.

The legacy of Rocellia Johnson and his work to inspire a Movement should not be romanticized around the warm memories of Rocellia or Bethany, as though relegated to a once-upon-a-time past. It should be held as a mantle that serves as a reminder of the work of evangelism and discipleship that must continue, because it involves God's mission. In his letter to the Phillipians, the Apostle Paul wrote, *"What you have learned and received and heard and seen in me—practice these things, and the God of peace will be with you"* (Php. 4:9). Thus, the work of ministry that has been learned and experienced should be put into actions that will continue beyond us.

The untraditional fire for evangelism that God ignited in and through Rocellia is still relevant and must be allowed to continue to burn bright and fresh and bold, from generation to generation, sparking new untraditional fires for God in the process. Whether you have experienced the movement first hand or have only learned about it in this book, I hope that you have been inspired by this special man of God's unconventional approach to the ministry of evangelism and discipleship, and that if you are a pastor or church leader, you will set out to become your own unique fire for the Lord.

Remarks

Pastor Johnson was my true hero and I know, beyond all shadow of a doubt, that I would not be (spiritually, mentally, morally) who I am or where I am today had I not had to blessed opportunity to sit and serve under his leadership and his clear preaching of the gospel. He is always in my heart!! As will beloved Dorothy!! Both were great, great servants of Lord!!

Deborah Augborne-Allen, 1975

I remember a time, I was so hurt. During a Gospel Marathon, Pastor Johnson was walking to his office with the Pastor that just finished preaching. I was sitting on the pew next to his office. Pastor Johnson saw the hurt look on my face; he came out of his office listened to me and gave me encouraging words. I will never forget it or him.

Vicki Kelley, 1974

I can think of so many times and events that took place at Bethany that Pastor Johnson's legacy will always be remembered, the 24-Hour Marathons, Workshops, Communion services, etc. However, what I remember most took place in such a small and insignificant gesture. My wife (Gail) and I were beginning students in Evangelism 101 taught by sister Norma Brown and Pastor Johnson. On this particular class night, we were informed that Pastor Johnson probably would not be at class that night because he was experiencing extreme back pains which most of the church knew about. When class started, Sister Brown who would do the first part and Pastor the second part, I said she would be teaching both parts of the class that night. Just as she was completing the first part of the class, Pastor Johnson walked in and we all could see he was in obvious pain even though he never complained. My wife and I looked at each other and thought that a man of his stature and resources could easily delegate his responsibility to anyone but his commitment to the ministry extended not just to other pastors, preachers, and teachers, but to little students like us, babes in Christ. I thought to myself, what kind of man is this. We left class that night with a complete understanding of what it really meant to be committed to God and the ministry in which he led and which we were called to serve.

Gail Stamps, 1970 and Perry Stamps, 1988

Pastor couldn't sing, but when he would sing "Without God, I could do nothing," it would make me cry.

Vicky Shipp, 1977

We love Pastor R. Johnson. We feel that Pastor was so advanced for his time in his teaching of his vision for evangelical training about how to bring people to the Lord. He was the first in history to conduct a 24-hour Gospel Marathon where people from all over would come to worship." He left a wonderful path to be followed.

Joanne & Weaverton Terrell, 1982

Pastor Johnson was like a second father to me. Partly because of Pastor Johnson's guidance, I obtained my Doctor of Education, I taught in the Bethany Christian Bible College (BCBC) for eight years, and I know the Word of God because Pastor told me to read my Bible daily. I loved him with all my heart.

Christine Wallace, 1967

My wife, Juanlyn and I were visiting L.A. and made an unannounced visit to Pastor's house. Sister [Dorothy] Johnson answered the door and was surprised and happy to see us. She took us to the back yard where Pastor was cleaning fish he had caught. He stopped everything and received us warmly. We talked and reminisced about an hour until sister Johnson came in saying a cat was in the back yard eating the fish he left out there. He rushed out to save his fish and came back in to finish our visit. It was a wonderful visit.

Gary Williams, 1982

My family belonged to Friendship Baptist Church in Seaside, CA where the Pastor was CL McFadden. They were from Oklahoma where they went to school together. When they both moved to California their churches fellowshipped together. When I was 19 I decided to move to Los Angeles and Rev McFadden told me to immediately connect with the Bethany Baptist Church. My training in evangelism and teaching at Bethany ignited the passion I still have for the word of God. I was married at Bethany and my children started their lives at Bethany, as well as some of the relationships that are the most precious in my heart.

Juanlyn Williams, 1979

I thank God for Pastor Rocellia Johnson. I am grateful that God gave Pastor Johnson the vision of Evangelism. At Bethany, I truly came into the saving knowledge of Jesus Christ as my Lord and Savior. Through Pastor Johnson's preaching and teaching, I was able to grow continuously. Pastor Johnson was a faithful and humble servant for the Lord. I was blessed to have him as my pastor.

Rhonda Wilson, 1981

I thank God for Pastor Johnson and his love for God's people that thought of others and their hope in Jesus. I remember when he first started and was going around to the churches and the conventions asking the leadership to join in, they didn't but it didn't stop him. I am so glad he didn't because God allowed me to become a product of the Evangelism Movement and get the opportunity to teach Evangelism 101 with him.

Ann Woodmore, St. Mark MBC
Evangelism 101 Instructor with Dr. Johnson, 2004

I feel honored to have been taught by some of Bethany's Sunday School Teachers (Annie Jefferson, RIH, Betty Richardson and Ernestine Wallace). Pastor, Dr. R. Johnson was a very down to earth preacher, Teacher and Counselor. He helped me handle some of my family issues! I will forever remember his, "Tell It like it really is" messages and the 24-hour Gospel Marathons and BCBC.

Karen Wright-Rahman, 1969

I learned the deeper meaning of scriptures from Dr. Rocellia "Rocky" Johnson. I was a member at little Bethany, but I met my husband Escoe Richardson at big Bethany forty-four years ago!

Annie Marie Wright-Richardson, 1969

About the Author

Harry A. Mitchell III is a husband and father that resides with his family in Southern California. Harry was a member of Bethany from 1976 to 1992. During his time at Bethany, Harry was a young deacon, a Sunday school teacher, an evangelism counselor and teacher. He is also a son of Pastor Rocellia Johnson in the ministry.

Harry is a graduate of Biola University and a graduate student of Theology and Ministry at Fuller Theological Seminary. He is the founder of *A Word Digital.com* a Christian publishing company and the author of several books, such as *Good Job! Developing a Biblical Perspective of Your Work, Reflections: Embracing God's Calling for Your Latter Years* and *Work. Pray. Bless: Discovering Your Work in God's Mission* and *The Wandering Life: A Wayward Journey to Understand My Work, Calling & Mission.*

Endnotes

1   "Without God I Could Do Nothing" song was originally released 1962-63. All rights reserved by Columbia Records, a division of Sony Music Entertainment. It was composed by Beatrice Brown, a long-time associate of Thomas A. Dorsey.

2   Elwell, W. A., & Comfort, P. W. (2001). In Tyndale Bible dictionary (p. 1192). Wheaton, IL: Tyndale House Publishers.

3   Elwell, W. A., & Comfort, P. W. (2001). In *Tyndale Bible dictionary* (p. 1192). Wheaton, IL: Tyndale House Publishers.

4   Hebrew word, *ra'ah*

5   Unger, M. F., Harrison, R. K., Vos, H. F., Barber, C. J., & Unger, M. F. (1988). In *The New Unger's Bible Dictionary* (Rev. and updated ed.). Chicago: Moody Press.

6   Stewart, R. A. (1996). Shepherd. In D. R. W. Wood, I. H. Marshall, A. R. Millard, J. I. Packer, & D. J. Wiseman (Eds.), *New Bible dictionary* (3rd ed., p. 1093). Leicester, England; Downers Grove, IL: InterVarsity Press.

7   Rocellia Johnson, source and event unidentified

8   Rocellia Johnson, source and event unidentified

9   Pastor Rocellia Johnson, *"It's Time"* Sermon, (Ro. 13:11-12), 1981 (Occasion and location unknown).

10   "Without God I Could Do Nothing" song was originally released 1962-63. All rights reserved by Columbia Records, a division of Sony Music Entertainment. It was composed by Beatrice Brown, a long-time associate of Thomas A. Dorsey.

11   Los Angeles Sentinel, "Homegoing Services Set for Rev. Rocellia Johnson, Founder of Bethany Baptist Church," (https://lasentinel.net/homegoing-services-set-for-rev-rocellia-johnson-founder-of-bethany-baptist-church.html), October 3, 2018.

12   Wood, A. S. (1981). Ephesians. In F. E. Gaebelein (Ed.), *The Expositor's Bible Commentary: Ephesians through Philemon* (Vol. 11, p. 58). Grand Rapids, MI: Zondervan Publishing House.

13   Rocellia Johnson, *It's the Time*, opening night remarks, Halifax Nova Scotia, Canada, 1988

14   Dale P. Andrews, *Practical Theology for Black Churches: Bridging Black Theology and African American Folk Religion*, (Westminster John Know Press: Louisville, KY), 2002, pg. 28 (Kindle version)

15 Dennis W. Wiley, The Black Church Studies Reader, Black Church Studies as Practical Theology, (Palgrave Macmillan: New York, NY), (https://doi.org/10.1057/9781137534552_16), 2016, pg. 163 (Viewed 9/26/20).

16 Rand, W. W. "Entry for 'SEER'". "American Tract Society Bible Dictionary"<http://classic.studylight.org/dic/ats/view. cgi?number=T1850>. 1859.

17 Bethany Baptist Church of West Los Angeles, *Coordination Board Report*, October 24, 1978

18 Bethany Baptist Church of West Los Angeles, Minutes of Evangelism Team meeting, 1982, p. 1

19 This is from a sermon by Pastor Johnson called *"The Church as Change Agent"* at an Evangelism Workshop in Port Arthur, Texas, August 1982. The scriptural text was from Rev. 3:14-18.

20 Faith & Leadership magazine, "Traditioned Innovation: A Biblical Way of Thinking," (https://faithandleadership.com/traditioned-innovation-biblical-way-thinking)

21 This is from a sermon by Pastor Johnson called *"The Church as Change Agent"* at an Evangelism Workshop in Port Arthur, Texas, August 1982. The scriptural text was from Rev. 3:14-18.

22 Pastor Rocellia Johnson, *"It's Time"* Sermon, (Ro. 13:11-12), 1981 (Occasion and location unknown).

23 Kenneth H. Hill. *Religious Education in the African American Tradition: A Comprehensive Introduction*, (Chalice Press: St. Louis, MO), pgs. 221-223, (Kindle Edition).

24 Pastor Rocellia Johnson, *"It's Time"* Sermon, (Ro. 13:11-12), 1981 (Occasion and location unknown).

25 Pastor Rocellia Johnson, Second Evangelism Teachers Training Workshop, Phoenix, Arizona, 1989.

26 Pastor Rocellia Johnson, *"It's Time"* Sermon, (Ro. 13:11-12), 1981 (Occasion and location unknown).

27 Notes from Annual Church Meeting (Leadership), 11/14/91.

28 Bethany Baptist Church Annual Church Meeting 1985

29 Easton, Matthew George. "Entry for 'Bethany'". "Easton's Bible Dictionary". <http://classic.studylight.org/dic/ebd/view. cgi?number=T545>. 1897. Viewed 11/16/20.

30 Historical Review, Part II, pg. 3

31 Historical Review, Part I, pg. 3

32 Historical Review, Part I, p. 2

33 Historical Review, Part II, p. 2

34 Bethany Baptist Church Annual Business Meeting, Coordination Board Report, (Prepared by Emilie Bowman), October 24-27 29, 1978.

35 Matthew 8:34; Revelations 22:17.

36 Reverend Rocellia Johnson, Thirty-Second National Evangelism Workshop in 2013.

37 Historical Review, Part III, p. 3

38 Historical Review, Part IV, p. 1

39 Kelly Simpson, KCET.org: "A Southern California Dream Deferred: Racial Covenants in Los Angeles" Article, (https://www.kcet.org/history-society/a-southern-california-dream-deferred-racial-covenants-in-los-angeles). February 22, 2012.

40 Historical Review, Part IV, p. 4

41 Historical Annex, Part V, p. 2

42 Historical Review, Part V, p. 4

43 Historical Review, Part V, p. 5

44 The name of the Bethany Christian Training Institute (BCTI) was changed to the Bethany Christian Bible College in 1992.

45 Rev. Rocellia Johnson, "The Church at Philippi" sermon, Bethany Baptist Church of West Los Angeles, December 7, 2007.

46 Bethany Baptist Church Annual Church Meeting 1985

47 Bethany Baptist Church Annual Church Meeting 1985

48 Bethany Baptist Church Course catalog.

49 Program…

50 Bethany Baptist Church Annual Church Meeting 1985

51 Reverend Brian Skinner now works as a certified Character Trainer and independent agent for *Character First Training* (https://charactersolutions.weebly.com)

52 Teaching a class that he called the "Universe of God," at the Bethany Baptist Church in April 1998.

53 The full title was "Take My Hand, Precious Lord," which she recorded in 1956 on her *Bless This House* album for Columbia Records and sang at Martin Luther King Jr's funeral in 1968. This song version was written by Thomas A. Dorsey in 1932. Aretha Franklin sang it at Mahalia Jackson's funeral in 1972.

54 Esther Kang, *Eddie Cole Doesn't Take His Legacy Lightly*, May 13, 2016 (https://lbpost.com/hi-lo/music/eddie-cole-doesn-t-take-his-family-legacy-lightly), Viewed 7/18/2020.

55 Bethany Baptist Church of West Los Angeles Annual Church Meeting November 1, 1985

56 Rocellia Johnson, source and event unknown

57 Los Angeles Times, *Gospel Wins Over Satan in 24-Hour Marathon* article, (https://www.google.com/amp/s/www.latimes.com/archives/la-xpm-1988-10-03-me-2539-story.html%3f_amp=true), October 3, 1988 (Viewed)

58 Paul Feldman, LA Times, *Gospel Wins Over Satan in 24-Hour Marathon* (https://www.latimes.com/archives/la-xpm-1988-10-03-me-2539-story.html) Published October 3, 1988, (Viewed 6.7.2020).

59 "It's Real," was written by the preacher and evangelist Homer L. Cox in 1907, (https://hymnary.org/person/Cox_HL), (Viewed 10/19/2020).

60 E.V. Hill, Wikipedia (https://en.wikipedia.org/wiki/E.V._Hill), Viewed March 15, 2020

61 Baker Evangelical Dictionary, "Covenant," Elwell, Walter A. "Entry for 'Church, the'". "Baker's Evangelical Dictionary of Biblical Theology". <http://classic.studylight.org/dic/bed/view.cgi?number=T139>. 1897.

62 Coordination Board Meeting, Annual Church Business Meeting and Evangelistic Services, October 1978, p.5

63 Ibid., pg. 4

64 Rocellia Johnson, source and event unknown

65 Evangelism Teachers Training Workshop, Phoenix, Arizona, 1989

66 Rocellia Johnson, source and event unknown

67 Pastor Johnson, Evangelism Teachers Training Workshop, Phoenix, Arizona, 1989 (Audio)

68 See pages 55, 57.

69 Pastor Johnson teaching "Introduction to Evangelism 101," event, location and date are unknown.

70 Quotes from Rhonda Wilson's class valedictorian speech from 1982 courtesy of Rhonda Wilson.

71 Pastor Johnson, Teachers Training Workshop, Phoenix, Arizona, 1989

72 D. James Kennedy, Evangelism Explosion: The Coral Ridge Program for Lay Witness, (Tyndale House Publishers: Wheaton, IL), 1976. The

Evangelism Explosion is an evangelism ministry that trains people how to share their faith in Christ and how to bring people from unbelief to belief. It utilizes a variety of components including prayer, actual on-the-job training where the experienced lead the inexperienced, and the principle of spiritual multiplication. (https://evangelismexplosion.org/about-us/what-is-ee/), Viewed 12/28/2020.

73 Pastor Johnson, Sidney Beach & Deloris Berry, *Evangelism Introduction* document, (September 1981)

74 Bethany Baptist Church, Introduction to Evangelism document, pg. 2

75 Evangelism Explosion, pg.

76 Bethany Christian Bible College Schedule of Classes, *Course Descriptions and Goals*, 1996-1997, pg. 18

77 Pastor Johnson, Teacher Training Workshop, Phoenix, Arizona, 1989

78 Pastor Johnson teaching "Introduction to Evangelism 101," event, location and date are unknown.

79 Pastor Johnson, Teachers Training Workshop, Phoenix, Arizona, 1989

80 Dr. D. James Kennedy, *Evangelism Explosion: The Coral Ridge Program for Lay Witness*, Tyndale House Publishers: Wheaton, IL), 1970.

81 Bethany Baptist Church, *Minutes of the Evangelism Team Meeting*, November 6, 1982.

82 This document which was entitled the "The History of the Movement: The History of the Bethany Baptist Church of West Los Angeles" was reportedly written by Karen Butler with sources which included Pastor Rocellia Johnson, Carolyn Lewis, Deloris Berry, Daniel Dawson and Debbie Thomas (Augborne-Allen). This document may have been written in the early eighties, but the actual date is unknown. The source for this document was Cheryl Warren.

83 The people that could clarify this issue had chosen not to participate in the project.

84 According to the Twenty-fifth Annual National Evangelism Movement program, in 1981 Pastor Washington became the first pastor to join the traveling Evangelism team.

85 Bethany Baptist Church, *Minutes of the Evangelism Team Meeting*, November 20, 1982.

86 Bethany Baptist Church, *Minutes of the Evangelism Team Meeting*, November 20, 1982.pg. 3

87 Reverend Rocellia Johnson, "Second Chance" sermon at Thirty-Second

National Evangelism Workshop in 2013 in Los Angeles.

88 "I want to Be A Follower of Christ" was written by J.W. Harris. The National Evangelism Movement claims no rights to this song.

89 Bethany Baptist Church Annual Church Meeting 1985.

90 Rocellia Johnson, source and event unknown.

91 Karen Butler, The History of the Movement: The History of the Bethany Baptist Church of West Los Angeles, probably written before 1989, pg. 4.

92 Bethany Baptist Church, Tenth Annual National Evangelism Workshop program, March 18-22, 1991, pg. 2

93 Courtesy of Karen Butler, National Evangelism Coordinator, NEM.

94 This information is based on the best verifiable information available at the time this book was written.

95 Karen Butler, *The History of the Movement: The History of the Bethany Baptist Church of West Los Angeles*, probably written before 1989.

96 Ibid., pg. 4.

97 Bethany Baptist Church, *Tenth Annual National Evangelism Workshop* program, March 18-22, 1991, pg. 2

98 Source: Twenty-fifth Annual National Evangelism Movement program conducted in July 2006 in Los Angeles.

99 This may not be a conclusive list of Workshops. Many of the church's evangelism records have been lost since the earthquake and relocation. These dates and locations were gathered from the actual Workshop program books courtesy of Emilie Duncan.

100 Tenth Annual National Evangelism Workshop program, pg. 3

101 Ibid., pg. 4

102 As of this writing, the Baptist Union of Trinidad and Tobago consists of twenty-one churches (www.baptunitt.wixsite.com).

103 The seed-plot scriptures were the key scriptures from the *Evangelism Explosion* used to share the Gospel message.

104 Karen Butler, *The History of the Movement: The History of the Bethany Baptist Church of West Los Angeles*, pg. 5

105 Teaching a class he called the "Universe of God" at the Bethany Baptist Church in April 1998.

106 Rocellia Johnson, "Second Chance" sermon at Thirty-Second National Evangelism Workshop in 2013 in Los Angeles.

107 Rocellia Johnson, Universe of God teaching series, April 19, 1998 at the

Bethany Baptist Church.

108 Teaching a class that he called the "Universe of God," April 1998

www.ingramcontent.com/pod-product-compliance
Lightning Source LLC
Chambersburg PA
CBHW030414100426
42812CB00028B/2956/J